# THE
# CHINESE
# GOURMET

FROM THE LIBRARY OF

Nicole          Love always
                Carmel

Nov 10 th 1997

# THE CHINESE GOURMET

RECIPES: *WILLIAM MARK*

TEXT: *HARRY ROLNICK AND JACKI PASSMORE*

## AUTHENTIC INGREDIENTS AND TRADITIONAL RECIPES FROM THE KITCHENS OF CHINA

**RAINCOAST BOOKS**

VANCOUVER

First published in Canada in 1994 by
Raincoast Book Distribution Ltd.
112 East 3rd Avenue
Vancouver, BC V5T 1C8

Produced by Weldon Russell Pty Ltd
107 Union Street, North Sydney NSW 2060, Australia

A member of the Weldon International Group of Companies

ISBN 1-895714-42-7

Publisher: Elaine Russell
General manager: Susan Hurley
Managing editor: Ariana Klepac
Project co-ordinator: Kayte Nunn
Assistant editor: Libby Frederico
Copy editor: Jill Wayment
US cooking consultant: Rosemary Rennicke
Designer: Stuart M<sup>c</sup>Vicar
Design concept: Judy Hungerford
Jacket design: Honor Morton
Illustrator: Kathie Smith
Food photographers: Andrew Furlong, Mark O'Meara,
  Bruce Peebles
Food stylists: Marie-Hélène Clauzon, Penny Farrell,
  Jacki Passmore
Indexer: Gary Cousins
Production: Dianne Leddy

Canadian Cataloguing in Publication Data

Mark, William, 1936-
  The Chinese gourmet

  Includes index.
  ISBN 1-895714-42-7

  1. Cookery, Chinese. I. Rolnick, Harry. II. Passmore, Jacki. III.
Title.
TX724.5.C5M37 1994      641.5951      C94-910107-9


Produced by Mandarin Offset, Hong Kong
Printed in China


A KEVIN WELDON PRODUCTION

*Front cover: Photographer: Rowan Fotheringham, Stylist: Suzie Smith*

*Back cover: Sin Ku Yu Kau (left, recipe page 100); Choi Chau Yu Pin
  (right, recipe page 101)*

*Opposite title page: Lijian Market, Yunnan, photograph: Robert Harding
  Picture Library*

*Title page: Jing Lung Har (left, recipe page 29); Lo Suen Dai Tze
  (right, recipe page 28)*

*Opposite contents page: water pots in a tea-house, Chengdu, photograph:
  China Tourism Photo Library/Wu Zhou Ming*

*Right: Sheung Dong Pa Ngarp (left, recipe page 139);
  Yeung Chung Ngarp (right, recipe page 138)*

# CONTENTS

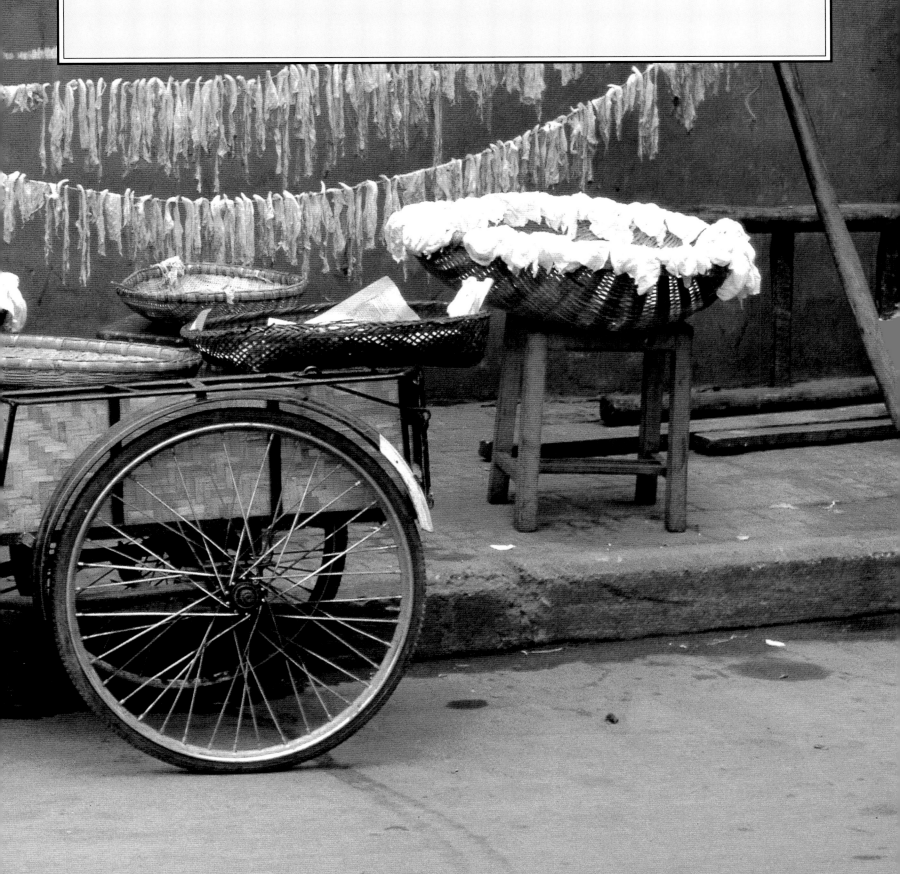

# INTRODUCTION

# INTRODUCTION

SINCE TIME IMMEMORIAL, FOOD IN CHINA HAS ENJOYED A STATUS THAT FAR TRANSCENDS ITS NUTRITIVE VALUE. ITS traditions, ingredients, preparation, serving, sharing, and eating are embedded deep in the heart and history of Chinese culture, linking the emperors, the peasantry, invaders, agriculture, trade, religion, philosophy, and medicine in a way that perhaps only French cuisine comes close to emulating.

¶ From earliest times, China was the world, the Middle Kingdom, and its produce was infinite. Chinese farmers had produce from countless fertile river valleys, mountains, and the endless steppes of Mongolia. And they were encouraged in their endeavors by emperors who researched new crops or instituted new farming techniques.

¶ The imperial court was a focus for the cuisine, where food was looked upon as the highest art. From the earliest dynasties, emperors would give countless banquets, at which courtiers would vie to present recipes with the rarest ingredients.

¶ The peasants, meanwhile, lived on rice, millet, local vegetables, and pork. In the South, though, so fertile was the land, so varied the seas, hills,

*Previous pages: Dried foods, including cabbage, are used in many Chinese dishes. In the days before refrigeration drying was an excellent method of preserving food, but the practice continues because of the fuller flavor it produces.*
ROBERT HARDING PICTURE LIBRARY/C C D TOKELEY

*Opposite: Eggplants (aubergines) for sale at a market in Kunming, Yunnan province. This small, thin variety of the vegetable is preferred in China for its more delicate flavor.*
ROBERT HARDING PICTURE LIBRARY/G & P CORRIGAN

savannahs, and lakes, that variety in their meals was inevitable. Their northern neighbors would have to save, pickle, conserve, and fear for drought or flood.

¶ Over the centuries came many culinary changes. The "primitive" Mongols brought sheep and barbecued dishes. Indian travelers introduced spices, like ginger and cilantro (fresh coriander). Later, Jesuits from Portugal planted great gardens that added European vegetables to the cuisine.

¶ During the twentieth century, Chinese food has undergone a revolution, not all of it positive. As the country has become more urbanized, the gospel of farm-fresh produce is giving way to that of frozen.

¶ Underlying all Chinese food (at least in principle) is the medical philosophy of *yin* and *yang*. Derived from ancient theories of chaos and order, the philosophy holds that in every aspect of life, the feminine quality or force (*yin*) must be in balance with the masculine (*yang*), if there is not to be chaos, disruption, destruction. Neither can exist without the other, and neither must dominate.

¶ *Yang*, the masculine quality, has foods which are sharp, positive, and usually more fattening such as red meat, chili, onions, fried foods, and red-cooked dishes. The *yin* was soothing, of course, but over time that soothing quality became dark, even black, negative. Some foods that have *yin* qualities are lettuce, fish, celery, steamed, and poached dishes. Only by intermarrying "positive" and "negative" foods can one enjoy the balance of bodily functions.

¶ In theory, a Chinese meal should follow these precepts, and this balance begins with the table. Porcelain should be of soft colors, the chopsticks preferably of wood. The table has a minimum of dishes. One rice bowl set on a saucer (the latter a receptacle for bones and gristle). One bowl ready for tea, sometimes a personal tea pot. In restaurants, a platter of steamed rice is placed in the center. At home, the hostess may dish out the rice to guests.

❡ The order of serving the various dishes of a meal should alway balance the qualities of *yin* and *yang*, the host or hostess providing the "correct" order of serving. At a restaurant, where meals are ordered in advance, the chef will give suggestions and make his own choice as to the order.

❡ For simple meals, all the dishes (usually a fish dish, a meat dish, and vegetables) will come together. In a dinner for six to eight people (hardly classified as a banquet), special dishes like Peking Duck will be offered separately, but the preceding dishes may be brought simultaneously. At a more formal dinner or banquet, platters are brought individually to be admired, then partaken of, as each dish should be savored for itself.

❡ But there are a few standard elements. First, no drinks will be served beforehand; tea is sufficient. Second, the opening course should be a cold dish; something like sliced chicken with sesame, or shredded jellyfish are all excellent.

❡ The usual equation for lunch or dinner is one dish per person, plus one other dish. But this is certainly changeable. One Beggar's Chicken, for example, is equal to three other courses. On the other hand, a vegetarian dinner could easily comprise eight platters for a party of four.

❡ In the parade of courses, spicy dishes (say, shrimp [prawns] in chili sauce) should alternate with mild dishes [chicken with almonds]; light dishes (pea tendrils or bean sprouts) with heavier dishes (pork with garlic); dark dishes (dried black Chinese mushrooms) with white dishes (fish with scallions [spring onions]).

❡ The final course may be noodles or soup. With Cantonese foods, which are (or should be) practically greaseless and light, noodles serve as a good contrast. For northern dishes, with their heavier cooking and noodle base, a clear soup is best, perhaps a broth with large black mushrooms. After this, a bowl of fruit, though guests may simply find a fresh pot of tea sufficient.

❡ For Westerners, knowledge of Chinese cuisine has been limited to that of two regions, Guangdong (Canton) in the South, and Beijing (Peking) in the North. Historically, the southerners were the first Chinese immigrants to America and Australia during

the nineteenth century. They left Macau to work in the goldfields and on the railroads, bringing with them not just industry and labor, but food as well.

**Guangdong (Canton)**

❡ With a coastline nearly 1,000 miles (1,600 kilometers) long and a subtropical climate all year round, this southern province is world-famous for its variety of foods. Fruits and teas grow in abundance; birds, swine, beef, and seafood are commonplace; and there is an endless variety of mushrooms. The emphasis is on variety and on fast cooking, bringing the freshest food to the peak of color and taste.

**Shanghai**

❡ Like New York or London, Shanghai has no real cuisine of its own. The metropolis has all the recipes of the Yangtze Valley, but it has absorbed the techniques of other areas of the country.

❡ Freshwater fish and shellfish are a specialty, with an emphasis on eel, shrimp (prawns), and crab. The resulting flavors are generally richer and heavier than those of Cantonese or Pekingese food. Preserved or pickled vegetables are often used, and noodles are served as frequently as rice.

❡ While most of its dishes come from different regions, Shanghai is supposedly home to Beggar's Chicken, Drunken Chicken, and Eight Treasure Duck, as well as preserved foods, like salted fish and dried bamboo shoots and mushrooms.

❡ Nearby are the provinces of Fujian, Jiangxi, and Zhejiang. The main method of cooking here, and in Shanghai, is stewing dishes in soy sauce, known as "red-cooking."

**Beijing and Mongolia**

❡ Bordering on and including the Mongolian desert, the cold dry climate of Beijing limits the availability of many ingredients used elsewhere. But two factors lie in Beijing's favor. First, the Mongols, who ruled China for so long, endowed the Chinese with their own special way of barbecuing and roasting. Second, the emperors welcomed other cuisines of China, and made them their own.

❡ Peking Duck is the most famous dish, but all meats are barbecued or roasted, originally over an open fire, a legacy of the Mongols. Thus there is Mongolian hot-pot, with a profusion of sauces around the lamb. A winter special is sizzling mutton, which comes bubbling to the table with whole scallions (spring onions) and cabbage.

❡ The major vegetable is cabbage, particularly Tianjin cabbage, which is added to soups, meats, and

*Planting rice in Sichuan province. Although not as popular in the North, rice is regarded as China's staple food and is an accompaniment to most dishes. China is the world's biggest producer of this important foodstuff.* LEO MEIER/WELDONS

fish. Since it can be stored during the cold weather, cabbage is practical, nutritious, and ubiquitous.

¶ The biggest contrast to southern cooking is the northern use of wheat and sorghum. Noodles, rolls, pancakes, and meat-filled turnovers originated here, with Tianjin dumplings famous throughout China.

¶ The Beijing people are the only ones who take pride in their desserts. Honeyed apples (or any other fruit coated with sugar and baked), chestnut purée with whipped cream and fruit salads are specials.

### Hangzhou

¶ Marco Polo extolled the variety and abundance of the markets of Hangzhou: "... an abundance of victuals, both wild game and fowls. All sorts of vegetables and fruits, ... huge pears weighing ten pounds [4.5 kilograms] a piece... raisins of excellent quality...every day a vast quantity of fish brought from the ocean...an abundance of lake fish, plump and tasty...spiced rice wine, fresh and cheap..."

¶ Hangzhou in May has the most beautiful aroma in all of China. This is when the Dragon Well tea blooms. Tea is used with delicate foods here, mainly shrimp (prawns), which are fried in tea leaves.

¶ The West Lake, in the center of the city of Hangzhou is China's most romantic spot, and tea-houses dot the islands of the lake. Here are served fish cooked in vinegar, duck with honey stuffing, and a noodle soup with mushrooms.

¶ Hangzhou has two unique culinary features. One is a vegetable that is difficult to obtain but well worth trying: *Shuen choi* is a slippery-smooth vegetable from the mallow family that grows around lakes. It has a mucilaginous coating and a delicate taste. In soups it has a highly sensuous texture. The second is a dish named after a poet, Tung Po pork (Su Tung Po). The pork is braised, then steamed, achieving the soft consistency of bean curd.

### Suzhou

¶ As Suzhou was traditionally the home of scholars, musicians, and talkers, it was inevitably the home of the tea-house *dim sum*, and sweets and pastries made from rice. There are about 50 kinds of pastries, variously colored by their ingredients: Red pastries are made with red rice, yellow with egg yolk, green with cabbage juice, and black with cocoa. Other ingredients include red bean paste, pine nuts, walnuts, sesame seeds and paste, sugar, bean curd, and preserved fruits. They are rarely offered as desserts, but serve as snacks any time of day.

¶ The squirrel fish comes "chattering" (actually sizzling with a pop-pop sound) to the table. Suzhou duck comes braised with almonds. Suzhou eel is topped with chunks of garlic.

¶ Suzhou has some of the most famous jasmine tea in China (60 percent of it is grown in the area), and Suzhou people drink it incessantly. For breakfast, Suzhou has a special "tea egg." The egg is steamed in soy sauce with jasmine tea!

### Sichuan and Hunan

¶ Sichuan food has a real balance of tastes. The hills of this province, bordering Tibet, have a plethora of spices and herbs. Here can be found star anise, fennel seed, chili, cilantro (fresh coriander), sesame, ginger, garlic, five-spice, and a wide selection of black and white peppers, as well as the renowned Sichuan peppercorn.

¶ Ingredients are simmered, stirred, steamed, and smoked. The meat and chicken dishes are often ground (minced), so that they soak up the relatively heavy sauces. The result is that the spices are fully integrated with the dishes.

¶ Chicken and pork are the main meat dishes, since there is little grazing land for lamb, sheep, or cows. In fact, the only beef dishes come from oxen which are used for haulage in the salt mines.

¶ Surprisingly, Sichuan recipes use much fish and shellfish, since the high mountains have great springs, rivers, brooks, and waterfalls, brimming with shrimp (prawns), crab, and fish of all kinds. The fish is steamed with all the spices available.

¶ The main ingredients are numerous. Besides chicken and pork, Sichuanese red rice, bamboo, wheat, corn, sweet potatoes, bananas, lemons, and oranges are abundant. Dumplings are also special, filled mainly with pork.

¶ Nearby Hunan province has good hearty, filling food, which, if anything, is hotter than Sichuan cooking. Typical is Emperor's Chicken with its profusion of ginger.

### Yunnan

¶ Yunnan is known for its Yunnan ham, mushrooms, and the picturesquely titled Crossing Over Bridge Noodles. This consists of noodles, mushrooms, and meats dumped into scalding hot water at the table.

### Teochiu

¶ Teochiu (Chiuchow) people are known as the Sicilians of China. Traders, and sailors, their food can be just as vigorous as they are.

¶ Teochiu restaurants stay open until dawn, mainly

*Tangerines (mandarins) from the South are just one of the ingredients of Chinese cuisine. This barge load of fruit will be sold at market in many parts of the country.* CHINA TOURISM PHOTO LIBRARY/PENG ZHENGE

because the thimble-sized Iron Buddha tea has probably more caffeine than coffee.

❦ The food is rich, sticky, almost sensuous. This is the land of goose heavily seasoned with soy or cooked in its own blood. Teochiu people have a style of satay sauce from their forays to Indonesia. They love sweet-and-sour dishes, deep-fried shrimp (prawn) balls, and crab meat rolls. Whelk is one of their specialties, along with shark fin. Typical of their wild contrasts of cooking are egg noodles, which are served with helpings of both sugar and vinegar.

❦ For dessert, sweetened bird's nest or sugary buns with red-bean fillings are served. They even have a recipe for taro root—covered and crystallized with sugar. Passionate food indeed!

**Overseas Chinese dishes**

❦ Every country has its own distinctive Chinese cuisine, some of it quite remarkable. The most "un-Chinese" Chinese food is that of the Chinese who in the nineteenth century settled in Malaya and Singapore. This is Nyonya food, which uses both Chinese cooking methods and spices from Southeast Asia. (The word "Nyonya" comes from an obscure Chinese word meaning "upper-class housewife.") Nyonya dishes are influenced by Thai and Malaysian cuisine, with chilis, lime, and tamarind pulp.

❦ Another hybrid is the cuisine of Portuguese Macau, which has been described as Mediterranean Chinese. The main influence is Cantonese Chinese but with a lot more: Portuguese port wine, cilantro (fresh coriander), Mediterranean codfish or sardines, pigeons raised in China. To a famous Portuguese stew are added Chinese cabbage leaves and chunks of pork with ginger and cilantro (fresh coriander). Local squid or crabs are stuffed with mild Portuguese cheese and ham.

❦ One could say that Hakka food is a style of "overseas Chinese," since Hakka people are constantly migrating from northern China. The cuisine, therefore, is usually pickled or preserved. The food is earthy peasant fare, simple but filled with ingenuity.

❦ Hakka people make a unique tripe dish. It is mildly curried, then placed in a betel-nut sauce. The taste is sweet, chewy—but awfully strange. More to common liking is a Hakka version of sauerkraut: sliced pork with cabbage, which is left to dry in the sun and then packed into jars to be pickled.

❦ Whatever the region, Chinese food creates its own atmosphere: For the eyes are the white of porcelain, for the nose is the aroma of jasmine tea. For the touch are wooden chopsticks. For the taste buds, one cannot begin to describe so many sensations. Even the sense of hearing is catered for: The chattering and sizzling of Chinese food is as music.

# OCCASIONS

# OCCASIONS

IKE RICE AND TEA, THE WORD "BANQUET" SEEMS SYNONYMOUS WITH CHINA. VISITING DIGNITARIES, DIPLOMATS, POP stars, and travel agents are inevitably treated to a Chinese banquet. New Year's Day is always celebrated with a family banquet. A meal in a Chinese restaurant for more than six people may also be called a banquet. The Chinese word actually suggests something modest: *Yin wui* which simply means "dinner gathering." But the result is far more extravagant than anything known in the West, and has an etiquette all its own.

¶ In the old days, the host would go around the table picking out the "best" parts of a dish for his guests. Today waiters serve this purpose for the first serving; after that, it's each guest for him- or herself. No one would dare take the final piece from a platter, which would be considered ill-mannered. When the host stands up, he is signifying that the banquet has ended. It would be improper to linger any longer at the table.

¶ While the main purpose of dinner banquets is to honor and impress the important guests, festive banquets are governed by ancient ritual. One week before Chinese New Year, for instance, the family gathers before their effigy or plaque representing the Kitchen God, and smears his lips with honey. This is to induce him to say only good things when he reports to Heaven on what has happened during the year. On New Year's Eve, a table is spread with special foods, so that the deity will get a good impression of the family. All New Year food must be prepared in advance, since no knives or scissors are allowed in use during the festivities; that would denote a martial atmosphere.

¶ The table itself is elaborate with symbols. Vegetarian dishes on the first-day feast are used to purify body and soul, a great nine-course banquet on the second (nine is a lucky number, signifying everlasting life and plenty). A rooster carved from vegetables might be the centerpiece, symbolizing New Year, and fertility. Or it might be a carp to symbolize persistence.

¶ Peaches also predominate. The peach is a symbol of marriage and of spring, and the Chinese name for the fruit is a pun on the word "million," so it also stands for prosperity. The New Year rice cake is sweet—to show an amiable disposition; sticky—to hold friends together, and round—to show the complete family circle.

¶ A rice cake, wrapped in bamboo leaves, not a banquet, is the food that symbolizes the annual Dragon Boat races, and in the fall, families celebrate the Moon Festival by going to the peaks of hills with the family to worship the moon. A golden-brown pastry filled with a purée of red beans, lotus paste, and salted duck egg, is the traditional Moon Cake for this festival.

## SHEUNG TONG DUNG CHEE

### SHARK FIN IN SUPERIOR BROTH

*A banquet without shark fin is not a banquet at all. It is the crowning glory. Nothing else need be said.*

1 lb (500 g) top-quality shark fin
15 cups (3¾ qt/3.75 l) water
4 oz (125 g) ginger
4 scallions (spring onions)
2 tablespoons Chinese rice wine
4 cups (1 qt/1 l) Superior Broth (see recipe, page 75), heated to boiling
2 tablespoons shredded Chinese or Virginia ham

SERVES 4–6

❡ Soak the shark fin in water to cover overnight.
❡ In a very large pan, bring the water to a boil and add the ginger, scallions, and wine. Add the shark

*Left: Sheung Tong Dung Chee; center: Sheung Tong Yin Wor; right: Sheung Tong Conpoy Dong Qua*

fin and simmer for 6 hours. Remove from the heat, cover, and let steep for 1 hour.

❡ Remove the shark fin from the pan and drain. By this time, the shark fin needles should be soft and easily broken with a fingernail.

❡ Place the shark fin in a large soup tureen with a cover. Add the broth and cover. Place the tureen on a steaming rack in a pan of boiling water and steam for 1 hour. Divide the soup into bowls, sprinkle the ham on top, and serve.

## SHEUNG TONG YIN WOR

### *BIRD'S NEST IN SUPERIOR BROTH*

*This is one of the more luxurious banquet dishes—and one of the most expensive, as birds' nests can cost up to $1,000 per pound (500 g). The nests come from the Gulf of Siam, and it is thought that the tradition of eating them started in the Ming dynasty, when the kings of Vietnam and Ayudhya (in Thailand) began sending tributes, including this rarity, to the emperors of China.*

*2 oz (60 g) dried superior-quality edible bird's nest, soaked in 2 cups (16 fl oz/500 ml) warm water for 12 hours and drained*
*4 cups (1 qt/1 l) Superior Broth (see recipe, page 75)*
*2 tablespoons shredded Chinese or Virginia ham*

*SERVES 4–6*

❡ Place the bird's nest on a plate and put the plate on a steaming rack in a pan of boiling water. Cover and steam for 30 minutes. Remove and set aside.

❡ In a separate large pan, bring the broth to a boil. Add the bird's nest and cook for 3 minutes. Divide the bird's nest and broth into bowls, sprinkle the ham on top, and serve.

## SHEUNG TONG CONPOY DONG QUA

### *WINTER MELON AND CONPOY IN SUPERIOR BROTH*

*This is one of those rare dishes that is fine enough to be served at a banquet and easy enough to enjoy at home. Winter melon is also known as wax melon and is good for "air-conditioning" the body during the summer.*

*1 lb (500 g) winter melon, peeled, seeded, and cut into ¼-inch (0.5-cm) slivers*
*4–6 large conpoy (dried sea scallops), soaked in warm water to cover for 4–5 hours, and drained*
*4 cups (1 qt/1 l) Superior Broth (see recipe, page 75), heated to boiling*
*1 teaspoon Chinese rice wine*

*SERVES 4–6*

❡ Blanch the winter melon in boiling water for 2 minutes. Remove and drain.

❡ Place the winter melon and conpoy in a large soup tureen with a cover. Add the broth and wine, and cover. Place the tureen on a steaming rack in a pan of boiling water and steam for 1 hour. Divide the soup into bowls and serve.

## FOOD AS MEDICINE

The Chinese concept of food-medicine is a powerful mix of legend, art, and actual curative powers. Thus, the wild herbs of the mountainsides have been extolled as much for their restorative powers as for their flavor. And because

the winds of the Gobi Desert in Mongolia are noted for being "healthier" than the winds of the cities, so meats hanging in shops traditionally face North.

The Chinese still preserve many of their ancient beliefs. Legends tell

of sages being magically cured of illnesses by drinking a potion of wild herbs. Today, Chinese herbal medicine is being recognized around the world for its efficacy. Thousands of years of research and detailed

documentation have been dedicated to this ancient craft, and medicinal properties have been discovered in the most unusual sources—herbs, mushrooms, horns, and antlers, "secret" roots and tubers, and insects. They

revolves around what is known as *yin* and *yang* — the masculine and feminine influences. It deals with the five energies of food: cold, hot, warm, cool, and neutral. But these adjectives rarely refer to sensations; rather they refer to the metaphysical properties of food.

Tea, for instance, has a cold energy. By drinking it, the heat of the body is cooled. Bamboo, bitter gourds, and most fruits also have a cold energy. Peppers are naturally hot, along with cinnamon bark and soy bean oil.

In ancient times, anyone suffering from, say, a bad cold would prepare a bowl of soup with ginger and drink it hot. The pungent flavor made them perspire, as the Chinese believe that ginger has a "warm" energy that heats the body. The ideal diet, then, is one that has a series of balances: the philosophical *yin* and *yang*, the medically cold and hot, the flavorful pungent and the bland, as well as a balance of colors, shapes, and textures.

Most of these rules were formulated informally from the earliest times, but in the T'ang dynasty, the encyclopedic *Pen T'sao* or "herbal" was written, specifying thousands of herbs, spices, meats, and vegetables to be used medically. In the back room of every Chinese herbalist, the pages of this tome are still consulted.

Today, the official Nutrition Research Institute of China develops recipes intended to enhance "beauty and strength." Their ingredients might be ordinary foods, but the

are dried and ground, shaved, chopped, or sliced to take, usually as an infusion, as the cure for a multitide of ailments.

The philosophy of Chinese food-medicine involves a series of equations. Basically it

combination of ingredients is designed to add or subtract the energy, warmth, cold, or pungency that causes disease.

Today's Chinese still use food as one aspect of medicine. They boil roots such as *dang gui*, and licorice with meats; they add seed pods, fruit, and nuts like wolfberry, red dates (jujubes), and lotus seeds to desserts.

Some of the more important ingredients are:

**Apricot seeds** (bitter almonds): The cure-all for coughs and asthma.

**Bird's nest:** Important for bronchial diseases, and good for the complexion.

**Black chicken:** Has noted aphrodisiac qualities.

**Carrot:** Improves the eyesight.

**Garlic:** The ultimate anti-rheumatism food, promoting regulation of the blood and digestive system.

**Ginger:** Excellent for the common cold.

**Ginseng:** For vitality, sexual energy, a cure for frigidity, a herb for recuperation.

**Mutton:** After childbirth, Chinese women will eat mutton for replenishment.

**Oysters:** Not, as the West opines, an aphrodisiac; in China they are considered a food to regulate the

metabolism.

**Pepper:** Effective in curing stomach troubles, and diarrhea.

**Pigeon:** Meat and eggs are taken by women during the menstrual cycle.

**Sea slugs:** Said to increase male virility.

**Snake bile:** A cure-all for a multitude of ailments.

**Tangerine (mandarin) peel, dried:** A "cool" food that neutralizes the unbalancing "poisons" of shellfish.

**Walnut:** Both the oil and the nut are used to compensate for general physical losses, a vitamin cure for weaknesses.

**White fungus:** Clears the complexion.

**Wine:** A few glasses of rice wine, with honey mixed in, is the cure for rheumatism, muscular spasms, and chest pains.

*1. walnuts; 2. bitter almonds; 3. wolfberries; 4. wormwood; 5. white fungus with wolfberries; 6. walnut cream pudding; 7. white fungus; 8. red dates (jujubes); 9. dried lotus root; 10. sea cucumber; 11. black mushrooms; 12. dried tangerine (mandarin) peel; 13. Chinese wine; 14. dried lotus seeds; 15. fish-stewed pigeon with dang gui; 16. ginger; 17. Chinese tea; 18. ginseng, 19. dang gui*

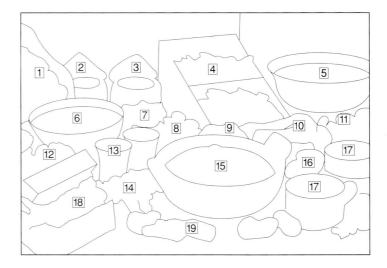

# KUM WAH YUK TSUI GAI

## *STEAMED CHICKEN AND HAM WITH KALE*

*Originally, this Cantonese dish was served with mustard greens, but I prefer kale. The vegetable, though, is mainly there as decoration, since this is a banquet dish and it must look as beautiful as it tastes.*

For the marinade:
*1 teaspoon salt*
*1 tablespoon Chinese rice wine*
*1 teaspoon sesame oil*
For the chicken:
*½ chicken, about 1½ lb (750 g)*
*3 oz (90 g) Chinese or Virginia ham, cut into 2 × ½-inch (5 × 1-cm) strips*
*3–4 tablespoons groundnut (peanut) oil*
*6 kale or mustard green stems, trimmed*
*salt*
*1 cup (8 fl oz/250 ml) water*
*1½ cups (12 fl oz/375 ml) chicken broth (stock)*
*1 tablespoon light soy sauce*
*1 teaspoon sugar*
*1 teaspoon Chinese rice wine*
*1 tablespoon cornstarch (cornflour)*

SERVES 4–6

¶ For the marinade: Combine all the ingredients in a bowl. Rub the marinade over the chicken. Bring a large pan of water to a boil, place a steaming rack in the middle, and steam the chicken over medium heat for 18–20 minutes. Remove the chicken from the pan. When cool, chop the chicken into 2 × ½-inch (5 × 1-cm) pieces. Arrange, alternating with ham, in 3 rows on a serving platter.
¶ Heat 2–3 tablespoons of oil in a wok or skillet (frying pan). Add the kale and stir-fry for 30 seconds. Add the salt and the water, and cook over medium heat for 3 minutes. Remove, drain, and place the kale beside the chicken and ham.
¶ Mix all the remaining ingredients in a bowl.
¶ Heat the remaining 1–2 tablespoons oil in the wok. Add the broth mixture and bring to a boil. Pour over the meats and kale, and serve.

# TSUI PAY GAI

## *CRISP CHICKEN*

*This is a popular restaurant dish, whose original name is "Crispy Skin Chicken." It is almost essential as a banquet dish in southern China, and most chefs will tell you it is*

---

### GINSENG
*A root vegetable, Panax ginseng often grows in the shade of oak or chestnut trees, or beneath bamboo mats that shade the plant from the sun. In China, ginseng is usually too expensive to be used merely for food. But it is sometimes made into a soup that is kept warm and sipped over a whole day. In parts of Manchuria and Korea, another luxury dish is made by stuffing a whole chicken with ginseng, then boiling it. The uses of ginseng, which contains B vitamins and enzymes, are varied: It is touted as everything from a general pick-me-up to a potent aphrodisiac.*

---

*impossible for an amateur to get the right balance between crisp skin and tender meat. While the process is not secret, it is long and tedious. Still, if you follow the recipe—with no shortcuts—it will assuredly come out right.*

*1 chicken, about 3 lb (1.5 kg)*
*1½ teaspoons salt*
*1 teaspoon five-spice powder*
*¼ cup (2 fl oz/60 ml) maltose or dark corn syrup*
*¾ cup (6 fl oz/185 ml) white vinegar*
*2–3 teaspoons aromatic red vinegar*
*⅓ cup (3 fl oz/90 ml) water*
*8 cups (2 qt/2 l) groundnut (peanut) oil*
*juice of 2 lemons*
For the dip:
*2 tablespoons salt*
*1 teaspoon five-spice powder*

SERVES 8–10

¶ Clean the chicken and pat dry. Tie a piece of string around the neck and hang to dry for 45 minutes.
¶ Baste the chicken with boiling water several times. Rub the salt and five-spice powder in the cavity.
¶ Melt the maltose with the vinegars and the water in a pan. Baste the chicken with the mixture until the surface is well covered. Hang for 2 hours.
¶ Heat the oil in a large pan over medium heat till lightly smoking. Fry the chicken for 6–7 minutes, turning frequently and avoiding direct contact with the bottom of the pot. Holding the string, lift the chicken out of the pot and baste with oil until the skin turns golden brown. Set aside and let cool.
¶ When cool, chop the chicken into bite-size pieces, arrange on a serving platter, and serve with the lemon juice and dip.
¶ For the dip: In a clean pan, stir-fry the salt until lightly browned. Remove from the heat, add the five-spice powder, and stir to mix.

*Top: Tsui Pay Gai; bottom: Kum Wah Yuk Tsui Gai*

# HOU TIN NGARP

### ROAST PEKING DUCK

*This recipe is the most practical way of preparing this classic dish at home. If you follow the directions carefully, this can taste just as good as the duck served in restaurants.*

1 duck, about 6 lb (3 kg), with the head attached
12–16 cups (3–4 qt/3–4 l) boiling water
½ cup (4 fl oz/125 g) aromatic or cider vinegar
1 cup (8 fl oz/250 ml) water

5 tablespoons honey
¼ cup (2 fl oz/60 ml) hoisin sauce
1 tablespoon sesame oil
48 pieces scallion (spring onion), white part only, 2 inches (5 cm) long
48 sticks cucumber, 2 inches (5 cm) long
36 Chinese Pancakes (see recipe, page 231)

SERVES 10–12

❡ Clean the duck inside and out, and pat dry.
❡ Close the cavity of the duck with a skewer. Cut off the wing tips. Make a cut in the neck. Insert a tube and blow, pulling the skin from the meat at the

*Top: Yeung Chung Ngarp; bottom: Hou Tin Ngarp*

same time, to inflate the duck skin. Tie a piece of string tightly beneath the opening on the neck.

❡ Place the duck on a rack in the sink. Pour one-fourth of the boiling water over the duck. Turn over and pour another fourth of the boiling water. Wait for 5 seconds. Repeat the process then rinse with cold water. Pat dry.

❡ Mix the vinegar, water, and honey in a bowl, and brush the mixture over the duck. Tie another piece of string around the neck and hang the duck to dry in a well-ventilated place for 10 hours or more.

❡ Preheat the oven to 400°F (200°C/Gas 6). Place the duck, breast side up, on a rack over a roasting

pan. Reduce the heat to 350°F (180°C/Gas 4). Turn the duck at 15-minute intervals and cook for 1 hour.

❡ Carve off the crispy skin, then carve the meat into thin slivers and place on a warm serving platter. To serve, spread 1 teaspoon of the *hoisin* sauce in the middle of a pancake. Add some skin and meat, and a piece of scallion and cucumber. Fold the pancake into an envelope and eat with the fingers.

## YEUNG CHUNG NGARP

*BRAISED DUCK STUFFED WITH ONION*

*This is a relatively complicated dish (though any Cantonese household could make it) and was probably reserved for a festival. The meat is steamed for several hours, making it tender enough to come right off the bone, and flavored with a light, natural sauce—a really beautiful dish.*

For the duck:
1 tablespoon salt
1 ½ teaspoons five-spice powder
1 teaspoon pepper
1 duck, about 4 lb (2 kg), cleaned and patted dry
2 tablespoons dark soy sauce
4 cups (1 qt/1 l) groundnut (peanut) oil
3 onions, cut into rings
For the sauce:
2 tablespoons oyster sauce
2 teaspoons dark soy sauce
2 teaspoons Chinese rice wine
1 tablespoon cornstarch (cornflour)

*SERVES 8–10*

❡ Rub the salt, five-spice powder, and pepper inside the cavity of the duck. Rub the dark soy sauce over the skin. Let dry for 2 hours.

❡ Heat the oil in a wok or skillet (frying pan) and fry the duck until browned, basting with the hot oil. Remove the duck from the pan and set aside.

❡ Drain all but 2 tablespoons oil from the wok and reheat. Add the onions, and stir-fry until translucent. Let cool, then stuff into the cavity of the duck.

❡ Place the duck in a deep dish. Put a steaming rack in a pan over boiling water and place the dish with the duck on top. Cover and steam over medium heat for 2 ½ hours. Reserve any liquid from the dish

❡ Remove the onions from the duck cavity and place on a serving platter. Chop the duck into bite-size pieces and place on top of the onion.

❡ In a small pan, mix the reserved liquid with the sauce ingredients and bring to a boil. Pour over the duck and serve.

## LO SUEN DAI TZE

---

### STIR-FRIED SCALLOPS WITH ASPARAGUS

*This is more of a Hong Kong than a Chinese recipe, as scallops have traditionally been very rare in China itself. The Chinese use their white asparagus, but I prefer the green kind in this recipe, which gives a stronger taste and texture.*

For the marinade:
1/5 egg white
1 teaspoon salt

1 teaspoon sugar
1 teaspoon cornstarch (cornflour)
For the scallops:
18 scallops
6 cups (1 1/2 qt/1.5 l) water
6 stalks fresh green asparagus, lower stem peeled, cut into
    1-inch (2.5-cm) lengths
3–4 tablespoons groundnut (peanut) oil
1 1/2 garlic cloves, finely chopped
1 1/2 slices ginger, finely chopped
6 tablespoons chicken broth (stock)
1 tablespoon light soy sauce

*Top: Jing Lung Har; bottom: Lo Suen Dai Tze*

1 teaspoon oyster sauce
½ teaspoon salt
½ teaspoon sugar
1 teaspoon cornstarch (cornflour)
1 teaspoon Chinese rice wine

*SERVES 4–6*

❡ For the marinade: Mix all the ingredients in a bowl.
❡ Marinate the scallops for 30 minutes.
❡ Bring the water to a rapid boil in a large pan. Add the scallops, reduce the heat to medium, and poach them for 30 seconds.

❡ Remove the scallops, drain, and set aside.
❡ Drain all but 2 cups (16 fl oz/500 ml) water from the pan and bring to a rapid boil. Add the asparagus and cook for 2 minutes. Remove, drain, and set aside.
❡ Heat the oil in a wok or skillet (frying pan) and add the garlic and ginger. When the aroma rises, add the scallops and asparagus. Stir-fry over very high heat for 30 seconds.
❡ Mix the broth, soy sauce, oyster sauce, salt, sugar, and cornstarch in a bowl. Add to the wok and stir-fry for 15 seconds. Add the wine and serve.

## JING LUNG HAR

### *STEAMED LOBSTER*

*We use spiny lobster in China, from the South China Sea, but the big-clawed lobsters from Europe and America are just as good. (But don't use frozen lobster, please.) There are many lobster dishes in China, but this one has a sauce, originating from Teochiu, which is sweet and has the aroma of the wine.*

1 live lobster, about 2 lb (1 kg)
6 cups (1½ qt/1.5 l) water
½ cup (4 fl oz/125 ml) groundnut (peanut) oil
2 garlic cloves, crushed
6 slices ginger
1 cup (8 fl oz/250 ml) chicken broth (stock)
1 tablespoon light soy sauce
1 teaspoon dark soy sauce
1½ teaspoons sugar
1 tablespoon Chinese rice wine
1½ teaspoons cornstarch (cornflour)

*SERVES 6–8*

❡ Two hours in advance, place the lobster in the freezer to kill it. Remove.
❡ Place the lobster on a cutting board, belly down, and cut off its tail. Turn the lobster over, split lengthwise in half and then chop into 1-inch (2.5-cm) pieces. Detach the large claws and split lengthwise in half. Arrange the pieces, shell side down, in a single layer on a large platter.
❡ Bring the water to a rapid boil in a wok or large pan. Place a steaming rack in the middle and set the platter with the lobster on top. Cover and steam over high heat for 10 minutes. Remove, drain all liquid from the platter, and set aside.
❡ Carefully heat the oil in a wok until smoking. Add the garlic and ginger, and pour over the lobster. Drain the excess oil from the platter and discard the ginger and garlic. Set aside.
❡ Mix all the remaining ingredients in a pan and bring to a boil. Pour over the lobster and serve.

# Herbs and Spices

Buddhist monks arriving in China in the third to the fifth centuries brought exotic spices with them from India. Middle Eastern countries, anxious to trade with China, introduced spinach, coriander, almonds, and hot peppers. Cloves and other fragrant spices came in from Vietnam and Indonesia. Indigenous species include a type of cardamom, Sichuan peppercorns, cassia bark, and star anise. Rarely is China's food as highly spiced as that of, for example, India. Instead, they prefer subtle intonations of aromatic spices in their food, and use cassia or cinnamon bark, Sichuan peppercorns, and several anise or licorice-flavored spices to achieve this. Herbs are not a dominant element of Chinese cooking. They rely mainly on various members of the onion family and the fresh pungency of cilantro (fresh coriander), and of course, ginger which is indispensable to good Chinese cooking.

## SPICES

**"Five spices"** (*beung nu fun*): Five-spice powder is used both as a flavoring and a condiment. It is an age-old formula which combines three spices native to China, star anise, cassia bark, and Sichuan peppercorns, together with fennel seeds and cloves from the nearby Spice Islands. As a condiment, it is mixed with salt that has been roasted in a dry pan, to make an aromatic dip for roasted meat.

**Star anise** (*bhat ghok*): These dried seed pods, gathered from a tree of the Magnolia family, are star shaped. When dried, the pods split open to reveal a single, flat, glossy brown seed in each point of the star. Star anise has a pronounced licorice flavor. It is added, whole or broken, to stewed, braised, and simmered dishes.

**Cassia** (*jou kuei*): The fragrant, rough bark of the cassia is used in braised and simmered dishes, and has extensive application in medicine. Cinnamon, which is more expensive, is also grown in southern China. It has smooth bark which curls into tight "quills" when dried.

**Sichuan peppercorns** (*faa jiu*): These are not related to black peppercorns, but are the aromatic, pink-brown seeds from the prickly ash tree (*xanthoxylum piperitum*). Chefs in Sichuan, their native province, prize them for their peppery taste, which if taken in excess can cause a numbing sensation on the tongue and lips. Ground, the powder can be sprinkled over a dish as a condiment, or mixed with heated salt to make an aromatic dip known as pepper-salt, for roasted meats.

**Salt:** The province of Sichuan has a number of natural salt deposits that provide a blackish, richly flavored salt. Certain dips, notably the pepper-salt that accompanies Sichuan roast duck, have a stronger, deeper flavor if Sichuan black salt is used.

**Ginger** (*sang keong*): In China, ginger classifies more as a herb than a spice, as it is used fresh, or pickled, never powdered. Vibrant, peppery, distinctive, it is one of the staples of the Chinese diet and is used in many dishes, sweet and savory. Fresh root ginger is peeled, then sliced, shredded, grated, or chopped, or just simply smashed with the side of a heavy cleaver to release its fragrant juices. It is also pickled in brine, rice wine, or rice vinegar, the later making it turn a light pink color, to use in cooking or as an accompaniment to roasted meats or 100-year-old eggs.

## HERBS

**Cilantro** (fresh coriander, *yuen sai*): The attractive leaves of cilantro resemble parsley, somewhat flattened. But there the similarity ends, for their flavor is pungent and strong, quite repellent to some, revered by others. Fronds of cilantro, with their long slender stems and sparse spread of leaves, make an attractive garnish which is used on many dishes. It marries well with fish, helping to overcome "fishy" odors, and is floated, chopped, in sauces and soups.

**Garlic chives** (*gau choi*): Because they are a member of the garlic family, garlic chives are good for invigorating the blood. *Gau choi* is used in fillings for dumplings or simmered in broths, and sometimes used, chopped, as a garnish. They are added to stir-fries, particularly with beef. It has attractive flower buds, shaped like miniature lotus blossoms, which are pickled in vinegar in the province of Shandong.

**Scallions/spring onions** (*kiu choi*): These slender onion shoots are invaluable in stir-fries as they cook quickly and their mild flavor does not overpower a dish. The green stems, sliced, shredded, or curled by soaking in iced water, are used as a garnish. Jiangxi is the main scallion-growing province in China.

## CHILIS/HOT PEPPERS

There are two schools of thought on how the chili pepper arrived in Asia. One theory is that chilis were brought by the Spanish, who acquired the New World plant after one of Columbus's journeys. Another says that the chili appeared around 1580, brought by the Portuguese to Macao. It became indispensable to the Sichuan style of cooking, and is used, in moderation, in most other parts of China. Throughout China, one can see peppers being sun-dried, spread on bamboo matting or hanging from rafters, to catch the sun and air.

The variety of chilis is vast, and they are used in several forms. The whole fresh, red or green pods are added directly to dishes, or are chopped and seeded for soups and stir-fries. In dried form, they are used whole, chopped, ground to a powder, or crushed to flakes. Chili, steeped in vegetable oil, makes the pungent bright amber-red chili oil, that adds tone and vibrancy to many dishes. Chili is mashed and combined with salt and fermented soy beans to make a chili paste, or mashed with garlic and salt to make a potent seasoning.

***Tse tin sui*** or "point to the sky peppers": The Chinese use these for their chili sauce which is very strong, though not quite to the potency of tabasco. The peppers cluster erect and slender, each about 1 1/4 inches (3 cm) long.

***Ngau kok tsui*** or "cow's horn peppers": More potent than *tse tin sui*, these hot chili peppers are used for flavoring pungent Sichuan dishes, and are also added to pickles.

*1. Cilantro; 2. garlic chives in bud; 3. garlic chives; 4. five-spice powder; 5. cassia bark; 6. Sichuan peppercorns; 7. fennel seeds; 8. dried chilis; 9. star anise*

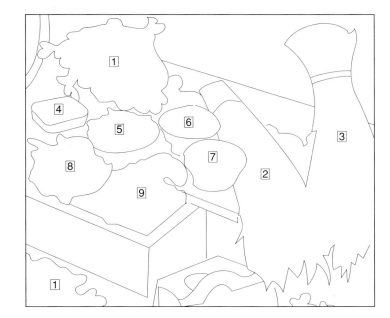

## JIN DAI HAR

*PAN-FRIED JUMBO SHRIMP*

*This is a classic dish, served all over China. I've given a Western-influenced version of it, adding ketchup. But since this has been used in South China for about a century, it is now almost authentic.*

4–6 uncooked jumbo shrimp (green king prawns)
2 cups (16 fl oz/500 ml) groundnut (peanut) oil
1 teaspoon finely chopped garlic
1 teaspoon finely chopped ginger
2 tablespoons chicken broth (stock)
1 tablespoon ketchup (tomato sauce)
1 tablespoon light soy sauce
1 teaspoon dark soy sauce
2¹⁄₂ teaspoons cornstarch (cornflour)
1 teaspoon Chinese rice wine

*SERVES 2–4*

❡ Cut the head and legs off the shrimp and discard. Clean, but don't peel. Cut the body into 2-inch (5-cm) pieces, pat dry, and dust with cornstarch. Set aside.
❡ Heat the oil until very hot in a wok or skillet (frying pan). Reduce the heat slightly and fry the shrimp for 2 minutes. Remove the shrimp from the wok and drain.
❡ Drain all but 1 tablespoon oil from the wok and fry the shrimp over medium heat until lightly browned on both sides. Add the garlic and ginger.
❡ Mix the broth, ketchup, soy sauces, and 1¹⁄₂ teaspoons of the cornstarch in a bowl. When the aroma rises from the wok, add the broth mixture and stir. Simmer over low heat for 15 seconds. Turn the heat to high. Add the wine and serve.

## HO YHU BOU PIN

*ABALONE SLIVERS IN OYSTER SAUCE*

*Boiling the abalone in the can helps remove the rubbery texture from the canned fish, which many people find objectionable. If you are lucky enough to buy abalone fresh, simmer it in water for about 4–5 hours. Even though abalone isn't even found in China (it comes from Japan and Mexico), it is considered one of the great delicacies of Chinese cooking.*

1 can (13¹⁄₂ oz/425 g) abalone
1 cup (8 fl oz/250 ml) cold water
1¹⁄₂ cups (12 fl oz/375 ml) chicken broth (stock)
4 slices ginger

¹⁄₂ teaspoon salt
¹⁄₄ cup (2 fl oz/60 ml) groundnut (peanut) oil
6 stalks fresh green asparagus, lower stem peeled
1 tablespoon oyster sauce
¹⁄₂ teaspoon sugar
1 teaspoon cornstarch (cornflour)
1 teaspoon finely chopped ginger
1 teaspoon finely chopped garlic
1 teaspoon Chinese rice wine

*SERVES 4–6*

*Top: Jin Dai Har; bottom: Ho Yhu Bou Pin*

❡ Put the can of abalone in a pan and add water to cover 3–4 inches (8–10 cm) above the can. Bring the water to a boil and boil for 2 hours over medium–low heat. (Do not let the water dry up, as it will cause the can to explode.) Remove the pan from the heat and remove the can when cool. Open the can and cut the abalone into ¼-inch (0.5-cm) thick slivers.

❡ Bring the cold water and ¾ cup (6 fl oz/185 ml) broth to a boil in a pan. Add the ginger, salt, 1 tablespoon oil, and the asparagus, and return to a boil. Lower the heat to medium, cover, and cook for

7 minutes. Remove and drain. Arrange the asparagus on a serving platter and set aside.

❡ Mix the remaining broth with the oyster sauce, sugar, and cornstarch in a bowl and set aside.

❡ Heat the remaining 3 tablespoons oil in a wok or skillet (frying pan). Add the ginger and garlic. When the aroma rises, add the broth mixture. Add the abalone, stirring until each slice is coated with sauce. Lower the heat and simmer for 30 seconds. Turn the heat to high and add the wine. Pour over the asparagus and serve.

# EQUIPMENT

The Chinese kitchen requires minimal equipment. In ancient times, cooks used just two pots: A *fu* or cauldron for boiling, and a *tseng* or steamer (used over the *fu*) for steaming or cooking grain. The wok only came into use around the tenth century, opening up new possibilities for cooking: Stir-frying, deep-frying, steaming, poaching, and boiling could all be done in this one versatile, fuel-efficient pan. Modern electric, aluminum, stainless steel, or copper woks seldom offer advantages over the old iron wok—they heat too slowly, burn quickly, do not disperse the heat evenly. A wok cover, dome-shaped, a long-handled square spatula and a wire or perforated metal scoop are essential equipment to partner the wok. A ladle and a pair of long wooden chopsticks, or normal eating chopsticks (*fi-tze*), complete the wok cooking requirements.

Gas heat is best with the wok, as the flame can be instantly adjusted to requirement. Electric stoves can be used by setting the wok on a metal ring adaptor over the element, but it is a poor second best. Flat-based woks are more suitable for use with an electric cooker.

The next acquisition for the Chinese kitchen would be bamboo steamers. Inexpensive and available in most Chinese stores, these baskets stack one atop the other for cooking several different foods at once. They are used in a wok, or in a large metal steamer. As the bamboo heats and moistens, it releases certain of its natural woody aromas, giving the food an extra dimension of flavor. Tiered aluminum steamers are useful for steaming whole chickens or fish, or plated foods. Steaming can also be done in a wok, the plate standing on a metal or bamboo rack.

Another essential piece of equipment is a sand or clay pot for making casseroles, soups, and dishes that require long cooking times. These pots, made of a light porous clay, come in many sizes. They should be soaked before the first use, and although they can withstand a gas or wood fire flame, may be unsuccessful over an electric element.

But before any food reaches the pans and steamers described above, they must first be prepared; and here the Chinese cleaver or "chopper" does its work. A skilled Chinese cook needs no more than one heavy-duty and one lightweight cleaver to perform all of the cutting, slicing chopping, peeling, mincing, smashing, and cubing needed in the kitchen. The speed at which this apparently unwieldly implement is manipulated, and the degree of accuracy in slicing and shredding, is astonishing. A soft wood chopping block accompanies the "chopper."

One piece of modern equipment that has invaded virtually every Chinese home is the electric rice cooker. It cooks perfect rice every time, so its main advantage is that it frees the cook to concentrate on the meat and vegetables.

Other items a cook might use include a double-boil pot or Yunnan steam pot for use inside a steamer; and a Mongolian hot-pot or *ho gu*. A range of twisted wire scoops and baskets for retrieving foods from soup or deep oil, or for heating noodles, a double "basket" fryer for making edible bird's nests and baskets from shredded yam, potato, or noodles, and a little metal or clay pot in which certain foods can be cooked and taken straight to the table, would complete a well-stocked Chinese kitchen.

*1. tiered steamer; 2. steamer baskets; 3. so po clay pots; 4. selection of cleavers; 5. vegetable parer; 6. Chinese scissors; 7. Chinese wok, stand, and wok utensils (spatula, ladle, chopsticks); 8. selection of wire and metal oil skimmers, noodle baskets, and "noodle nest" basket*

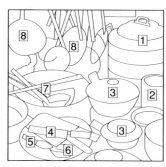

*Top: For Tsui Juen Pak; bottom: Hai Wong Sin Ku*

# FOR TSUI JUEN PAK

### BRAISED CHINESE CABBAGE WITH HAM

*An easy, lovely dish. In the old days, we used to think that the fat of the ham was the most important part. But now we use lean ham.*

3–4 tablespoons groundnut (peanut) oil
3–4 slices ginger
2 garlic cloves, crushed

1 lb (500 g) Chinese cabbage, cleaned and cut into
   ¹⁄₂- x 4-inch (1- x 10-cm) strips
2 cups (16 fl oz/500 ml) chicken broth (stock)
2 oz (60 g) Chinese or Virginia ham, cut into
   ¹⁄₈- x 2 ¹⁄₂-inch (0.25- x 6-cm) slices
1 teaspoon cornstarch (cornflour), diluted in
   1 tablespoon water
¹⁄₂ teaspoon dark soy sauce
1 teaspoon Chinese rice wine

*SERVES 4–6*

Heat the oil in a wok or skillet (frying pan) and fry the ginger and garlic until it is lightly browned. Add the cabbage and stir-fry over high heat for a few minutes, until it becomes soft. Add the broth and place the ham on top. Bring to a boil, cover, and simmer over medium heat until the liquid is reduced by one-third.

Remove the ham and set aside.

Mix the cornstarch and soy sauce, and stir into the wok. Add the wine. Transfer the cabbage to a serving platter, arrange the ham on top, and serve.

## HAI WONG SIN KU

*STIR-FRIED MUSHROOMS WITH CRAB MEAT AND CORAL SAUCE*

*If you have trouble obtaining coral (roe), just do without. But do not substitute caviar (hot caviar is terrible!).*

*1 live female crab, about 12 oz (375 g)*
*1 tablespoon Chinese rice wine*
*6 cups (1 1/2 qt/1.5 l) water*
*1 lb (500 g) straw mushrooms*
*6 tablespoons groundnut (peanut) oil*
*1 1/2 teaspoons finely chopped garlic*
*1 1/2 teaspoons finely chopped ginger*
*1 tablespoon oyster sauce*
*1 teaspoon salt*
*1 cup (8 fl oz/250 ml) chicken broth (stock)*
*1 tablespoon light soy sauce*
*1 teaspoon aromatic or cider vinegar*
*1/4 teaspoon pepper*
*1 teaspoon cornstarch (cornflour)*
*1 egg white*

*SERVES 4–6*

Place the crab, belly up, on a cutting board and, using a sharp knife, make an incision in the middle to kill it. Lift the shell, remove the lung (the chrysanthemum-like substance) and discard. Remove the coral (roe), place in a bowl and set aside. Chop the crab into 6 pieces, crack the claws, and place on a plate. Set aside.

Mix the wine with the coral and set aside.

Bring 4 cups (1 qt/1 l) of water to a boil in a wok or large pan. Place a steaming rack in the middle and set the plate with the crab on top of the wok. Cover and steam for 15 minutes. Remove the crab meat when cool and set aside.

Bring 2 cups (16 fl oz/500 ml) water to a boil in a large pan. Add the mushrooms and cook for 1 minute. Remove, drain, and set aside.

Heat 3 tablespoons oil in a wok or skillet (frying pan) and add half of the garlic and ginger. When the aroma rises, add the mushrooms to the wok. Add the oyster sauce and salt, and stir-fry over high heat for 1 minute. Transfer to a serving platter, cover, and set aside.

Mix the broth, soy sauce, vinegar, pepper, and cornstarch in a bowl.

Heat the remaining oil in the wok and add the remaining ginger and garlic. When the aroma rises, add the crab meat and the broth mixture. Bring to a boil and stir in the coral. When it returns to a boil, stir in the egg white. Pour over the mushrooms and serve.

## VEGETABLE CARVING

The orange phoenix spreading its wings above a platter of appetizers; the coiled dragon that perches in the center of a wide platter of tidbits, each scale clearly outlined, each claw long and sensuous, its wide gaping mouth emitting puffs of smoke; these are the sight that can greet diners at a Chinese banquet. They look too perfect to be anything but molded from plastic. But closer inspection reveals the telltale texture and grain of carrot, yam, or turnip. For festivals and banquets, the Chinese chef will carve elaborate centerpieces from vegetables, to decorate the most important dishes.

Symbolism rules here. The creatures of legend or myth, shapes that invite longevity and prosperity, messages of joy and good health are intricately carved, using techniques that have been

*...iece carved by Adam Kong; onion chrysanthemums, carrot roses, onion lotus blossom*

and ham; then to the fanned tail which spreads across the platter made from foods arranged to depict the brilliant colors and shape of the tail feathers.

Each plate of food for the banquet will also be garnished with an array of vegetables carefully sculpted into floral or animal motifs. It is an art to which only a dedicated few aspire to its highest form, and these skills can ensure a respected position in the kitchens of major restaurants.

A simple, but impressive, example of vegetable carving can come to the table at either the soup or dessert course. A round melon—winter melon for soup, watermelon for dessert—is cut open at the top, the flesh scooped for use in the dish, then the exterior of the shell carved, each cut revealing light green flesh to contrast with the jade green of the exterior.

On a day-to-day basis, the Chinese home cook rarely bothers to decorate plates of food, save for a sprig of cilantro (fresh coriander) or a wisp of scallion (spring onion). But most good restaurants will use at least some form of carved vegetable decor on their serving plates. Simplest are shapes stamped from carrots and cucumber, using metal vegetable cutters or by carving indents the length of the whole vegetable which, when sliced, reveal simple shapes such as leaves and flowers. Next step up the scale is to carve pieces of carrot, yam, or turnip into flower shapes, which may be dyed with food colorings. Onions, too, are carved to resemble lotus blossoms and chrysanthemums, traditional motifs of importance to the Chinese. Tomatoes, cucumbers, and radishes are subject to transformation into fans, goldfish, turtles, rabbits, and other simple shapes. Carved cucumber motifs often decorate the rim of a plate. A thick slice of cucumber with skin is cut closely into a comb shape to fan onto the plate in a number of traditional patterns. Even within a dish, you may discover aesthetically worked slices of vegetable with floral or animal motifs. Sometimes these have a symbolism reflecting the occasion, or they may be purely decorative. Perhaps less impressive, but often used, are simple garnishes such as leek or scallion (spring onion) "brushes."

A highly skilled vegetable carver may be able to work with just one small, well sharpened knife, but a whole vegetable-carving kit is sold in China, for the enthusiast. It includes a dozen small sharp knives with blades of different shapes for specific tasks; a collection of vegetable stamp cutters; tools with v-shaped or curved blades for serrating and shaping; digging and gouging tools, scrapers and scalpels. In all, over fifty pieces of various equipment are included in one convenient kit, for the intricate task of vegetable carving.

handed down over the centuries—together with well honed skills and hours of patience.

At a major banquet, the first course is usually a massive platter of hors d'oeuvres presented as a clever motif. The carved white radish head of a peacock (dyed or hand-painted in the appropriate colors), for instance, may progress to a body composed of slivers of chicken, egg, mushrooms,

## JING LUNG LEE

*STEAMED SOLE*

*The most important ingredient in this recipe is experience. Only experience can teach you how long to cook a certain size and thickness of fish (you can also substitute pomfret, turbot [flounder] or sea bass [groper] for the sole). This dish is usually prepared for festive occasions, when only the freshest fish is expected by merrymakers.*

For the sauce:
*1 teaspoon dark soy sauce*
*1 tablespoon light soy sauce*
*1 teaspoon sugar*
*1 teaspoon salt*
*1/3 teaspoon pepper*
*1 teaspoon sesame oil*
*1 teaspoon Chinese rice wine*
For the sole:
*2 scallion (spring onion) stems*
*1 lb (500 g) whole sole, washed, cleaned, and patted dry*
*1 tablespoon shredded ginger*
*2–3 tablespoons groundnut (peanut) oil*
*1 tablespoon chopped scallion (spring onion)*

*SERVES 4–6*

❡ For the sauce: In a bowl, mix all the ingredients well.
❡ Place the two scallion stems on a long platter. Put the sole on top and sprinkle with the ginger.
❡ Bring 4 cups (1 qt/1 l) of water to a rapid boil in a large pan. Place a steaming rack in the middle and put the platter with the fish on top. Cover and steam for 8 minutes.
❡ Remove the platter and drain any liquid.
❡ Heat the oil in a separate pan, add the chopped scallions, and fry for 10 seconds. Add the sauce and cook for 10 seconds. Pour over the fish and serve.

## TONG CHO WONG YU

*FRIED YELLOW CROAKER*

*I have chosen croaker here, but any fish with relatively large bones will do. If you use a small-boned fish, you will have to pluck out the bones with your chopsticks (which is difficult) or spit them into your side-bowl (which is uncouth).*

For the marinade:
*1 tablespoon light soy sauce*
*1 teaspoon salt*
*1 teaspoon sugar*
*1 teaspoon pepper*

For the fish:
*1 yellow croaker or rock cod, 1 1/2–2 lb (750 g–1 kg), scaled, cleaned, and patted dry*
*2 tablespoons cornstarch (cornflour)*
*6 cups (1 1/2 qt/1.5 l) groundnut (peanut) oil*
*1 teaspoon chopped ginger*
*1 tablespoon chopped garlic*
*1 tablespoon chopped scallion (spring onion)*
*1 red chili, seeded and shredded*
*1 green chili, seeded and shredded*
*2 cups (16 fl oz/500 ml) Sweet-and-sour Sauce (see recipe*

*for Sweet-and-sour Pork Chiuchow-syle, page 150)*
*1 teaspoon Chinese rice wine*
*2 tablespoons chopped cilantro (fresh coriander)*

*SERVES 6–8*

❡ For the marinade: Mix all the ingredients in a bowl.

❡ Score the fish with 6 diagonal cuts on both sides and marinate for 30 minutes. Rub the dry cornstarch on both sides.

❡ Heat the oil in a wok or skillet (frying pan) until very hot. Add the fish and reduce the heat to medium. Fry for 7–8 minutes. Remove the fish from the wok and drain.

❡ Reheat the oil until very hot. Return the fish to the pan and fry for 1 minute. Remove the fish from the wok, drain, and transfer to a serving platter.

❡ Drain all but 2–3 tablespoons of the oil from the wok and reheat. Add the ginger, garlic, scallion, and chilis. When the aroma rises, add the Sweet-and-sour Sauce and bring to a boil. Add the wine.

❡ Pour the sauce over the fish, sprinkle with cilantro, and serve.

*Top: Tong Cho Wong Yu; bottom: Jing Lung Lee*

*Left: Sheung Ku E-Fu Min; right: Chiu Chau Chau Fan*

## SHEUNG KU E-FU MIN

*E-FU NOODLES WITH FRESH AND BLACK MUSHROOMS*

*While E-fu noodles are found all over China, they are usually associated with Teochiu, where they are eaten for dessert with vinegar and sugar. Legend holds that they were "invented" in a mandarin household: A man named Mr E (E-fu means "the house of E") had a servant, who was supposed to*

*dump noodles in water; instead, he put them in boiling oil. Voilà! Fluffy, deep-fried noodles. This recipe is Cantonese, and the E-fu noodles are perfect for soaking up the flavor of the oyster sauce and mushrooms.*

For the sauce:
*1 tablespoon light soy sauce*
*2 tablespoons oyster sauce*
*1 teaspoon Chinese rice wine*
*1 teaspoon sesame oil*
*2 cups (16 fl oz/500 ml) chicken broth (stock)*

For the sauce: Combine all the ingredients in a bowl.

❡ Steam the black mushrooms for 15 minutes and then set aside.

❡ In a small pan, cook the fresh mushrooms in the boiling water for 1 minute. Remove from the heat, drain, and set aside.

❡ Place the noodles in a large pan of boiling water. Cook until soft, about 2–3 minutes. Remove from the heat, drain and set aside.

❡ Heat the oil in a wok or skillet (frying pan). Add the ginger, fresh mushrooms, and black mushrooms, and cook for 1 minute. Add the sauce and the noodles. Cook, stirring constantly, until the liquid has almost evaporated. Serve.

## CHIU CHAU CHAU FAN

*FRIED RICE YANG CHOW-STYLE*

*When you hear that a certain chef comes from Shanghai, you can be pretty sure that he actually comes from Yang Chow, a town northwest of that port city, where many of China's great gourmet recipes have been born. The reason for Yang Chow's culinary fame is that the salt merchants of China had their homes here in the middle of the nineteenth century, and these wealthy businessmen naturally had some of the best chefs in the country. Fried rice may be a common dish, but it originated in Yang Chow, where it was considered quite a delicacy.*

*3–4 tablespoons groundnut (peanut) oil*
*1 tablespoon shredded ginger*
*3–4 slices cooked ham, cut into 1/4-inch (0.5-cm) squares*
*4 oz (125 g) peeled and cooked shrimp (prawns)*
*1 1/3 cups (10 oz/315 g) rice, cooked and cooled*
*1 tablespoon light soy sauce*
*1 teaspoon dark soy sauce*
*1 1/2 teaspoons salt*
*2 eggs, beaten*
*2 tablespoons chopped scallions (spring onions)*
*3–4 tablespoons chicken broth (stock)*

*SERVES 4–6*

❡ Heat the oil in a wok or skillet (frying pan) and add the ginger, ham, and shrimp. Add the rice, about 1/2 cup (1 3/4 oz/50 g) at a time, stirring to separate the grains. Continue stirring over high heat for 1 minute.

❡ Add the soy sauces and salt, and stir over high heat for 1 minute. Add the eggs and stir over high heat for 1 minute.

❡ Add the scallions and broth. Stir to mix, and serve.

For the noodles:
*3 dried black mushrooms, soaked in water to cover for 1 hour, drained, and thinly shredded*
*6 oz (185 g) fresh straw or button mushrooms (champignons), stems discarded*
*2 cups (16 fl oz/500 ml) boiling water*
*8 oz (250 g) E-fu noodles*
*3–4 tablespoons groundnut (peanut) oil*
*1 tablespoon shredded ginger*

*SERVES 4–6*

## THE CHINESE BANQUET

Murals from the Han dynasty, two thousand years ago, show the host of a banquet seated on a couch surrounded by his friends. Before them is a low table on which dozens of dishes have been placed. To the side are groups of servants broiling (grilling) meats and pouring wines. As each dynasty tried to outdo its predecessor in the number of dishes and their elaborateness, banquets became exaggerated excesses in the impossible and vulgar. In the late 1800s, the Empress Dowager would, even when dining alone, sometimes order nearly 100 dishes.

The dishes chosen by the seventeenth-century emperor, from Manchuria, were labeled the Man Banquet. In the South, the ethnically different Chinese also had their own style of banquet, known as the Han Banquet. Eventually, the two traditions were blended to create what is looked back on now as the Man Han Banquet.

Slightly less extravagant were the banquets held during the reign of Emperor Kang-hei during the eighteenth century. Leaving the confines of Beijing to tour the South, the emperor would bring with him a retinue of consorts, wives, and hundreds of officials and palace servants. Wherever the emperor stopped, an enormous tent would be set up for his entourage and for the local Mandarin officials,

dishes—one for each day of the year. Many of these dishes were set out for display, and not meant to be eaten.

The banquet tradition continues today, though the proportions have been tempered to suit the times. A typical Man Han Banquet would have dishes from all the major regions of China. Among them might be:

**Teochiu, hors d'oeuvres:** Traditional snacks from the southern coastal region, including deep-fried mashed shrimp (prawn) balls, sliced braised goose with vinegar; steamed crab cakes, and braised whelks.

**Canton (Guangdong), suckling pig:** Charcoal roasted suckling pig judged by the texture of its skin. The meat would not be eaten at a banquet.

**Manchuria, bear's paw:** Though today the cooking of bear's paw is generally banned, it was an important part of a banquet in the past.

**Fujian, monk jumping over the wall:** Two centuries ago, an apprentice monk, hungry for meat (monks were strict vegetarians), would sneak outside his monastery to collect food and put whatever delicacies he found into a soup pot. The aroma of the soup was so enticing that the Chief Abbot put aside his fury at the monk's insubordination and jumped over the wall to try the soup. Today there are countless variations of this delicious soup, which may contain abalone, kidneys, ham, and herbs.

**Sichuan, pan-fried jumbo freshwater shrimp (king prawns) in chili sauce:**

and a lavish meal would be served featuring foods of the North and South.

By the early nineteenth century, banquets had been codified into six classes. Such details as the required quantities of food and the order of importance of the guests were spelled out with great precision. The Man Banquet should have 365

These river shrimp (prawns) are prepared with bell peppers (capsicums), garlic, and spices of the province.

**Beijing/Manchuria, Peking duck:** The most famous dish from China, eaten sandwiched within a small soft crêpe.

**Hangzhou, beggar's chicken:** The most honored guest will be invited to crack the crust, releasing a heavenly aroma.

**Sichuan, braised bean curd:** This is a famous dish which dates back to the sixteenth century, hot with local chili.

**Mongolia, Mongolian hot-pot:** This dish is served with a profusion of sauces for dipping.

**Beijing, handmade noodles:** At the end of the nineteenth century, the Empress Dowager discovered these noodles when she heard the sounds of a noodle-maker outside her palace. He was called before the empress to demonstrate how he made noodles, and warned that if his noodles did not justify the disturbance he was making, an unspecified fate would befall him. Since he lived to tell the tale, his noodles were a success.

**Fung Shing, pan-fried glutinous rice:** When

prepared for a banquet, the glutinous rice is cooked with sausages and mushrooms.

There would be a famous dessert, such as double-boiled bird's nest from Teochiu, sweetened with honey, and double-boiled with lotus seeds and coconut milk, and the banquet would conclude with Chinese petit fours, including: Peking mashed date cookies (biscuits), Cantonese peony delights, Teochiu crystal cakes, and Sichuan deep-fried fresh milk fritters. Aromatic teas such as Dragon Well, or Iron Goddess of Mercy (*tit kuan yin*) would be served. Other drinks included China's most famous wine, the fiery *Mao tai*; rice distilled *haw tiao*; and *tung hua*, a white hock introduced to China by nineteenth-century German missionaries.

*1. watercress soup; 2. braised pork with cabbage; 3. abalone and black mushrooms in oyster sauce; 4. date pastries; 5. poached chicken; 6. crisp beef with tangerine (mandarin) peel and Sichuan peppercorns; 7. 100-year-old eggs; 8. braised shark's fin; 9. steamed fish; 10. "long-life" noodles; 11. hors d'oeuvres; 12. steamed snail bread*

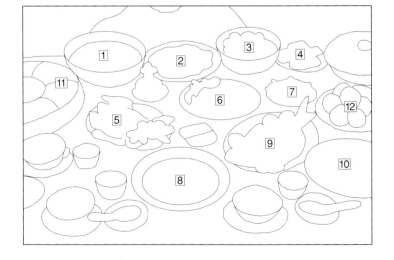

## SUET YI LIN TZE GONG

### WHITE FUNGUS AND LOTUS SEED SWEET SOUP

*White, or silver, fungus was at one time more expensive than bird's nest, and it is still a costly ingredient. This sweet soup is very popular for its health value (the fungus and the lotus seeds are both good for clearing out the respiratory system) and its taste. The contrast between the soft lotus seeds and the slightly crispy fungus is delightful. This soup can be served either hot or cold.*

*½ oz (15 g) white fungus*
*6 oz (185 g) lotus seeds, peeled and halved*
*8 cups (2 qt/2 l) water*
*1 cup (8 oz/250 g) sugar*

*SERVES 4–6*

¶ Soak the white fungus in warm water to cover until soft. Drain and tear into bite-size pieces.
¶ Soak the lotus seeds in warm water to cover for 2 hours. Drain.
¶ Bring the water to a boil in a large pan. Add the lotus seeds and cook over medium–low heat until the seeds become soft, about 1 hour. Add the sugar, stirring to dissolve. Add the fungus and boil for 10 minutes. Serve.

## JIN FUN GOR

### FRIED DUMPLINGS

*The dumplings can be pan-fried or deep-fried for a good dish to end a big meal. Traditionally, we might eat fried dumplings by themselves, or dunk them in chicken soup. Either way, it is an informal, delicious way to give a complicated dinner a simple home-style ending.*

For the dumplings:
*8 oz (250 g) uncooked shrimp (green prawns), heads removed, peeled, deveined, patted dry, and finely chopped*
*2 oz (60 g) pork fillet, ground (minced)*
*1 oz (30 g) cooked pork fat, ground (minced)*
*2 oz (60 g) bamboo shoots, minced*
*1½ teaspoons salt*
*1 teaspoon pepper*
*¼ teaspoon sesame oil*
*1 teaspoon cornstarch (cornflour)*
*4 cups (1 qt/1 l) groundnut (peanut) oil*
*2 tablespoons chopped cilantro (fresh coriander)*
*1 recipe dough (see Shrimp Dumplings recipe, page 52)*

*4 cups (1 qt/1 l) chicken broth (stock)*
*1 tablespoon light soy sauce*
*1 teaspoon Chinese rice wine*

*SERVES 6–8*

¶ Mix together the shrimp, pork, pork fat, bamboo shoots, salt, ½ teaspoon of the pepper, sesame oil, and cornstarch. Heat 1 tablespoon of the groundnut oil in a wok or skillet (frying pan). Sauté the shrimp

mixture over medium heat for 1½ minutes. Remove and set aside. When cool, add the cilantro.

❡ Roll the wrapper dough into a long sausage shape and divide into pieces the size of 2 teaspoons. Press each piece with the side of a lightly greased cleaver to form wrappers approximately 2½ inches (6.5 cm) in diameter. Cover with a cloth.

❡ Place a wrapper on a flat surface and place about 1 tablespoon filling in the center. Fold up and press the edges to form a crescent shape. Repeat with the remaining wrappers.

❡ Heat the remaining oil in the wok until very hot. Add the dumplings and lower the heat to medium–high. Fry until golden brown. Remove, drain, and transfer to a serving platter.

❡ Bring the broth to a boil and add the remaining ingredients. Divide among soup bowls and serve with the fried dumplings.

*Top: Suet Yi Lin Tze Gong; bottom: Jin Fun Gor*

# DIM SUM

# D I M  S U M

THE POETIC TRANSLATION OF DIM SUM IS "LITTLE HEARTS" OR "TO TOUCH THE HEART." LITERALLY IT CONJOINS "SPOTS" or "particles" and "heart" to describe tiny snacks that are meant to please the palate without overfilling the stomach.

❡ *Dim sum* are popular as a light lunch, brunch, or between-meal snack. Having *yum cha* means to eat *dim sum* accompanied by a constantly replenished pot of Chinese green jasmine tea, or the darker tea *po lei* or *pu erh*, which is both refreshing and digestive. Near infinite in variety, *dim sum* can be steamed and fried dumplings, soft dough buns, chewy glutinous rice cakes and all manner of steamed diced meat and meatballs, sliced roasted meats, crisp-fried or braised spicy meats and seafoods. They are fresh, wholesome, inexpensive, and ordering them is easy. When a waiter wheels a cart to your table piled high with little bamboo steamer baskets or plates of fried *dim sum*, you simply select whatever looks appealing; at the end of the meal, the number of empty dishes then determines your bill.

❡ Working hard behind the scenes, the *dim sum* chef prepares the skins and stuffs each morsel using just a few special implements of the trade: A *so choi*, a wooden hammer for making doughy wrappers or "skins"; a metal *juat do* for shaping dumplings; and a *ba pei do*, a blunt metal spatula for making the semi-transparent rice wrappers for *har gau*, or steamed shrimp (prawn) dumplings.

❡ The history of *dim sum* is woven into many legends. One story tells of the noblemen of Suzhou and Hangzhou in the fourteenth century, who would spend their afternoons in ornate tea-houses. There, they were would gossip, drink tea, and be entertained by "sing-song girls." Their valets and the proprietors of the tea-houses would concoct an endless array of delicacies to please them: Pastries, buns, dumplings, tiny meatballs, shaped noodles, and stewed spiced pork. The recipes for these dishes have been passed down through the centuries and many are now found on *dim sum* menus in China and elsewhere today.

❡ Another tale relates that *dim sum* was created for grand imperial banquets. The main courses were so huge and many were virtually inedible, meant to impress the eye or the honor rather than the palate. The affairs dragged on for so long, that the emperors called for tasty culinary *intermezzi* that they could actually enjoy.

❡ The styles of *dim sum* vary from province to province and kitchen to kitchen. In Hong Kong, some restaurants have gone back to basics, offering only a selection of the simple, traditional dishes. Other restaurants take pride in serving two dozen different *dim sum* daily, and still others have taken an opulent approach, using such exotic ingredients as shark's fin and abalone.

*Previous pages: The varieties of* dim sum *are potentially as extensive as the imagination of the chef. Many dishes are tasty morsels of meat or vegetables enclosed in a thin, flour-based wrapper.* BRUCE PEEBLES

*Opposite: A stall selling steamed buns in Kunming, Yunnan province. These delicious meat-filled snacks are part of the* dim sum *tradition — daytime nibbles which are eaten in tea-houses and on the street.* CHINA TOURISM PHOTO LIBRARY/PENG ZHENGE

# HAR KAU

### SHRIMP DUMPLINGS

*These dumplings, known as* har kau, *are the most famous of all* dim sum *dishes. If visitors to Hong Kong can say only four words, they are* dim sum *and* har kau. *Less known is tang flour, which is flour from which all the gluten has been removed. The dough should be rolled as thin as filo pastry.*

For the filling:
8 oz (250 g) uncooked shrimp (green prawns), heads removed, deveined, cleaned, patted dry, and cut into ½-inch (0.5-cm) pieces
2 oz (60 g) cooked pork fat, finely chopped
2 oz (60 g) bamboo shoots, finely shredded
1½ teaspoons salt

½ teaspoon pepper
¼ teaspoon sesame oil
1 teaspoon cornstarch (cornflour)
For the dumplings:
½ cup plus 1 tablespoon (5 fl oz/155 ml) water
1 cup (4 oz/125 g) tang or Chinese dumpling flour
2 teaspoons cornstarch (cornflour)
½ teaspoon lard
6 cups (1½ qt/1.5 l) cold water

*SERVES 8–12*

❡ For the filling: Place all the ingredients in a bowl and stir to mix well. Refrigerate for 30 minutes.
❡ For the dumplings: Bring the water to a rapid boil in a pan. Mix together the flour and cornstarch, and add to the water. Stir rapidly until the mixture becomes transparent. Cover for 5 minutes. Remove from the pan and knead, adding in the lard.

*Top: Har Kau; left: Siu Mai; right: Chuen Kuen*

Continue kneading until the dough becomes firm.

❡ Roll the dough into a long sausage shape. Pull off about 1½ teaspoons and press with the side of a lightly greased cleaver to form wrappers 2 inches (5 cm) in diameter. Cover with a cloth.

❡ Place a wrapper on a flat surface and put about 1½ teaspoons of the mixture in the center and fold up, with the upper flap larger than the lower one. Make 7–9 small pleats in the upper flap and press to seal. Place on a lightly greased platter. Repeat with the remaining wrappers.

❡ Bring the cold water to a rapid boil in a wok or large pan. Place the dumplings in a lightly greased steamer and set the steamer in the wok. Cover and steam over high heat for 5 minutes. Remove the steamer from the wok. Uncover and let cool for 2 minutes. Remove the dumplings when the wrappers become slightly firm, and serve.

## CHUEN KUEN

### SPRING ROLLS

*Spring rolls, which were traditional to the Spring Festival, were once a do-it-yourself recipe at the table. The wrappers and a variety of pork, chicken, or vegetables for the filling would be served, and each person would make his or her own rolls, which would be heated individually. That is messy and time-consuming, so you may want to use this recipe instead.*

For the marinade:
*2 teaspoons light soy sauce*
*1 teaspoon oyster sauce*
*1 teaspoon cornstarch (cornflour)*
For the spring rolls:
*4 oz (125 g) chicken breast, shredded*
*4 cups (1 qt/1 l) groundnut (peanut) oil*
*2 dried black mushrooms, soaked, drained, stems discarded, and shredded*
*4 oz (125 g) bamboo shoots, shredded*
*2 oz (60 g) chives, cut into 1-inch (2.5-cm) lengths*
*16 spring roll wrappers*

*SERVES 4–6*

❡ For the marinade: Mix all the ingredients in a bowl.

❡ Marinate the chicken for 15 minutes.

❡ Heat 1–2 tablespoons oil in a wok or skillet (frying pan). Add the chicken and mushrooms, and stir-fry over medium heat for 1 minute. Add the bamboo shoots, and stir-fry for 30 seconds. Add the chives and mix well. Transfer to a dish and let cool. Drain any liquid.

❡ Place one spring roll wrapper on a flat surface

and place a portion of the filling in the center. Fold both ends towards the center. Then fold up the lower flap and roll the wrapper into a tube shape. Wet the end flap with water, and seal. Repeat with the remaining wrappers.

❡ Heat the remaining oil in a pan until very hot. Add the rolls, a few at a time, and fry until golden brown, about 30 seconds. Remove and drain.

❡ Serve immediately.

## SIU MAI

### PORK AND SHRIMP DUMPLINGS

*This is one of the most popular dim sum, comparable to Shrimp Dumplings. In Hong Kong, the dumplings are sometimes decorated with crab roe, although carrot purée will do as well.*

For the marinade:
*1 tablespoon light soy sauce*
*½ teaspoon salt*
*½ teaspoon sugar*
*¼ teaspoon pepper*
*1 tablespoon cornstarch (cornflour)*
For the dumplings:
*4 oz (125 g) pork fillet, finely diced*
*1 oz (30 g) pork fat, finely diced*
*4 oz (125 g) uncooked shrimp (green prawn) meat, finely diced*
*2 dried black mushrooms, soaked, drained, stems discarded, and finely diced*
*24 won ton wrappers, trimmed into circles*
*2 tablespoons well-cooked carrot purée*
*6 cups (1½ qt/1.5 l) water*

*SERVES 4–6*

❡ For the marinade: Mix all of the ingredients together in a bowl.

❡ Place the pork, pork fat, and shrimp in a bowl. Add the marinade and stir with a fork until sticky. Add the mushrooms and stir to mix well. Refrigerate for 30 minutes.

❡ Hold a wrapper in the palm of one hand. Place some of the pork mixture in the center. Push it down with a spoon and squeeze gently to make an open dumpling. Add a bit of carrot purée on top. Place on a lightly greased platter. Repeat with the remaining ingredients.

❡ Bring the water to a boil in a wok or large pan. Set a steamer on top. Place the dumplings on the steamer and steam over high heat for 10 minutes.

❡ Serve immediately.

*Left: Kau Choi Kau; top: Gai Bau; bottom: Ngau Yuk Kou*

## NGAU YUK KOU

### BEEF BALLS

*You have to use good-quality beef here — no cheap cuts. This is because I won't use any kind of meat tenderizer, which would alter the taste; this dish is too delicate for that kind of change.*

5 ½ cups (1 ⅓ qt/1.3 l) water
1 teaspoon salt
6 oz (185 g) Chinese cabbage, cut into ½- × 2-inch
　(1- × 5-cm) pieces
8 oz (250 g) beef fillet, ground (minced)
1 tablespoon light soy sauce
½ teaspoon sugar

1 egg white
1 tablespoon cornstarch (cornflour)
2 oz (60 g) cooked pork fat, ground (minced)
2 teaspoons groundnut (peanut) oil
2 tablespoons water

SERVES 6

❡ Bring 1½ cups (12 fl oz/375 ml) of the water to a boil and add ½ teaspoon salt. Add the cabbage and cook for 5 minutes. Remove, drain, and set aside.
❡ Place the beef in a bowl and add the remaining salt and the soy sauce. Stir with a fork to mix well. Add the sugar, egg white, and cornstarch. Stir until very sticky. Add the remaining ingredients and stir to mix well. Form the mixture into 12 balls and set aside.
❡ Divide the cabbage among 6 saucers, each 4 inches (10 cm) in diameter. Place 2 balls on each saucer.
❡ Bring the remaining water to a boil in a wok or large pan. Set a steaming rack on top and place the saucers on the steamer. Cover and steam for 5–6 minutes. Serve.

# KAU CHOI KAU

## FRIED CHIVE DUMPLINGS

*The Chinese use two kinds of chives: green chives,* gao choi, *and white chives,* kao wong. *This recipe uses green chives, for a* dim sum *dish with lots of taste.*

12 oz (375 g) Chinese green chives, chopped
2 oz (60 g) dried shrimp (prawns), soaked for 30 minutes, drained, and chopped
2 tablespoons ground (minced) pork fat
½ teaspoon salt
1 teaspoon sugar
1 teaspoon Chinese rice wine
2 cups (8 oz/250 g) all-purpose (plain) flour
¾ cup (6 fl oz/185 ml) boiling water
6 cups (1½ qt/1.5 l) cold water
3–4 tablespoons groundnut (peanut) oil

SERVES 6–8

❡ Mix together the first six ingredients in a bowl and set aside.
❡ Sift the flour into a separate bowl, add the boiling water, and stir to make a thick dough. Cover with a cloth and set aside for 30 minutes.
❡ Knead the dough for about 3 minutes, until smooth. Roll into a long sausage shape and cut into 2 pieces. Cover 1 piece with a cloth and set aside.

Divide the other piece of dough into about 20 pieces and roll each into a round wrapper, about 3 inches (8 cm) in diameter.
❡ Place 1½ tablespoons of the chive mixture in the middle of a wrapper. Fold in half to form a crescent shape and press the edges together to seal. Place on a lightly greased platter, leaving space between the dumplings. Repeat with the remaining dough.
❡ Bring the cold water to a boil in a wok or large pan. Place a steaming rack over it and place the platter with the dumplings on the rack. Cover, and steam for 10 minutes. Remove and set aside to cool.
❡ Heat the oil in a wok or skillet (frying pan) and fry the dumplings until golden brown on the bottom. Serve.

# GAI BAU

## STEAMED CHICKEN BUNS

*This is a hearty, filling dish from Shanghai, where chefs seem to understand how to handle the crunchy, healthy bamboo shoot. Always use bamboo shoots, and thinly slice them for best results.*

For the marinade:
1 tablespoon oyster sauce
1 teaspoon salt
1 teaspoon sugar
1 teaspoon Chinese rice wine
2 teaspoons cornstarch (cornflour)
½ teaspoon pepper
¼ teaspoon sesame oil
For the buns:
10 oz (315 g) chicken leg meat, cut into ½-inch (1-cm) cubes
2 oz (60 g) pork fat, diced
2 oz (60 g) bamboo shoots, thinly sliced
3 dried black mushrooms, soaked, drained, stems discarded, and diced
1 tablespoon shredded ginger
1 tablespoon chopped scallion (spring onion)
1 recipe Chinese Steamed Bread dough (see recipe, page 232)

SERVES 12

❡ For the marinade: Mix all the ingredients in a bowl.
❡ Marinate the chicken and pork fat for 15 minutes.
❡ Add the bamboo shoots, mushrooms, ginger, and scallion. Work with the fingers to mix well.
❡ To make and steam the buns, see Ground Pork and Cabbage Buns (page 60).

## JIN HUP TZE

### PAN-FRIED MEAT BOXES

*"Meat boxes" are like ravioli—variations on the traditional dumpling with two pieces of wrapper. The leek and garlic give them that special flavor.*

1 oz (30 g) pork fat, ground (minced)
6 oz (185 g) beef fillet, ground (minced)
3 oz (90 g) leek, finely chopped
2 tablespoons chopped cilantro (fresh coriander)
1 tablespoon light soy sauce
¼ teaspoon salt
½ teaspoon sugar
¼ teaspoon sesame oil
1 teaspoon Chinese rice wine
1 teaspoon cornstarch (cornflour)
48 dumpling wrappers, about 2 inches (5 cm) in diameter
    (see Fried Chive Dumplings, page 55)
4–6 tablespoons groundnut (peanut) oil
¼ cup (2 fl oz/60 ml) chicken broth (stock)

*SERVES 6–8*

❡ Place the pork, beef, leek, and cilantro in a bowl. Add the soy sauce, salt, sugar, sesame oil, wine, and cornstarch, and work with the fingers to mix well. Remove the mixture from the bowl and throw it back in. Repeat for 1 minute until the mixture becomes smooth and firm. Set aside.
❡ Lay a dumpling wrapper on a flat surface and place about 1 tablespoon of the mixture in the middle. Place another wrapper on top and pinch the edges to seal. Place on a lightly greased plate. Repeat with the remaining ingredients.
❡ Heat a wok or skillet (frying pan) until very hot. Add 2 tablespoons of oil and rotate the wok to coat the bottom well. Add the meat "boxes," 12 at a time, and fry over medium–high heat until the bottoms are golden brown.
❡ Add 2 tablespoons broth. Reduce the heat to low, cover, and cook for 4–5 minutes. Turn the boxes over and cook over medium–high heat for 1 minute. Transfer to a serving platter and cover to keep warm. Repeat with the remaining meat boxes and serve hot.

## WOR TIP

### POT-STICKERS

*Pot-stickers, also known as pan-stickers, come from the North of China. They must be served scaldingly hot. The sauce of shredded ginger and vinegar is meant to cool them down—although only relatively.*

For the pot-stickers:
8 oz (250 g) pork fillet, ground (minced)
2 oz (60 g) pork fat, very finely chopped
4 oz (125 g) cabbage, finely chopped
2 oz (60 g) chives, chopped
1 tablespoon light soy sauce
1 teaspoon salt
1 teaspoon sugar
¼ teaspoon pepper
¼ teaspoon sesame oil
1 tablespoon cornstarch (cornflour)
36 dumpling wrappers (see Fried Chive Dumplings, page 55)
3–4 tablespoons groundnut (peanut) oil
3 tablespoons chicken broth (stock)
For the dip:
2 tablespoons shredded ginger
2 tablespoons aromatic or cider vinegar
1 tablespoon light soy sauce

*SERVES 6–8*

❡ Put the pork, pork fat, cabbage, and chives in a bowl. Add the soy sauce, salt, sugar, pepper, sesame oil, and cornstarch. Work with the fingers to mix well. Remove the mixture from the bowl and throw it back in. Repeat the process until the mixture becomes smooth and firm.
❡ Place a wrapper on a flat surface and put 1 tablespoon of the mixture in the center. Shape into a crescent and make 8–10 pleats on the upper flap to seal. Place on a lightly greased platter. Repeat with the remaining mixture.
❡ Heat a wok or skillet (frying pan). Add 2 tablespoons of oil and rotate the wok to coat well with oil. Arrange the dumplings in the wok, leaving space between them so they don't stick together. Fry over medium heat until the bottoms of the dumplings are lightly browned, about 1 minute.
❡ Add the broth, cover, and cook over low heat for 5 minutes. Drain the liquid. Add the remaining oil. Turn the dumplings over and fry over medium heat for 1 minute. Serve.
❡ Mix together the ginger, vinegar, and soy sauce, and serve as a dip.

## JAI KAU

### VEGETARIAN DUMPLINGS

*I use groundnut (peanut) oil here, because most Cantonese like their vegetarian dumplings in this rather heavy oil. But camellia oil, which is hard to find outside central China, would be best for the first step. By the way, almost any fresh (not frozen) vegetables will do.*

*2–3 tablespoons groundnut (peanut) oil*
*1 teaspoon finely chopped ginger*
*1 teaspoon finely chopped garlic*
*2 oz (60 g) bamboo shoots, chopped*
*2 oz (60 g) carrot, chopped*
*2 oz (60 g) green peas*
*2 oz (60 g) button mushrooms (champignons), chopped*
*3 dried black mushrooms, soaked, drained, stems discarded, and chopped*
*½ oz (15 g) dried cloud ear fungus, soaked, and coarsely chopped*
*6 tablespoons chicken broth (stock)*
*1 tablespoon light soy sauce*
*1 teaspoon sugar*
*1 teaspoon salt*
*1 teaspoon oyster sauce*
*1 teaspoon Chinese rice wine*
*1 teaspoon cornstarch (cornflour)*
*2 tablespoons chopped cilantro (fresh coriander)*
*36 dumpling wrappers (see Fried Chive Dumplings, page 55)*

*SERVES 6–8*

❡ Heat the oil in a wok or skillet (frying pan) and add the ginger and garlic. When the aroma rises, add the vegetables, mushrooms, and fungus. Stir-fry over high heat for 1 minute.

❡ Mix the broth, soy sauce, sugar, salt, oyster sauce, wine, and cornstarch. Add to the wok and stir-fry over medium heat for 1 minute. Add the cilantro and mix well.

❡ Spread the mixture on a plate and drain any liquid. Let cool.

❡ Place a dumpling wrapper on a flat surface and put 1 tablespoon of the vegetable mixture in the center. Shape into a crescent and make 8–10 pleats on the upper flap to seal. Place on a lightly greased plate. Repeat with the remaining mixture.

❡ Bring 6 cups (1 ½ qt/1.5 l) of water to a rapid boil in a wok or large pan and set a steamer on top. Arrange the dumplings on the steamer, leaving space between them so they don't stick together.

❡ Steam the dumplings over high heat for 10 minutes and serve immediately.

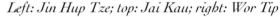

*Left: Jin Hup Tze; top: Jai Kau; right: Wor Tip*

*Top: Won Ton Tong; left: Jar Won Ton; right: Har Dor Sze*

## WON TON TONG

*WON TON IN SOUP*

*This is a good* dim sum *dish, especially at the end of a banquet—not an imperial-style banquet, but a special family dinner. This recipe is from Shanghai, not Canton. The green cabbage and mixed meat make the dish much lighter than the Cantonese version, in which some noodles are added to the soup.*

*8 oz (250 g) pork fillet, ground (minced)*
*2 teaspoons salt*
*1 teaspoon sesame oil*
*1 teaspoon cornstarch (cornflour)*
*4 oz (125 g) bamboo shoots, washed, dried, and finely chopped*
*1 lb (500 g) Chinese cabbage, washed, dried, and finely chopped*
*48 won ton wrappers*
*6 cups (1½ qt/1.5 l) boiling water*
*1 cup (8 fl oz/250 ml) cold water*
*4 cups (1 qt/1 l) chicken broth (stock)*
*1 teaspoon Chinese rice wine*
*1 tablespoon light soy sauce*
*½ teaspoon pepper*

*SERVES 4–6*

❡ Place the pork, salt, sesame oil, and cornstarch in a bowl and stir to mix well. Add the bamboo shoots and cabbage, and mix well.
❡ Spoon about 1½ teaspoons of the mixture in the center of a wrapper. Wrap up and squeeze lightly. Repeat with the remaining wrappers.
❡ Drop the *won tons* into a large pan with the boiling water. Add the cold water. When the water returns to a boil and the *won tons* float to the surface, remove and drain. Divide the *won tons* among soup bowls.
❡ Bring the chicken broth to a boil in a large pan and add the wine, soy sauce, and pepper. Pour over the *won tons* and serve.

## JAR WON TON

*DEEP-FRIED WON TON WITH SWEET-AND-SOUR SAUCE*

*Many Chinese words about food have origins unconnected with their culinary meanings. Won ton literally means "cloud and swallow," and originally the two words together denoted a blur or vagueness, like a bird flying across a cloud. Nowadays, won ton is seen as something that encases the mixture of elements inside it.*

4 cups (1 qt/1 l) groundnut (peanut) oil
36 won tons (see Won Ton and Noodles in Soup, page 230)
1 teaspoon finely chopped garlic
1 teaspoon finely chopped red chili
1 cup (8 fl oz/250 ml) Sweet-and-sour Sauce (see Sweet-
   and-sour Pork Chiuchow-Style, page 150)

*SERVES 4–6*

❡ Heat the oil in a wok or skillet (frying pan) until
very hot. Add the *won tons* (about 10 at a time),
lower heat slightly, and fry until golden brown.
Remove the *won tons* from the wok, drain, and place
on a serving platter.
❡ Drain all but 1 tablespoon oil from the wok. Add
the garlic and chili. When the aroma rises, add the
sauce. Bring to a boil and serve in a bowl as a dip.

## HAR DOR SZE

*SHRIMP TOAST*

*This popular dim sum recipe is made with ordinary white
bread and is a savory, delicious dish.*

For the marinade:
½ teaspoon salt
¼ teaspoon pepper
1 teaspoon cornstarch (cornflour)
½ egg white
For the toast:
6 oz (185 g) uncooked shrimp (green prawn) meat
1 oz (30 g) pork fat, finely diced
1 oz (30 g) Chinese or Virginia ham, finely diced
½ onion, chopped
4 slices white bread, about ¼-inch (0.5-cm) thick,
   trimmed of crusts
4 eggs, beaten
4 cups (1 qt/1 l) groundnut (peanut) oil

*SERVES 4*

❡ For the marinade: Mix all the ingredients in a bowl.
❡ Place the shrimp, pork fat, ham, and onion in a
bowl and add the marinade. Stir with a fork until
sticky. Set aside. Cut the bread slices diagonally in
half. Spread the shrimp mixture on one half and
cover with the other. Brush the egg on both sides.
❡ Heat the oil until hot in a wok or skillet (frying
pan). Add the bread, 4 pieces at a time and fry over
low heat until golden brown. Remove and drain.
❡ Serve hot.

*Clockwise from top: duck eggs; hom tan on charcoal; P'i tan in rice husks*

## HUNDRED-YEAR-OLD EGGS

Rather than being dug up
from an ancient tomb, as
the name might suggest,
"100-year-old eggs," or as
some call them "1000-year
eggs," are actually
preserved for only 100
days at most. Fresh duck
eggs are mixed with
various preservative
compounds that permeate
the shell and alter the
consistency of the egg.

There are two main
methods for preserving
eggs in China: *P'i tan* are
coated with an alkaline
mud and then covered in
ash, rice husks, or tea
leaves, before storing in
large crocks for 100 days.
The yolk becomes creamy
and very pungently
flavored, the white turns an
amber-gray color and
coagulates into a firm,
gelatin-like consistency.

They are shelled and the
egg sliced to serve as an
*hors d'oeuvre* with slivers of
preserved ginger and a
vinegar dip.

*Hom tan* are preserved in
brine and saltpeter, or a
mixture of finely ground
charcoal and brine. The
yolk hardens to a firm,
grainy texture and acquires
a pleasing salty taste. These
must be cooked before they
are ready to eat, as a snack
with a splash of sesame oil
and vinegar and a sliver of
ginger, or to add, sliced, to
*congee*. The yolks are an
ingredient in the fillings of
many sweet pastries.

Hundred-year-old eggs
are valued not only for
their taste, but also for
their medicinal value. The
preservation process raises
their alkalinity, making
them a good antidote for
ulcers and other conditions
caused by hyper-acidity.
They are also considered a
cure for hangovers.

## MA TI GO

*WATER CHESTNUT CAKE*

*If you have any of this mouth-watering dessert left over (which is doubtful!), you can store it in the refrigerator, where it will last for two or three days. Then take it out and pan-fry it for a few minutes; this will caramelize the sugar, giving the cake a totally different taste.*

*10 cups (2 ½ qt/2.5 l) water*
*1 cup plus 2 tablespoons (9 oz/280 g) sugar*
*2 cups (6 oz/185 g) water chestnut flour*
*1 cup plus 2 tablespoons (9 oz/280 g) water chestnuts, peeled and diced*
*3 tablespoons groundnut (peanut) oil*

*SERVES 8–10*

❡ Bring 4 cups (1 qt/1 l) of the water to a boil in a large pan. Add the sugar and let it dissolve completely. Turn off the heat and stir in the flour. Mix well.
❡ Add the water chestnuts and stir to mix well.
❡ Transfer the mixture to a greased 8- × 8- × 2-inch (20- × 20- × 5-cm) cake pan and set aside.
❡ Bring the remaining water to a boil in a wok or large pan. Set a steaming rack on top and place the cake pan inside the steamer. Cover and steam for 30 minutes. Let cool. Refrigerate.
❡ Cut into 2-inch (5-cm) squares. Serve cold, or pan-fry in the oil until lightly browned on both sides and serve hot.

## CHOI YUK BOU

*GROUND PORK AND CABBAGE BUNS*

*This is my favorite recipe for this dish, but you can adjust the proportion of meats and vegetables to your own taste. I prefer more vegetables, which makes the buns lighter and more refreshing, but you might like something a bit heavier and meatier.*

For the marinade:
*½ teaspoon pepper*
*½ teaspoon sesame oil*
*1 teaspoon cornstarch (cornflour)*
For the buns:
*6 oz (185 g) pork fillet, finely diced*
*2 oz (60 g) pork fat, finely diced*

*Top left: Ma Ti Go; top right: Choi Yuk Bou; bottom: Cha Yip Darn*

## Dim Sum Dishes

*Dim sum* is not all dumplings and buns. Often, the tiny steamer baskets reveal bite-size fragments of *pai gwat* (pork), or *ngau tao* (tripe) braised and steamed, or steamed with black beans, garlic, and chili, or beef balls flavored with a hint of lime and cilantro (fresh coriander). There are beancurd-skin wrapped batons of pork or chicken, tender braised squid or chickens' feet.

The sliced cold meats that might precede a Chinese banquet are an enjoyable element of *yum cha*. Cold sliced roast duck, its skin burnished a glorious amber; rectangular slivers of bubbly pork crackling over pink tender meat; finely sliced red-edged *cha siu* pork; chicken poached in soy sauce; finely sliced seasoned pork or beef, and terrine-like meat compounds are beautifully presented on small oval plates for selection from the dim sum cart. There are also salad-style dishes like fine strips of cold steamed chicken bathed in creamy sesame dressings spiked with a touch of chili.

*1. roast suckling pig; 2. roast duck; 3. soy poached chicken; 4. cold shredded chicken with sesame dressing; 5. glutinous rice dough cakes with sweet mung bean filling; 6.* cha siu

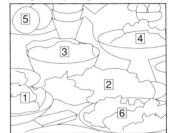

1 lb (500 g) Chinese white cabbage, washed and
    coarsely chopped
3 dried black mushrooms, soaked, drained, stems discarded,
    and very finely chopped
1 recipe Chinese Steamed Bread dough (page 230)
6 cups (1½ qt/1.5 l) water

SERVES 12

❧ For the marinade: Mix all the ingredients in a bowl.
❧ Marinate the pork and pork fat for 15 minutes.
❧ Wrap the chopped cabbage in a clean, dry towel and twist to absorb the excess moisture.
❧ Mix the pork, cabbage, and mushrooms together in a bowl.
❧ Roll the dough into a long sausage shape and divide into 24 portions. Flatten each with the palm and place 1 tablespoon filling in the middle of each. Wrap the dough around the filling, making pleats all around and leaving a small hole in the middle. Stick a piece of waxed (greaseproof) paper on the bottom. Repeat with the remaining ingredients and set aside to let rise for 10 minutes.
❧ Bring the water to a rapid boil in a wok or large pan. Set a steamer in the wok and place the buns in the steamer, leaving space between them so they don't stick together. Steam over high heat for 12 minutes and serve.

## Cha Yip Darn

### SPICY TEA EGGS

*The Chinese generally make this with only cinnamon and star anise. But five-spice powder really gives it more complexity and taste. It can be used as* dim sum, *for breakfast, or for a bedtime treat.*

1 dozen eggs
5 tablespoons black tea leaves
1 tablespoon five-spice powder
¼ cup (2 fl oz/60 ml) dark soy sauce
1 tablespoon salt
½ teaspoon sugar

SERVES 6–12

❧ Put the eggs in a large pan and add water to cover. Bring to a boil over medium heat, then reduce the heat and simmer for 15 minutes. Remove the eggs and let cool.
❧ Tap the eggs with a spoon to crack the shells all over and place them in a large pan. Add some water to cover them completely and then add all the remaining ingredients. Bring to a boil and simmer for about 3 hours. Drain and let cool.
❧ Shell the eggs and cut each into 6 wedges. Serve.

## JIN DARN KOK

*EGG DUMPLINGS WITH PORK AND ONION FILLING*

*This recipe is very easy, but it is also time consuming. Nevertheless the result is worth the labor, as you will never be able to taste this dish in a restaurant. It must be served steaming hot, and no restaurant will want the trouble of preparing it on the spot.*

For the marinade:
½ teaspoon salt
¼ teaspoon sesame oil
½ teaspoon Chinese rice wine
½ teaspoon cornstarch (cornflour)
2 teaspoons water
For the dumplings:
4 oz (125 g) pork fillet, ground (minced)
6–8 tablespoons groundnut (peanut) oil
1 medium onion, chopped
½ teaspoon salt
3 eggs, beaten

*SERVES 4–6*

❧ For the marinade: Mix all of the ingredients together in a bowl.
❧ Marinate the pork for 15 minutes.
❧ Heat 1 tablespoon oil in a wok or skillet (frying pan). Add the onion and sauté until translucent. Transfer to a bowl and set aside.
❧ Heat 2 tablespoons oil in the wok. Stir-fry the pork over medium heat until quite dry. Add it to the onion together with the salt and mix well.
❧ Reheat the wok. Add 1 tablespoon oil and coat the wok evenly. Add 1 tablespoon egg to form a small, thin pancake. Remove it from the wok and place about 1½ teaspoons of the pork and onion mixture, in the center. Fold the pancake into a crescent while it is still moist and press lightly to seal. Repeat with the remaining ingredients and serve.

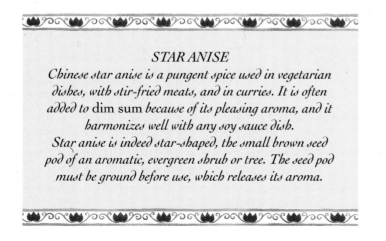

### STAR ANISE

*Chinese star anise is a pungent spice used in vegetarian dishes, with stir-fried meats, and in curries. It is often added to* dim sum *because of its pleasing aroma, and it harmonizes well with any soy sauce dish.*
*Star anise is indeed star-shaped, the small brown seed pod of an aromatic, evergreen shrub or tree. The seed pod must be ground before use, which releases its aroma.*

## JAR YU KOU

*FRIED DACE BALLS*

*You can use any kind of fresh white fish for this recipe, or even buy ground (minced) fish from your fishmonger. The success of the dish depends on how it is stirred: It is necessary to stir the mixture very slowly and carefully until the paste is very sticky.*

*Left: Jin Darn Kok; right: Jar Yu Kou*

1 lb (500 g) dace (or other white-fleshed fish) fillet, chopped
1 scallion (spring onion), finely chopped
1 1/2 teaspoons salt
1/2 teaspoon pepper
2 tablespoons water
1 tablespoon cornstarch (cornflour)
4 cups (1 qt/1 l) groundnut (peanut) oil
2 tablespoons hoisin sauce

SERVES 4–6

❡ Place all the ingredients except the *hoisin* sauce in a bowl. Stir with a fork until the mixture is very sticky and forms a ball.
❡ With wet hands (to avoid mixture sticking), form the paste into balls about 3/4 inch (2 cm) in diameter and place on a lightly greased platter.
❡ Heat the oil in a wok or skillet (frying pan) until hot. Lower the heat slightly and add the fish balls, a few at a time. Fry until golden brown and expanded. Remove and drain. Serve with the *hoisin* sauce as a dip.

# JING PAI GUI

### STEAMED PORK SPARE-RIBS

*This can be served as a dim sum or as a main course. In Hong Kong, it is always on the dim sum menu.*

1 red chili, finely chopped
1 tablespoon finely chopped garlic
1 tablespoon fermented black beans, mashed
1 tablespoon light soy sauce
1 teaspoon dark soy sauce
1 teaspoon chili oil (optional)
1 teaspoon sugar
1 teaspoon Chinese rice wine
2 teaspoons cornstarch (cornflour)

12 oz (375 g) pork spare-ribs, chopped into bite-size pieces
12 slices ginger
12 pieces scallion (spring onion), about 1½ inches (4 cm) long, white part only
4 cups (1 qt/1 l) water

*SERVES 6*

¶ Mix the first nine ingredients in a bowl. Add the spare-ribs and marinate for 1 hour.
¶ Divide the ribs among 6 saucers, each 4 inches (10 cm) in diameter. Place 2 ginger slices and 2 scallion pieces on top of each. Set aside.
¶ Bring the water to a boil in a wok or large pan. Set a steaming rack on top and place the saucers on the steamer. Cover and steam for 15 minutes.
¶ Serve immediately.

*Jing Pai Gui*

## DIM SUM SKINS

Chinese chefs have developed a special knack for making the edible "skins" or wrappers, to encase the bite-size dumplings and buns served as *dim sum*. Some are prepared fresh in the restaurant or home kitchen, others are factory produced.

The simplest is the *won ton* skin, made in the same way as pasta dough by combining flour and egg. The dough is kneaded and worked until it is smooth and elastic, then rolled paper-thin and cut into 2³⁄₄-inch (6-cm) squares. Sold fresh or frozen, in packages of about 36, *won ton* skins can be stored in

the refrigerator for about 4 days, or frozen, well wrapped, for a month or so. *Won tons* are dumplings with their fillings completely enclosed by the wrappers. They can be steamed, boiled in a soup, or deep-fried. *Siu mai* use the same wrapper, but their filling is exposed at the top. They are usually steamed, but can also be fried.

The near-transparent wrappers that enclose delicate *dim sum* such as *har gau* and *fun gor* are made from a special gluten-free wheat starch. Always made fresh, the flour is mixed with boiling water to produce a soft, white dough which is shaped into

thin, round wrappers.

Spring roll skins are quite tough, dry to the touch, and paper-thin. Made from rice flour, they are usually factory-produced to sell in packs of a dozen or so, in both small and large sizes. They are usually sold frozen, as the fresh skins will very quickly dry out, becoming brittle and unusable.

A fine parchment-like skin made from beancurd residue encases certain dumplings. These cream-colored skins come in large flat sheets which are folded, and must be dipped into warm water to soften for wrapping. Beancurd skins can be stored, in a

sealed container, in the pantry virtually indefinitely.

Dumpling wrappers made from wheat flour dough are sold in blocks of about 36 pieces. They are whiter in color than *won ton* wrappers, and are usually round in shape.

*1. dumpling wrappers; 2. bean curd skins; 3. spring roll skins; 4. har gau dough and wrappers; 5. wheat flour dumpling skins*

## MIN FA GAI

### STEAMED CHICKEN WITH FISH MAW

*This is a common* dim sum *dish. I recommend eel maw, but you can get ling (greenling) or croaker (rock cod) at your grocery or fishmonger.*

For the marinade:
$1/2$ teaspoon salt

2 teaspoons light soy sauce
1 teaspoon Chinese rice wine
$1/2$ teaspoon sugar
$1 1/2$ teaspoons cornstarch (cornflour)
For the chicken:
2 chicken legs, cut into bite-size pieces
6 dried black mushrooms, about 1 inch (2.5 cm) in
    diameter, soaked, drained, stems discarded
1 piece puffed conger-eel or fish maw, soaked in cold water
    for 4–5 hours

*Left: Min Fa Gai; right: Chuen Darn Siu Mai*

8 cups (2 qt/2 l) water
6 slices ginger

*SERVES 6*

❧ For the marinade: Mix all of the ingredients together in a bowl.
❧ Marinate the chicken and mushrooms for 30 minutes.
❧ Split the conger-eel maw and cut into 2-inch (5-cm) lengths. In a large pan, bring 4 cups

(1 qt/1 l) of the water to a boil. Add the maw and boil for 10 minutes. Remove and rinse under tap water. Squeeze dry.
❧ Divide the maw among 6 saucers, each 4 inches (10 cm) in diameter. Place the chicken and mushrooms on top and add the ginger.
❧ Bring the remaining water to a boil in a wok or large pan. Set a steaming rack on top and place the saucers on the steamer. Cover and steam for 15 minutes. Serve.

## CHUEN DARN SIU MAI

### *QUAIL EGGS ON PORK DUMPLINGS*

*Quail eggs are inexpensive, but pigeon eggs are tastier, so you may want to try them for this recipe. Either sort makes an attractive complement to the rich pork dumplings.*

For the marinade:
1 tablespoon light soy sauce
1 teaspoon salt
$1/2$ teaspoon sugar
$1/4$ teaspoon pepper
1 tablespoon cornstarch (cornflour)
2 tablespoons chicken broth (stock)
For the eggs and dumplings:
4 oz (125 g) pork fillet, ground (minced)
1 oz (30 g) pork fat, ground (minced)
4 oz (125 g) uncooked shrimp (green prawn) meat, ground (minced)
2 dried black mushrooms, soaked, drained, stems discarded, and finely chopped
1 tablespoon chopped cilantro (fresh coriander)
12 quail eggs, boiled and shelled
6 cups ($1 1/2$ qt/1.5 l) water

*SERVES 6*

❧ For the marinade: Mix all the ingredients in a bowl.
❧ Place the pork, pork fat, and shrimp in a bowl. Add the marinade and stir with a fork until sticky. Add the mushrooms and stir to mix well. Refrigerate for 30 minutes.
❧ With wet hands (to avoid the mixture sticking), divide into 12 equal portions and form into egg-shaped dumplings. Place a bit of the cilantro and a quail egg on each dumpling. Place 2 dumplings on a saucer, about 4 inch (10 cm) in diameter. Repeat with the remaining dumplings.
❧ Bring the water to a rapid boil in a wok or large pan. Set a steamer in the wok and place the saucers on the steamer. Cover and steam over high heat for 12–15 minutes. Serve.

# S O U P

# S O U P

THE FIRST QUESTION OFTEN ASKED ABOUT CHINESE SOUP IS: DO YOU EAT IT AT THE BEGINNING, MIDDLE, OR END OF THE MEAL? This is not a problem for the Chinese themselves, as most food is served at the same time and one can sip soup along with the rice, meat, and vegetables; there is no "order" per se. Even at banquets, soup is not limited to a specific course: It may be served throughout the meal, acting as a palate-cleanser between dishes.

❡ The next question, then, is: What is soup? The Chinese distinguish between light soups (clear broth with some meat and onions added) and heavy soups. The latter are meals in themselves, the broth is rich, the vegetables and meats are chosen with care, and the simmering process can take hours.

❡ One version of Mongolian Hot-pot consists of bubbling chicken broth (stock), in which meats and vegetables are boiled and eaten separately. But by the end of the meal, the broth (stock) contains bits and pieces of all the ingredients and is drunk like a soup. This idea of "leftover" soup is also the basis of

*Previous pages: Soup in China is much more than just a first course. It is either used consommé-style during and after a meal as a refreshing contrast to heavy or spicy dishes, or as a noodle, meat, and vegetable-based main dish. This Tibetan family in Sichuan Province are eating thick soup as a substantial part of their meal.* LEO MEIER/WELDONS

*Opposite: Patrons enjoying their noodles and soup at one of Beijing's many eating stalls. These outdoor establishments provide inexpensive and satisfying meals at virtually any time of the day.* HUTCHISON LIBRARY/TREVOR PAGE

the third use of Peking Duck. Imperial families would only eat the prized skin of the duck and others would eat the meat. But for the thousands slaving in the royal kitchens, the bones would be boiled up for a hearty duck soup.

❡ No region in China lacks a famous soup. From the "accidental" soups of Mongolian Hot-pot to sizzling Snake Soup accompanied by dishes of white chrysanthemum petals, mushrooms, and shreds of fish, the range and variety demonstrate how much the Chinese appreciate soup.

❡ The Cantonese make vegetable-filled dumplings to flavor possibly the most famous of Chinese soups, *Won Ton*. Soups play an important part in the cooking of Sichuan; the plethora of spices from this region, including the Sicuan peppercorn, combine to make the famous Hot and Sour Soup. In the far North, the broth (stock) is flavored with soy sauce, garlic, and oils, and in the winter, it is mixed with cabbage leaves and possibly mutton, lamb, or beef. These northern soups are considered to be the most nutritious in China.

❡ When preparing soup for a banquet, the rarer and more expensive the ingredients the better. In the richest banquet soup, it is the combination of shark fin texture, abalone chunkiness, the right vinegar, and the long, long, simmering time that makes the soup a national treasure. Traditionally served to the Emperor, "palace soups" or *dat tsai* (literally "big dishes") would be thick shark-fin soups combined with flesh from the rarest animals and fish. When Southeast Asian monarchs gave tribute to Chinese emperors they would inevitably include bird's nest, which was sweetened and made into the now famous soup.

## SAI WU NGOR YUK

*WEST LAKE BEEF SOUP*

*West Lake is the major lake in Hangzhou and, with its lit-
tle islands dotted with tea-houses, is considered one of the
most beautiful lakes in China. This soup is a Cantonese
dish, but it is so simple and lovely that it was named after
the Hangzhou site.*

For the marinade:
*1 teaspoon salt*
*1 teaspoon sugar*
*2 teaspoons cornstarch (cornflour)*
*1 tablespoon water*
For the soup:
*4 oz (125 g) ground (minced) beef fillet*
*2 cups (16 fl oz/500 ml) water*
*4 cups (1 qt/1 l) Secondary Broth (see recipe, page 75)*
*1 tablespoon shredded ginger*
*1 tablespoon chopped scallion (spring onion)*

*1 tablespoon light soy sauce*
*1/2 teaspoon pepper*
*1 teaspoon sesame oil*
*1 teaspoon Chinese rice wine*
*2 tablespoons cornstarch (cornflour), diluted in 2
    tablespoons water*
*2 egg whites*
*1 tablespoon chopped cilantro (fresh coriander)*

*SERVES 4–6*

❡ For the marinade: Combine all of the ingredients
in a bowl.
❡ Marinate the beef for 15 minutes.
❡ Bring the water to a boil in a pan. Add the beef,
stirring to separate. When the beef turns white,
remove it from the pan, drain, and set aside.
❡ Bring the broth to a boil in a separate pan. Add
the ginger, scallion, soy sauce, pepper, sesame oil,
wine, and cornstarch. Stir in the egg whites. Add
the beef and cilantro, and heat through.
❡ Serve immediately.

*Top: Sai Wu Ngor Yuk; bottom: Suen Lat Tong*

*Yunnan steam pot containing chicken and Chinese herbs in soup, with small serving pots.*

## Yunnan Steam Pot

Chinese cooks employ several techniques to extract flavor from ingredients they use in soups, and to ensure the ingredients are cooked to succulent tenderness. One is the method of "double-boiling," in which the ingredients are cooked in a sealed pot inside a steamer. Pots can be as simple as a length of bamboo, plugged at both ends and are often used when cooking pork or pigeon. Tiny pots and cups made from brown unglazed clay are used for soups and for some famous rich, fat-pork dishes. Straight-sided vitreous china pots with double lids are used in most parts of China in restaurants and the home kitchen, but in the central provinces they prefer the Yunnan steam pot.

Usually made of a dense clay, the steam pots have an inner, narrow chimney inside, rather like an inverted funnel. The soup begins with just the meat and vegetables, and little or no liquid. As the water in the steamer heats to boiling, the chimney draws the steam up from below to condense inside the pot and run down the sloped sides of the funnel to form a soup inside the pot. This method is particularly suitable for slow cooking.

## Suen Lat Tong

### *SOUR AND PEPPERY SOUP*

*This soup is made in restaurants (in fact, no Sichuan restaurant is without it), at banquets, and at home, and there are as many variations on the recipe as there are cooks. It was originally made with chicken blood, but this is hardly necessary; the success of the dish comes primarily from the balance between the pepper and vinegar.*

For the marinade:
*2 teaspoons salt*
*1 teaspoon sugar*
*1 tablespoon cornstarch (cornflour)*
*2 tablespoons water*
For the soup:
*2 oz (60 g) pork fillet, cut into slivers*
*2 oz (60 g) uncooked shrimp (green prawns), peeled and deveined*
*2 cups (16 fl oz/500 ml) water*
*4 cups (1 qt/1 l) Secondary Broth (see recipe, page 75)*
*12 pieces cloud ear fungus, soaked in cold water for 30 minutes and drained*
*1 piece bean curd, shredded*
*2 oz (60 g) bamboo shoots, sliced*
*1 tablespoon shredded ginger*

*1 tablespoon chopped scallion (spring onion)*
*2 tablespoons aromatic or cider vinegar*
*1 teaspoon chili oil*
*1/2 teaspoon pepper*
*1 teaspoon sugar*
*2 tablespoons cornstarch (cornflour), dissolved in 2 tablespoons water*
*1 egg, beaten*
*1 teaspoon Chinese rice wine*
*2 teaspoons dark soy sauce*

*SERVES 4–6*

❡ For the marinade: Combine all the ingredients in a bowl, then divide the mixture equally into two bowls.
❡ Marinate the pork and shrimp in separate bowls for 15 minutes.
❡ Bring the water to a boil in a pan. Add the pork and cook for 1 minute. Add the shrimp and cook for 1 minute. Drain and set aside.
❡ Bring the broth to a boil in a separate pan. Add the fungus, bean curd, bamboo shoots, ginger, scallion, vinegar, chili oil, pepper, and sugar.
❡ When the broth returns to a boil, add the pork and shrimp. Stir in the cornstarch. Add the egg and stir. Add the wine and soy sauce, and heat through before serving.

*Top: Sheung Tong; center: Choi Hung Hoi Sinn Tong; bottom: Tung Ku Kai Tong*

## CHOI HUNG HOI SINN TONG

### RAINBOW SEAFOOD SOUP

The recipe for this dish was devised around the 1970s, probably by an enterprising Hong Kong hotel chef. The fact that it was developed for tourists, however, makes it no less appetizing—in fact, it is part of a tradition. In the seventeenth and eighteenth centuries, Cantonese chefs were often invited to Beijing to create masterpieces for Manchu "tourists."

For the marinade:
2 teaspoons salt
2 teaspoons sugar
2 teaspoons cornstarch (cornflour)
1 teaspoon sesame oil
1 tablespoon water

For the soup:
6 conpoy (dried sea scallops)
4 oz (125 g) raw shrimp (green prawns), peeled and
    deveined, washed and patted dry
4 oz (125 g) sea bass fillet, diced
4 cups (1 qt/1 l) water
4 cups (1 qt/1 l) Secondary Broth (see recipe, page 75)
1 tablespoon shredded ginger
2 oz (60 g) carrots, thinly sliced
1 tablespoon light soy sauce
1 teaspoon Chinese rice wine
2 tablespoons cornstarch (cornflour), dissolved in
    2 tablespoons water
2 oz (60 g) cucumber, thinly sliced
1 tablespoon chopped cilantro (fresh coriander)

SERVES 4–6

❡ For the marinade: Combine all of the ingredients in a bowl.

❡ Marinate the *conpoy*, shrimp, and sea bass for 15 minutes.

❡ Bring the water to a boil in a large pan and add the seafood. When the water returns to a boil, remove the seafood from the pot immediately, drain, and set aside.

❡ Bring the broth to a boil in a separate large pan. Add the ginger and carrots, and cook for 2 minutes. Add the seafood and cook until the broth returns to a boil.

❡ Add the soy sauce and wine. Stir in the cornstarch. Sprinkle the cucumber and cilantro on top and serve.

## TUNG KU KAI TONG

### *CHICKEN AND BLACK MUSHROOM SOUP*

*This is an extrtemely easy, tasty, and healthy soup—but its simplicity doesn't mean that you can ignore the directions. You must be very careful in timing the cooking of the chicken: If it's overcooked, it can become stringy and will ruin a good soup.*

For the marinade:
*½ teaspoon salt*
*½ teaspoon sugar*
*1 teaspoon cornstarch (cornflour)*
*1 tablespoon water*
*1 teaspoon Chinese rice wine*
For the soup:
*2 cups (16 fl oz/500 ml) water*
*4 oz (125 g) chicken breast, cut into 2- × 1-inch (5- × 2.5-cm) strips*
*4 dried black mushrooms, soaked in warm water for 1 hour, drained, and stems discarded*
*½ teaspoon salt*
*½ teaspoon sugar*
*1 teaspoon Chinese rice wine*
*4 cups (1 qt/1 l) Secondary Broth (see recipe, opposite)*
*1 tablespoon shredded ginger*
*1 tablespoon light soy sauce*
*¼ teaspoon sesame oil*

*SERVES 4–6*

❡ For the marinade: Combine all of the ingredients in a bowl.

❡ Marinate the chicken for 15 minutes.

❡ Bring the water to a boil in a pan and add the chicken. When the chicken has turned white,

remove, drain and set aside.

❡ Cut the mushrooms into thin slivers. Mix with the salt, sugar, and wine, place on a steaming rack in a pan of boiling water, and steam for 10 minutes. Remove from the pan and set aside.

❡ Bring the broth to a boil in a large pan and add the ginger. Add the chicken and mushrooms. Add the soy sauce and sesame oil, and heat through.

❡ Serve immediately.

## SHEUNG TONG

### *SUPERIOR BROTH*

*Superior Broth is the soul of great Chinese cooking, comparable in aroma, depth and complexity to a vintage wine. It is used in only the finest dishes, especially in conjunction with such expensive ingredients as shark fin, which is prized for its texture, but has a bland taste. Because the Chinese chef never throws anything away, any leftovers from making Superior Broth can be used for Secondary Broth, which is more than adequate for most everyday recipes.*

*2½ lb (1.25 kg) chicken*
*2½ lb (1.25 kg) lean pork*
*2 lb (1 kg) Chinese or Virginia ham*
*15 cups (3¾ qt/3.75 l) water*
*4 oz (125 g) ginger, lightly crushed*
*6 scallions (spring onions)*
*3 pieces dried orange peel*

*YIELDS 10 CUPS (2½ qt/2.5 l)*

❡ Chop the meats into large pieces and place them in a pan. Add water to cover, bring to a boil, and cook for 10 minutes. Drain and rinse the meats.

❡ Bring the water to a boil in a very large pan. Add the meats and all the remaining ingredients. When the mixture returns to a boil, lower the heat and simmer uncovered for 5 hours. Strain the liquid and discard the other ingredients (or save for use in Secondary Broth).

### *SECONDARY BROTH*

*YIELDS 10 CUPS (2½ qt/2.5 l)*

❡ Reserve all of the solid ingredients used for Superior Broth and place them in a large pan. Add 12 cups (3 qt/3 l) water and bring to a boil. Lower the heat and simmer uncovered for 2½ hours. Strain the liquid and discard the other ingredients.

# JUG YU LO PAK TONG

### CARP AND SHREDDED TURNIP SOUP

*This is a mild Sichuan dish, offering good nutrition and wonderful flavor. I like to use carp, but any local fish can be substituted without a sacrifice in taste.*

1–2 white turnips, about 1 lb (500 g), peeled and cut into
  2-inch (5-cm) shreds
1 carp, about 1 lb (500 g), cleaned and patted dry
2–3 tablespoons groundnut (peanut) oil
4 cups (1 qt/1 l) Secondary Broth (see recipe, page 75)
4 slices ginger
1 tablespoon chopped cilantro (fresh coriander)
1 teaspoon pepper

SERVES 4–6

❡ Place the turnips in a pan with water to cover and cook for 5 minutes. Remove, drain, and set aside.
❡ Heat a wok or skillet (frying pan) and add the oil. Fry the fish until lightly browned on both sides. Wrap with cheesecloth and set aside.
❡ Bring the broth to a boil in a large pan. Unwrap the fish and add it to the pan with the turnips and ginger. When the broth returns to a boil, lower the heat and simmer for 30 minutes. Divide the soup into bowls, add the cilantro and pepper, and serve.

*Below: Jug Yu Lo Pak Tong*

*Premier grade shark's fin tips*

soaked in cold water for up to 3 days, then simmered until the skin peels away. The flesh must be removed by further soaking over several days until soft enough to remove from the cartilage, which is finally ready for drying. In the kitchen, shark's fins must be processed further, usually by simmering with ginger, scallions (spring onions), and rice wine. Shark's fin is traditionally served as filaments in a delicious soup in which it is simmered slowly until sublimely tender. More expensively, the fins can be braised whole, absorbing the accompanying seasonings but retaining a chewy texture that is highly regraded by Chinese connoisseurs.

Shark's fin is classified into grades:

"Most superior" means from the fin tip, and may be in the form of fine threads or the whole triangular fins.

"Very superior" comes from the middle of the fin.

"Superior" comes from the part nearest the body.

"Premier" denotes flakes of fin that have broken off in the cleaning process; these are good only for mixing, usually with crab, onions and eggs.

# SHARK'S FIN

Shark's fin is the thread-like dried cartilage taken from the fins of certain sharks, in particular the hammerhead and the tiger sharks. The former yields long, smooth threads, the latter short, thick threads.

Overfishing has, these days, forced fishermen as far as Mexico and South Africa in search of this delicacy, the second-most expensive seafood in China after abalone.

As with many exotic ingredients used in Chinese cooking, shark's fin is prized for its perceived "medicinal" value, it being described in the ancient pharmacopoeia as a tonic for good skin. It perhaps the "truffle" of China, its presence in a dish enhancing the flavor of whatever it is cooked with.

## PREPARATION
Shark's fin requires meticulous and lengthy preparation. The whole fin is removed from the fish,

## NOTE
Because shark's fin is so expensive, it has inspired some unscrupulous restaurateurs to use counterfeit ingredients in their dishes. A foolproof test for authenticity is to rub a tiny strand on a table: The fake fin will disintegrate into powder, while the real thing remains whole.

## LING MOWN DUN NGARP

*DOUBLE-BOILED DUCKLING AND PICKLED LIME SOUP*

*The Teochiu people love pickled lime, because it is a "cooling" ingredient. And this summer soup, with its distinctive citrus taste, is highly refreshing in hot weather.*

1 duckling, about 3 lb (1.5 kg)
4 cups (1 qt/1 l) water
1 pickled lime
4 slices ginger
1 tablespoon Chinese rice wine
4 cups (1 qt/1 l) boiling Secondary Broth ( recipe, page 75)

*SERVES 4–6*

❡ Chop the duckling into 6 pieces, clean thoroughly, and place in a large pan. Add the water and bring to a boil. Cook the duck for 5 minutes, remove, and drain.
❡ Place the duck, lime, ginger, and wine in a large soup tureen with a cover. Add the broth and cover. Place the tureen on a steaming rack in a pot of boiling water and steam for 3 hours. Divide the soup into bowls and serve.

## HI YUK SUK MAI GUNG

*CRAB MEAT AND CORN SOUP*

*This is a common soup in Cantonese restaurants, and is sometimes disappointing. However, using real Secondary Broth will make this dish much more flavorful.*

1 crab, about 12 oz (375 g)
1 tablespoon groundnut (peanut) oil
1 tablespoon shredded ginger
3 cups (24 fl oz/750 ml) Secondary Broth (see recipe, page 75)
1 can creamed corn (sweetcorn)
1 tablespoon chopped cilantro (fresh coriander)
1 teaspoon Chinese rice wine

*SERVES 4–6*

❡ Place the crab belly up on a cutting board and cut in half. Clean thoroughly and steam in a pan for 15 minutes. Remove the meat from the shell and set aside.
❡ Heat the oil in a pot and add the ginger. When the aroma rises, add the broth and corn, stirring to mix well. Bring the mixture to a boil, add the crab meat, and stir. When it returns to a boil, add the cilantro and wine. Divide the soup into bowls and serve.

*Left: Hi Yuk Suk Mai Gung; right: Ling Mown Dun Ngarp*

## CHING QUA YUK PEEN TONG

### SLICED PORK AND CUCUMBER SOUP

This soup has an interesting mix of flavors — with refreshing cucumber, savory pork, and an extra little kick of vinegar.

For the marinade:
1 teaspoon sugar
1/4 teaspoon sesame oil
2 teaspoons cornstarch (cornflour)
1 tablespoon water
For the soup:
6 oz (185 g) pork fillet, cut into 2- × 1-inch
   (5- × 2.5-cm) strips
3 cups (24 fl oz/750 ml) water
4 cups (1 qt/1 l) Secondary Broth (see recipe, page 75)
6 slices ginger
1/2 teaspoon sesame oil
1 teaspoon aromatic or cider vinegar
1 teaspoon salt
1 teaspoon Chinese rice wine
1/2 teaspoon pepper
1 cucumber, seeded and cut into slivers

SERVES 4–6

❡ For the marinade: Combine all of the ingredients in a bowl.
❡ Marinate the pork for 15 minutes.
❡ Bring the water to a boil in a pan and add the pork. When the water returns to a boil, remove the pork and set aside.
❡ Place the broth and ginger in a large pan and bring to a boil. Add the sesame oil, vinegar, salt, wine, and pepper. Add the pork and cucumber and heat through.
❡ Divide amongst 4–6 bowls and serve.

## LIN NGOU NGOR NAM TONG

### BRISKET OF BEEF AND LOTUS ROOT SOUP

North China is famous for its beef briskets, but this is a Cantonese dish, in which beef is paired with lotus root soup. Add some steamed rice for a satisfying single meal.

2 lb (1 kg) beef brisket, cut into 1 1/4-inch (3-cm) cubes
2 oz (60 g) ginger, crushed

Opposite: top: Lin Ngou Ngor Nam Tong; bottom: Ching Qua Yuk Peen Tong

12 cups (3 qt/3 l) water
6 red dates, pitted
1/3 piece dried tangerine (mandarin) peel, soaked in cold
   water for 30 minutes and drained
1 lotus root, about 1 lb (500 g), cleaned and cut crosswise
   into 1/4-inch (0.5-cm) thick pieces
2 teaspoons salt
For the sauce:
3–4 tablespoons groundnut (peanut) oil
6 cloves garlic, crushed
6 slices ginger
2 tablespoons oyster sauce
1 tablespoon dark soy sauce
1 tablespoon Chinese rice wine
1 1/2 tablespoons cornstarch (cornflour)
2 cups (16 fl oz/500 ml) beef broth (stock)

SERVES 6–8

❡ Place the beef in a large pan and add water to cover. Bring to a boil and cook for 3 minutes. Remove the beef from the pan, drain, and set aside.
❡ Heat a wok or large skillet (frying pan), and add the ginger and beef. Sauté over medium heat until all of the beef juices have evaporated. Set aside.
❡ Put the water in a large pan. Add the dates, orange peel, and lotus root, and bring to a boil. Add the beef and ginger.
❡ When the water returns to a boil, lower the heat and simmer for 2 hours. Remove from the heat, cover, and let steep for 1 hour. Return to the heat and bring to a boil. Reduce the heat and simmer for 2 hours.
❡ Remove the beef and lotus root from the pan and set aside. Add the salt to the pan, divide the soup into bowls, and serve.
❡ For the sauce: Heat the oil in a wok or skillet (frying pan), and fry the garlic and ginger until aroma rises. Add the beef and lotus root. Mix the remaining ingredients in a bowl and add to the wok. Stir over high heat for 1 minute and serve separately.

*Hot-pot surrounded by prepared ingredients and dipping sauces*

# CHINESE HOT-POTS

Communal eating is an important element of Chinese society. In some instances dishes are cooked at the table, with each diner looking after himself. Elegant brass "hot-pots," comprising a circular "moat" around a central chimney which sits atop a charcoal brazier, are used for cook-at-the-table meals, under such fanciful names as "chrysanthemum fire pot," "Mongolian hot-pot," and "ten varieties hot-pot."

The raw ingredients, which include cabbage or other vegetables, scallions (spring onions), bean curd, meatballs, finely sliced meat, seafood, and noodles, are presented on plates set around the hot-pot. Each diner selects his or her choice of ingredient to dip into the bubbling stock in the moat. Before eating, each mouthful is dunked into one of the accompanying spicy sauces, or into beaten raw egg. When all of the main ingredients have been eaten, the noodles are added to the hot-pot, which, when cooked, are eaten as a soup with the intensely flavored broth.

In Sichuan province, their famous communal hot-pot is a two-part wok inset into a table-top over a heat source. One container holds oil, the other a potently seasoned stock in which chilis bob in profusion. The ingredients are threaded onto thin bamboo skewers, to suspend in the hot liquid until cooked.

*Top: Pi Quuk Cheung Yu Pak Choi Tong; bottom: For Tu Chun Pak Tong*

## PI QUUK CHEUNG YU PAK CHOI TONG

*PORK RIBS, OCTOPUS, AND CABBAGE SOUP*

*The Chinese eat a lot of octopus, usually dried. It isn't expensive, and its taste is more concentrated than that of squid.*

2 lb (1 kg) pork spare-ribs
12 cups (3 qt/3 l) water
2 oz (60 g) ginger, chopped
¹/₃ piece dried tangerine (mandarin) peel, soaked in cold
    water for 30 minutes and drained
1 dried octopus, 3–4 oz (90–125 g), soaked in cold water for
    1–2 hours, and drained
1¹/₂ lb (750g) green cabbage
3 dried figs

*SERVES 6–8*

❡ Place the ribs in a large pan, add water to cover, and bring to a boil. Cook for 5 minutes. Remove the ribs, rinse, drain, and set aside.
❡ Place the water, ginger, and tangerine peel in a large pan and bring to a boil. Add the ribs and all the remaining ingredients. When the water returns to a boil, lower the heat, and simmer for 3 hours.
❡ Divide the soup into bowls and serve.

## FOR TU CHUN PAK TONG

*HAM AND CABBAGE SOUP*

*Although this sounds very much like an Irish soup, it is actually a dish that the Beijing people enjoy all year round. After all, the markets are filled with all varieties of cabbages for 12 months of the year, and this soup is a tasty way to consume the vegetable, as well as to savor some good ham.*

2–3 tablespoons groundnut (peanut) oil
4 slices ginger
1 lb (500 g) shredded Chinese cabbage
4 cups (1 qt/1 l) Secondary Broth (see recipe, page 75)
2 oz (60 g) Chinese or Virginia ham, thinly sliced

*SERVES 4–6*

❡ Heat the oil in a large wok or skillet (frying pan) and add the ginger and cabbage. Stir over high heat for 2 minutes.
❡ Add the broth. When it comes to a boil, lower the heat to medium, cover, and cook for 15 minutes. Add the ham and cook for 5 minutes.
❡ Divide the soup into bowls and serve.

*Top: Cho Chiu Yu Tong; bottom: Conpoy Daun Far Tong*

# CHO CHIU YU TONG

### *AROMATIC VINEGAR AND FISH SOUP*

This should be made at the same time as the recipe for Fillet of Sole in Wine Sauce, on page 103. First you make that dish, then you can use the leftovers and the fish bones to make this very rich soup. Use Superior Broth to make it really special. The flavor is rich, and the vinegar and pepper lend it extra savor.

1¹/₂ lb (750 g) sole, sea bass, or groper
2–3 tablespoons groundnut (peanut) oil
4 cups (1 qt/1 l) Secondary Broth (see recipe, page 75)
6 slices ginger
3 scallions (spring onions)
1 tablespoon aromatic or cider vinegar
1¹/₂ teaspoons pepper
1 teaspoon Chinese rice wine
¹/₂ teaspoon sesame oil

Remove the fish from the pot, place on a serving dish, and serve.

¶ Drain the soup into another pan and bring to a boil. Add the vinegar, pepper, wine, sesame oil, and cilantro. Adjust taste with salt. Divide the soup into bowls and serve separately.

## CONPOY DAUN FAR TONG

*CONPOY AND EGG-DROP SOUP*

*People always associate egg-drop soup with the Chinese — and for good reason. As an ingredient, it's like the punch line to a comic's opener, "We were so poor that...." Indeed, the ancient Cantonese were often so poor that they would have to make soup from spring water, a pinch of onion — and, for flavor, some drops of beaten egg. This dish is still delicious and is easy enough to make for a quick meal.*

*4 conpoy (dried sea scallops)*
*1 teaspoon Chinese rice wine*
*1/2 teaspoon sesame oil*
*4 cups (1 qt/1 l) Secondary Broth (see recipe, page 75)*
*1 tablespoon shredded ginger*
*2 eggs, beaten*
*1 tablespoon chopped scallions (spring onions)*

*SERVES 4–6*

¶ Soak the *conpoy* in a small bowl with water to cover for 2 hours. Add the wine and sesame oil. Place the bowl on a steaming rack in a pan of boiling water and steam for 20 minutes. Let cool, reserving any liquid in the bowl. Tear the *conpoy* into shreds and set aside.

¶ Place the broth and ginger in a large pan and bring to a boil. Add the *conpoy* and the reserved liquid. Stir in the egg and add the scallions. Divide into bowls and serve.

*1 tablespoon chopped cilantro (fresh coriander)*
*salt to taste*

*SERVES 4–6*

¶ Cut the fish into pieces, wash, and pat dry. Heat the oil in a wok or skillet (frying pan), and fry the fish until lightly browned. Set aside.

¶ Place the broth, ginger, and scallions in a large pan and bring to a boil. Add the fish, and cook, covered, over medium–low heat for 30 minutes.

---

*SEAWEED*
*The Chinese use two varieties of seaweed: purple, which usually turns up in soups; and white, which is multi-purpose. The seaweed is sold packaged in long, dry strips. Preparing either type of seaweed is simple. It should be placed in boiling water for about 10–15 minutes, then washed in cold water until the surface no longer feels sticky. Finally, it should be wiped dry with a clean cloth. Seaweed is used in certain duck or pork appetizers, and also as a salad vegetable, mixed with cucumbers and bean sprouts.*

---

## BOU PEEN DOU MIU TONG

### SLICED ABALONE AND PEA TENDRIL SOUP

*This is a banquet dish (abalone has always been too expensive for the commoner), but not an imperial banquet dish, as royalty would never use the ingredient in a simple soup. Nonetheless, the soup is still very special: The aroma of the pea tendrils gives a special taste to the abalone, whose texture is as smooth and beautiful as any food in the world.*

4 cups (1 qt/1 l) Secondary Broth (see recipe, page 75)
4 slices ginger
1 can , 13½ oz (425 g), abalone, cut into slivers
1 teaspoon Chinese rice wine
¼ teaspoon sesame oil
salt
2–3 tablespoons groundnut (peanut) oil
2 cups (16 fl oz/500 ml) water
8 oz (250 g) pea tendrils

SERVES 4–6

❡ Bring the broth and ginger to a boil in a large pan. Add the abalone, wine, and sesame oil. Adjust taste with salt.
❡ Heat the groundnut oil and a pinch of salt in a large pan. Add the water and bring to a boil. Add the pea tendrils and stir. When the water returns to a boil, remove the pea tendrils, drain, and divide into soup bowls.
❡ Pour the soup over the pea tendrils and serve.

## SHEUNG TONG CHUK SANG GARP DAN

### BAMBOO FUNGUS AND PIGEONS' EGGS IN SUPERIOR BROTH

*It is the addition of rare bamboo fungus that makes this a special banquet dish. Pigeon egg is always a delicacy. It is soft, slightly glutinous, and has a special meaning: The egg is considered a potent aphrodisiac in China.*

8–12 pieces bamboo fungus
3 cups (24 fl oz/750 ml) boiling water
4–6 pigeon eggs
2 cups (16 fl oz/500 ml) cold water
1 teaspoon Chinese rice wine
4 cups (1 qt/1 l) Superior Broth (see recipe, page 75)
1–1½ tablespoons shredded Chinese or Virginia ham

SERVES 4–6

❡ Cut off and discard the net, tip, and heads of the fungus. Soak the remaining fungus in warm water to cover for 2 hours.
❡ Blanch the fungus in the boiling water for 3 minutes. Remove, drain, and set aside.

❡ Place the eggs and the cold water in a pan. Bring slowly to a boil and cook for 15 minutes. When cooked, remove the eggs and let them cool Peel and set aside.
❡ Place the fungus, eggs, and wine in a large soup tureen that has a cover. Add the broth and cover. Place the tureen on a steaming rack in a pan of boiling water and steam for 30 minutes.
❡ Divide the soup into bowls, sprinkle the ham on top, and serve.

*Left: Bou Peen Dou Miu Tong; right: Sheung Tong Chuk Sang Garp Dan*

# Fish and Seafood

# FISH AND SEAFOOD

WITH OVER 3,000 MILES (4,800 KILOMETERS) OF COASTLINE, A PROFUSION OF LAKES, RIVERS, man-made and natural canals, and temperatures ranging from sub-zero to tropical, China probably has more marine and riverine fish and shellfish than any country in the world. Ancient records show that fishing and fish-breeding go back thousands of years. But, of course, the art of cooking fish is timeless.

For the modern Chinese gourmet, there is only one rule for fish: absolute freshness. While frozen foods are becoming more prevalent, fish in Chinese markets are, whenever possible, purchased live. Shoppers go to the markets with bags in which fish and water can be carried home. In the kitchen the fish is placed on a wooden board, and killed with one knock on the head from the flat edge of a cleaver.

When unable to buy fish live, the Chinese housewife or chef will look for telltale signs of freshness. The eyes should be clear, not filmy. The gills should be pink to red. The flesh should be firm (touching is not taboo) and odorless.

Once cleaned and scaled, the fish is generally cooked whole, though a fillet or steak may be

*Previous pages: Like many other foods, fish is often hung for wind-drying. The flavor, even after soaking or steaming, is strong and distinctive and much loved by the Chinese.*
BRUCE COLEMAN LIMITED/FRASER HALL

*Opposite: A young fisher-girl from Canton (Guangdong) province holds a large salted fish. Salting is a widely used preserving process in China, and the intense taste that results when the fish is fried is favored by many.*
CHINA TOURISM PHOTO LIBRARY/CHAN YAT NIN

acceptable for a casserole or a mixed seafood dish. It may be cooked by many methods, but by far the most respected is steaming. This traditionally keeps fragrance and color and tastes as natural as possible.

The Chinese look askance at many saltwater fish. To them, these fish have too brackish a taste. River fish like various members of the carp family, are their favorites and they prize the rock and black carp above others. But *shek paan*, the grouper or garoupa is one marine exception that all Chinese respect for its tender meat. The flat, silver-white *paak cheong* or pomfret and *hung yu*, red snapper, are both fish that suit the Chinese taste and cooking methods.

From the ocean also come shellfish—almost all types of which are consumed with great relish. But freshwater shrimp (prawns) and crabs are also caught in China's many lakes and the massive rivers that dissect this huge country. Eels, too, are an abundant food source and highly regarded, especially by the Shanghainese, who serve it braised in a rich brown sauce, and liberally doused with white pepper before coming, sizzling, to the table.

"Drunken shrimp" is a culinary frivolity in the best Chinese tradition. Live shrimp in their shells are placed in a bowl of Chinese warm wine, over a tiny, low fire. The combination of wine, heat, and lack of oxygen causes a slow death just at the point of eating.

It is true that the Chinese enjoy eating virtually any creature that can be caught or harvested from the sea that is not poisonous. Thus many strange creatures of the deep—sea slugs, eels, abalone, clams, floating creatures like giant jellyfish and octopus, and free swimming sea life such as squid, cuttlefish, sharks, and turtles have their prescribed place in the kitchen and the cooking pot.

## HEUNG LARK JIN YU

### PAN-FRIED FISH WITH RED CHILI SAUCE

*The most esteemed quality in Cantonese cooking is fresh-
ness. But when the ingredients cannot all be fresh, you can
hide the fact with a rich sauce. The fish for this dish can
have been chilled or frozen, but it will still taste good because
of the red chili and garlic.*

For the sauce:
*1 tablespoon light soy sauce*
*1 teaspoon dark soy sauce*
*1 teaspoon sugar*
*2 teaspoons Chinese rice wine*
*½ cup (4 fl oz/125 ml) chicken broth (stock)*
*½ cup (4 fl oz/125 ml) water*
For the fish:
*1 lb (500 g) whole perch (redfin) or sea bass (groper),
    washed, cleaned, and patted dry*
*1 tablespoon cornstarch (cornflour)*
*4–6 tablespoons groundnut (peanut) oil*
*1 tablespoon shredded ginger*
*1 tablespoon chopped scallion (spring onion)*
*1 tablespoon seeded and chopped red chili*
*1 teaspoon chopped garlic*

*SERVES 4–6*

❡ For the sauce: In a bowl, mix all the ingredients
together well.
❡ Coat both sides of the fish with cornstarch.
❡ Heat the oil in a wok or skillet (frying pan), add
the fish, and fry over medium heat for 3 minutes on
each side. Remove the fish and set aside.
❡ Drain all but 1–2 tablespoons of oil from the wok
and reheat. Add the ginger, scallions, chili, and
garlic. Stir-fry for 15 seconds.
❡ Return the fish to the wok. Pour the sauce over
the fish, cover, and cook over medium–low heat for
2 minutes. Serve.

## SZE JUP JING YU

### STEAMED SALMON STEAK WITH BLACK BEAN SAUCE

*What a combination! The rich, moist salmon and thick,
strong black bean sauce complement one another to yield an
entirely new flavor. In some recipes, black bean sauce is
paired with delicately flavored fish, but this is always a
mistake, as the fish is overwhelmed by the sauce. Salmon,
however, can hold its own and balance the presence of the
black beans.*

For the sauce:
*2 tablespoons fermented black beans, chopped*
*1 tablespoon light soy sauce*
*1 teaspoon sugar*
*1 teaspoon sesame oil*
*2 teaspoons Chinese rice wine*
*2 teaspoons cornstarch (cornflour)*
*1 tablespoon water*

For the salmon:

*2 salmon steaks, 8 oz (250 g) each*
*2 scallion (spring onion) stems*
*3–4 tablespoons groundnut (peanut) oil*

*SERVES 4–6*

❦ For the sauce: In a bowl, mix all the ingredients well. Place the scallion stems on a long platter and put the fish on top. Spread the sauce evenly over the fish.

❦ Bring 3–4 cups (24 fl oz–1 qt/750 ml–1 l) of water to a rapid boil in a large pan. Place a steaming rack in the middle of the pan and put the platter with the fish on top. Cover and steam over high heat for 7–8 minutes. Remove and set aside.

❦ Heat the groundnut oil in a small pan, pour over the fish, and serve.

*Top: Sze Jup Jing Yu; bottom: Heung Lark Jin Yu*

## CHUEN MAI GONE SIU YU

### BRAISED COD WITH FAVA BEAN SAUCE

*This is a Sichuan dish—very pungent. The hot fava (broad) bean paste has a lot of garlic and chili, giving this dish a punch that is the hallmark of Sichuan cooking. Cod is very common, but any fish can be substituted here, even trout if you don't mind the bones.*

For the marinade:
*1 tablespoon light soy sauce*
*1 teaspoon sugar*
*1 teaspoon pepper*
*2 teaspoons cornstarch (cornflour)*
For the fish:
*2 pieces cod steak, about 1 lb (500 g)*
*4–5 tablespoons groundnut (peanut) oil*
*1 tablespoon chopped ginger*
*1 tablespoon chopped garlic*
*1 tablespoon chopped scallion (spring onion)*
For the sauce:
*1 tablespoon light soy sauce*
*2 tablespoons hot fava (broad) bean paste*
*1 teaspoon sugar*
*1 cup (8 fl oz/250 ml) chicken broth (stock)*

*SERVES 4–6*

❡ For the marinade: Mix all the ingredients together in a bowl.
❡ Marinate the cod for 15 minutes.
❡ For the sauce: Mix all the ingredients in a bowl and set aside.
❡ Heat 2–3 tablespoons of the oil in a wok or skillet (frying pan) and fry the cod until browned on both sides. Remove, drain, and set aside.
❡ Heat 2 tablespoons of the oil in the wok and add the ginger, garlic, and scallion. When the aroma arises, add the sauce. Return the fish to the wok and cook over medium–low heat for 5 minutes.
❡ Serve immediately.

## SHEUNG DONG YU LAU

### BRAISED COD WITH MUSHROOMS AND BAMBOO SHOOTS

*Cod can be bland, so give it extra zing with this rich sauce. The mushrooms, wine, and ginger add flavor that the fish does not have on its own. Don't worry if you need to use frozen fish—braising in the sauce disguises the fact that the fish may not be fresh.*

For the marinade:
*1 teaspoon salt*
*1 teaspoon sugar*
*1 teaspoon sesame oil*
*1 tablespoon cornstarch (cornflour)*
For the fish:
*1 lb (500 g) cod fillet, cut into 1- × 1/2 -inch (2.5- × 1-cm) pieces*
*3 cups (24 fl oz/750 ml) groundnut (peanut) oil*
*1 teaspoon finely chopped garlic*
*2–3 pieces ginger*
*2 scallions (spring onions), white part only, cut into 1 1/2 -inch (3-cm) lengths*
*6 dried black mushrooms, soaked in warm water for 1 hour, drained, and stems discarded*
*2 oz (60 g) bamboo shoots, cut into slivers*
*1 1/2 cups (12 fl oz/375 ml) chicken broth (stock)*
*1 tablespoon oyster sauce*
*1 teaspoon dark soy sauce*
*1 teaspoon Chinese rice wine*

*SERVES 4–6*

❡ For the marinade: Combine all of the ingredients in a bowl.
❡ Marinate the cod for 15 minutes.
❡ Heat the oil in a wok or skillet (frying pan) and fry the cod until lightly browned. Remove, drain, and set aside.
❡ Drain all but 2–3 tablespoons of oil from the wok and reheat. Add the garlic, ginger, scallions, mushrooms, and bamboo shoots. Stir-fry for 1 minute. Return the cod to the wok and add the broth. Cover and cook over medium–low heat for 7 minutes.
❡ Add all the remaining ingredients. Stir to mix well and serve.

*Left: Chuen Mai Gone Siu Yu; right: Sheung Dong Yu Lau*

*Left: Chiuchow Chu Yu; right: Hung Siu Yu*

# CHIUCHOW CHU YU

## FISH STEW CHIUCHOW-STYLE

*When Chiuchow people sit down for a hearty stew, they have a ritual. Everybody dips a spoon into the central bowl and if they like the soup, they nod and smack their lips in approval. This is a typical Chiuchow stew, and the sea bream is extremely tasty.*

For the seasoning:
1 teaspoon salt
1/2 teaspoon pepper
2 teaspoons cornstarch (cornflour)
For the fish:
1 lb (500 g) sea bream fillet, cut into 1- x 1 1/2 -inch
    (2.5- x 3-cm) pieces
2–3 tablespoons groundnut (peanut) oil
2 cups (16 fl oz/500 ml) chicken broth (stock)
2–3 slices ginger
1 Chinese celery stalk, or fine stalk of celery, cut into
    1 1/2 -inch (3-cm) lengths
1 tablespoon fish sauce
1 tablespoon pickled vegetables
1 teaspoon Chinese rice wine

SERVES 4–6

❧ For the seasoning: Combine all of the ingredients in a bowl and mix well.

❧ Coat the fish with the seasoning, and set aside for 15 minutes.
❧ Heat the oil in a wok or skillet (frying pan) and sauté the fish for about 1 1/2 minutes. Remove, drain, and set aside.
❧ Bring the broth to a boil in a pan and add the ginger and celery. Add the fish to the pan, cover, and cook over medium heat for 5 minutes. Add the fish sauce, pickled vegetables, and wine.
❧ Serve immediately.

# HUNG SIU YU

## BRAISED FISH SHANGHAI-STYLE

*Carp, yellow croaker, or rock cod, or even sea bass or groper are suitable for this rich dish. The aroma is enticing, with the vinegar giving a bit of a sting. People from Shanghai like sugar in their sauces, and this gives it a distinctive flavor.*

For the marinade:
1 1/2 teaspoons salt
1/2 teaspoon pepper
1 1/2 tablespoons cornstarch (cornflour)
1 1/2 tablespoons water
For the fish:
2 lb (1 kg) yellow croaker, carp, or rock cod, scaled, washed,
    cleaned, and patted dry
1 cup (8 fl oz/250 ml) groundnut (peanut) oil
6 garlic cloves
2–3 slices ginger
2 scallions (spring onions), chopped
1 tablespoon light soy sauce
1 tablespoon dark soy sauce
2 teaspoons sugar
1 teaspoon aromatic or cider vinegar
3 cups (24 fl oz/750 ml) chicken broth (stock)
1 teaspoon Chinese rice wine

SERVES 4–6

❧ For the marinade: Combine all of the ingredients in a bowl and mix well.
❧ Marinate the fish for 30 minutes.
❧ Heat the oil in a wok or skillet (frying pan) and pan-fry the fish until lightly browned on both sides. Remove the fish from the wok, drain, and set aside.
❧ Drain all but 3–4 tablespoons of oil from the wok and reheat. Add the garlic, ginger, and scallions, and sauté for 1 minute. Add the soy sauces, sugar, vinegar, and broth. Return the fish to the wok, cover, and cook over medium–low heat for 15 minutes. Add the wine and serve.

# FISH AND SEAFOOD TYPES

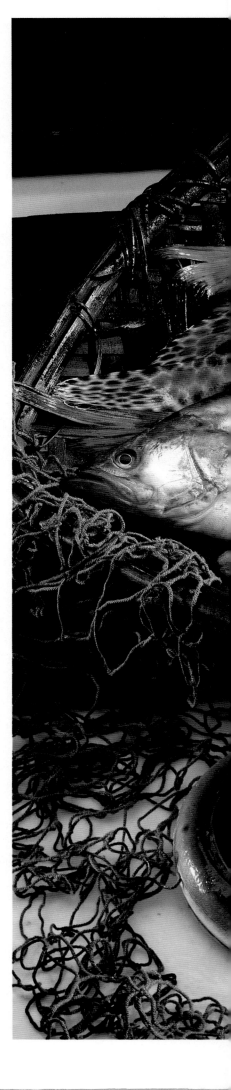

The massive Yangtze that meanders across central China, and the Huang (Yellow) River which flows North through Shandong province, are well stocked with fish, eels, turtles, and even several kinds of freshwater shellfish. Similarly, the scenic West Lake and China's many other lotus-covered lakes are an excellent breeding ground for carp and other fish, and some unique mollusks.

At night, along the picturesque Li River in the South, narrow craft slide over the still surface that reflects the towering mountains on each side. Perched on the front are trained cormorants whose nightly duty is to dive for fish and return to the boats to release them from deep inside their long necks into the fishermen's baskets. In the Chinese language, the word for fish is "*yu*." With a different inflection, this word can also mean abundance.

**Carp:** Most prized are carp, which are netted daily in massive quantities. The small crucian or common carp (*jug yu*) is a meaty little fish with tender flesh. It is popular throughout the country and cooked many different ways, from hot and spicy in the fiery Sichuan chili and vinegar sauces to blandly steamed with egg.

**Grass carp** (*wan yu*): This has a long meaty body and thick tail. It is often marinated before cooking, so the flavors penetrate the soft flesh right down to the bones. One unusual way of cooking this fish is to

bundle it inside a bamboo tube and grill it over glowing coals.

**Rock carp:** These have small heads, thick bodies, and small bones. Their rich, sweet meat is complemented by intense seasonings, and sweet-and-sour combinations.

**Big-headed chub fish:** These are prized for their meaty heads, which account for at least one-fourth of their body weight. They are simmered for hours into delicious milky soup-stews.

Over the generations, many elaborate preparations for fish have been devised. One that particularly impresses is "Fish in the shape of a bunch of grapes," where a meaty fillet still in its skin is deeply scored, floured, and fried to curl and part into golden "grape" shapes. It is served with a sweet-tart grape juice-based sauce.

Perhaps China's most famed fish dish is Westlake Carp, named for the scenic, lotus-covered West Lake in Hangzhou. The fish are cooked in woks so hot they glow red. Just a few moments in the pan to sear, then braised in wine and ginger and lastly glazed with a sweet and tangy golden sauce.

**Mandarin fish** (*kwai yu*): These are, next to carp, the most frequently consumed fish in China. Their flesh is akin to a perch or sea bass.

**Other small fish:** Snake head (*sang yu*) and dace (*lang yu*), tench, and catfish are eaten in quantity.

**Rock cod and groper (garoupa)** (*sheek pan*):

These are two favorite Chinese sea fish.

**Golden thread**, *hung sam*: Has a pink body, yellow stripes, and thread-like extension from its tail, and is one of the most abundant fish in South China waters.

**Pomfret:** With their leathery silver skin, pomfret are treated to aromatic smoke before frying or steaming, to serve red-brown and fragrant.

**Salt and freshwater eels:** These are sold live in Chinese fish markets, where they are scooped from plastic tubs into plastic bags to carry, still wriggling, back to the kitchen for preparation.

**Squid and cuttlefish:** These appear in many Chinese dishes, and the clever Chinese chef has devised a way of preparing the chewy white flesh to make it both tender and attractive. Using his cleaver held at an angle, he makes a series of close scores across the flesh, then he turns and cuts across these scores. The flesh then cooks into "pine cone" curls.

*1. cuttlefish; 2. grass carp (wan yu); 3. rock cod; 4. mandarin fish (kwai yu); 5. big head (dai yu); 6. yellow egg (wong sin); 7. squid; 8. white eel (pak sin); 9. snake head (sang yu); 10. dace (lang yu); 11. common carp (jug yu)*

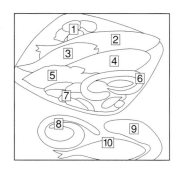

*Top: Fu Qua Mun Yu; bottom: Jum Yu*

## JUM YU

### POACHED SALMON STEAK

*While salmon is available in China, it is not commonly served. The problem is that salmon is a seasonal dish, and the Chinese like to eat their favorites all year long. The cilantro (fresh coriander) gives this Cantonese dish an extraordinary aroma.*

For the marinade:
*1 teaspoon salt*
*1 teaspoon sugar*
*1/2 teaspoon sesame oil*
*1 tablespoon cornstarch (cornflour)*
For the fish:
*1 lb (500 g) salmon steak, about 1/2-inch (1-cm) thick*
*8 cups (2 qt/2 l) water*
*2 scallions (spring onions)*
*4–6 slices ginger*
*1 tablespoon Chinese rice wine*

*1 tablespoon salt*
*2 tablespoons groundnut (peanut) oil*
*2 tablespoons light soy sauce*
*1 teaspoon sugar*
*1 teaspoon sesame oil*
*1 cup (8 fl oz/250 ml) chicken broth (stock)*
*1 tablespoon finely chopped cilantro (fresh coriander)*

*SERVES 4–6*

¶ For the marinade: Combine all of the ingredients in a bowl.
¶ Marinate the salmon for 15 minutes.
¶ Place the water, scallions, ginger, wine, and salt in a large pan and bring to a rapid boil. Add the salmon. When the water returns to a boil, lower the heat, and simmer for 15 minutes. Remove, drain, and transfer the salmon to a serving platter.
¶ In a wok or skillet (frying pan), heat the groundnut oil. Add the soy sauce, sugar, sesame oil, and broth. Bring to a boil and pour over the salmon. Sprinkle the cilantro over the top and serve.

# FU QUA MUN YU

### BRAISED POMFRET WITH BITTER MELON

*Pomfret is popular in Cantonese cooking and, during the tropical summers, the combination of pomfret and bitter melon is a welcome "cooler." It may seem to be a strange mixture, but the flavors do harmonize.*

For the seasoning:
*1 teaspoon salt*
*1 teaspoon sugar*
*1 tablespoon cornstarch (cornflour)*
For the fish:
*1 lb (500 g) pomfret, sea bass, or groper, scaled, washed, cleaned, and patted dry*
*1 lb (500 g) bitter melon, seeds discarded, sliced lengthwise, and cut into thin slivers*
*4 cups (1 qt/1 l) boiling water*
*1 cup (8 fl oz/250 ml) groundnut (peanut) oil*
*2 tablespoons fermented black beans*
*2 garlic cloves, finely chopped*
*1 tablespoon light soy sauce*
*1 teaspoon dark soy sauce*
*1 teaspoon sugar*

*4 cups (1 qt/1 l) chicken broth (stock)*
*1 teaspoon Chinese rice wine*

*SERVES 4–6*

❡ For the seasoning: Combine all the ingredients in a bowl.
❡ Coat the fish with the seasoning, and set aside for 30 minutes.
❡ Blanch the melon in the boiling water for 2 minutes. Drain and set aside.
❡ Heat the oil in a wok or skillet (frying pan) and fry the fish until lightly browned on both sides. Remove the fish from the wok, drain, and set aside.
❡ Drain all but 2–3 tablespoons of oil from the wok and reheat. In a bowl, mash together the black beans and garlic, and add to the wok. Cook the mixture over low heat for 1 minute, then add the soy sauces and sugar.
❡ Add the bitter melon and stir-fry over high heat for 1 minute. Add the broth and bring to a boil. Return the fish to the wok, cover, and cook over medium–low heat for 12 minutes. Remove the fish and melon to a serving platter and cook the sauce over high heat to reduce slightly. Add the wine and pour the sauce over the fish. Serve.

*Dried and reconstituted sea cucumbers*

# SEA CUCUMBER

The common "spiky" sea cucumber (*chee sum*), bêche de mer, or trepang, is one of the most prized ingredients in the Chinese gourmet's cupboard.

Though the flavor is nearly non-existent and the texture is fleshy and gelatinous, the sea cucumber is deemed a potent aphrodisiac. Like shark fin, it soaks up the flavors of the rich sauces in which it is cooked.

In certain parts of China and in Hong Kong, this little marine animal can be purchased fresh and ready for cooking at fish markets. Dried sea cucumbers require a very lengthy soaking or a very slow simmer overnight to soften their rigid forms. They are then cut open, any remnants of their innards scraped out, and soaked in cold water for a further half hour. Once ready to cook, they can be refrigerated for up to a week, if the water is changed daily. An additional boiling, with sliced ginger, helps to remove any fishy taste and improves the flavor. Sea cucumber is cooked on its own, or added to soups and stews. The rarer "smooth" sea cucumber *tok sum* is also sold for eating.

*Dried, salted strips of jellyfish and whole, flat sun-dried mantles; upper right: fresh jellyfish*

## JELLYFISH

When the sun rises on the tiny beach of Hatchao, Thailand, boats anchor along the shore, their nets dispersing some of the ugliest creatures of the sea. Hatchao Samran is a major port for fishing jellyfish, *phopilema esculenta*—a delicacy prized by the Chinese who now have to seek it far from Chinese waters where stocks have been depleted.

After being cleaned and dried, the flat white mantles of the jellyfish are sliced wafer-thin and loaded onto cargo ships for transportation to China and Hong Kong.

Jellyfish is, like shark fin and other Chinese delicacies, appreciated for its texture rather than its bland taste. It is served cold as an appetizer, its texture tender, crunchy, and elastic, and is sometimes added to a stir-fried chicken dish.

Jellyfish is sold dried in disks of around 15 inches (about 38 cm) in diameter. As long as it is kept in a sealed container, it will last indefinitely. To prepare, soak the flat sheets in cold water for three or four hours, then drain. Pour on hot water and pour off immediately. No further cooking is required if the jellyfish is to be used in a salad. If it is to be stir-fried, scald very briefly in an extremely hot wok.

## SIN KU YU KAU

### STIR-FRIED FILLET OF FISH WITH FRESH MUSHROOMS

*This dish uses substantial chunks of fish that contrast with the button mushrooms, which have a robust taste.*

For the marinade:
*1 teaspoon sugar*
*1 teaspoon salt*
*1/2 teaspoon sesame oil*
*1 teaspoon cornstarch (cornflour)*
*1 1/2 tablespoons groundnut (peanut) oil*
For the fish:
*12 oz (375 g) rock cod or salmon fillet, cut into 1 1/2- × 1-inch (3- ×2.5-cm) pieces*
*10 oz (315 g) button mushrooms (champignons)*
*3 cups (24 fl oz/750 ml) boiling water*
*1 cup (8 fl oz/250 ml) groundnut (peanut) oil*
*1 teaspoon chopped garlic*
*1 teaspoon chopped ginger*
*1/2 teaspoon salt*
*1 tablespoon oyster sauce*

*1 teaspoon dark soy sauce*
*1/2 teaspoon sesame oil*
*1 teaspoon cornstarch (cornflour)*
*1 cup (8 fl oz/250 ml) chicken broth (stock)*
*1 teaspoon Chinese rice wine*
*1 tablespoon chopped scallions (spring onions)*

*SERVES 4–6*

❡ For the marinade: Combine all the ingredients in a bowl.
❡ Marinate the fish for 15 minutes.
❡ Blanch the mushrooms in the boiling water for 1 minute. Drain and set aside.
❡ Heat the oil in a wok or skillet (frying pan) and add the fish, stirring to separate. Fry the fish over medium heat for 2 minutes. Remove the fish from the wok, drain, and set aside.
❡ Drain all but 2–3 tablespoons of oil from the wok and reheat. Add the garlic and ginger. Add the mushrooms and fish, and stir-fry over high heat for 1 minute. In a bowl, mix together the salt, oyster sauce, soy sauce, sesame oil, cornstarch, and broth, and add to the wok. Bring to a boil and add the wine. Sprinkle the scallions on top and serve.

# CHOI CHAU YU PIN

## STIR-FRIED FILLET OF CARP WITH FLOWERING CABBAGE

*Cantonese housewives know the secret of this dish, which is rarely served in restaurants. The secret is in the heat: High, medium and then high again, each for a few seconds. The timing must be accurate, to ensure the best taste.*

For the marinade:
3/4 teaspoon salt
3/4 teaspoon sugar
1 teaspoon cornstarch (cornflour)
2–3 tablespoons groundnut (peanut) oil
For the fish:
10 oz (315 g) carp, rock cod, or flake fillet, cut into 1/8-inch (0.25 cm) thin slices
1 cup (8 fl oz/250 ml) groundnut (peanut) oil
2–3 slices ginger
1/2 teaspoon salt
1 lb (500 g) Chinese flowering cabbage, flowers and stems discarded, chopped
1 cup (8 fl oz/250 ml) chicken broth (stock)
1 teaspoon finely chopped ginger
1 teaspoon finely chopped garlic

1/2 tablespoon oyster sauce
1/2 tablespoon light soy sauce
1 teaspoon sugar
1 teaspoon cornstarch (cornflour)
1 teaspoon Chinese rice wine

SERVES 4–6

❧ For the marinade: Combine all of the ingredients in a bowl.
❧ Marinate the fish for 15 minutes.
❧ Heat the oil in a wok or skillet (frying pan). Add the ginger, salt, and cabbage, and stir-fry over high heat for 1 minute. Add 1/4 cup (2 fl oz/60 ml) of the broth, cover, and cook over medium heat for 1 minute. Transfer the cabbage to a serving platter, cover, and set aside.
❧ Heat the remaining oil in a wok. Add the fish and stir-fry quickly over high heat for 30 seconds. Remove the fish from the wok, drain, and set aside.
❧ Drain all but 1–2 tablespoons of oil from the wok and reheat. Add the ginger and garlic. Return the fish to the wok and stir-fry over high heat for 15 seconds. In a bowl, mix together the oyster sauce, soy sauce, sugar, cornstarch, and remaining broth, and add to the wok. Bring to a boil and add the wine. Pour over top of cabbage and serve.

*Top: Choi Chau Yu Pin; bottom: Sin Ku Yu Kau*

## TUNG CHOI JING YU

### STEAMED POMFRET AND PICKLED VEGETABLES

*The Chiuchow people love pickled vegetables for their strong flavor, and they also enjoy contrasts in their food. In this dish, the pomfret is complemented by the tung choi, which means garlic stems. This is another of the "soupy" dishes so beloved in the region.*

3 scallions (spring onions)
1 pomfret or sea bream, about 1½ lb (750 g)
2 tablespoons pickled vegetables, washed and squeezed dry
1 tablespoon shredded ginger
1 tablespoon shredded chilis
3–4 tablespoons groundnut (peanut) oil
1 tablespoon light soy sauce
1 teaspoon sugar
1 teaspoon Chinese rice wine
1 cup (8 fl oz/250 ml) chicken broth (stock)

SERVES 4–6

❡ Place the scallions on a platter and place the pomfret on top. Spread the pickled vegetables, ginger, and chilis evenly over the pomfret.
❡ Place a steaming rack in a wok or round-bottomed pan and add enough water to reach nearly to the top of rack. Bring the water to a rapid boil and place the platter with the pomfret on the rack. Cover, and steam over high heat for 10 minutes. Remove the pomfret and set aside. Drain the wok.
❡ Heat the oil in the wok until very hot and pour over the pomfret.
❡ Mix all the remaining ingredients in the wok and bring to a boil. Pour over the pomfret and serve.

## SZE CHIU JING YU

### STEAMED COD WITH SOYBEAN PASTE AND CHILIS

*The chili, garlic, and cilantro (fresh coriander) in this recipe are combined with soybean paste for a vigorous taste.*

For the marinade:
1 teaspoon salt
1 teaspoon sugar
1 teaspoon sesame oil
2 teaspoons cornstarch (cornflour)
For the fish:
1 lb (500 g) cod steaks, about ¾-inch (1.75-cm) thick
3 scallions (spring onions)
2 tablespoons soybean paste
3 garlic cloves, finely chopped

*Top: Tung Choi Jing Yu; bottom: Sze Chiu Jing Yu*

1 teaspoon sugar
1 teaspoon hot chili oil
1 teaspoon cornstarch (cornflour)
1 teaspoon Chinese rice wine
1 tablespoon water
1 tablespoon shredded chilis
1 tablespoon shredded ginger
1 tablespoon chopped cilantro (fresh coriander)
3–4 tablespoons groundnut (peanut) oil

SERVES 4–6

❡ For the marinade: Combine all the ingredients in a bowl. Marinate the cod for 15 minutes.
❡ Place the scallions on a platter and place the cod on top. In a bowl, mash together the soybean paste and garlic, and mix with the sugar, chili oil, cornstarch, wine, and water. Spread the paste evenly over the cod. Sprinkle the chilis and ginger on top.
❡ Place a steaming rack in a wok or round-bottomed pan and add enough water to reach nearly to the top of the rack. Bring the water to a rapid boil and place the platter with the cod on the rack. Cover and steam over high heat for 10 minutes.
❡ Remove the cod from the wok and drain the liquid. Sprinkle the cilantro over the cod.
❡ Heat the oil in the wok until very hot. Pour over the cod and serve.

## SANG MUN YU

### BRAISED SEA BASS WITH SHREDDED PORK AND BLACK MUSHROOMS

*It is best to use fresh pork in this dish, even though only a small amount is required, as it is an important flavoring.*

For the seasoning:

*1 teaspoon salt*

*1 teaspoon sugar*

*1 tablespoon cornstarch (cornflour)*

For the fish:

*1 sea bass, sea perch, or groper, about 1½ lb (750 g)*

*1 cup (8 fl oz/250 ml) groundnut (peanut) oil*

*6 garlic cloves*

*3 scallions (spring onions), cut in half*

*3–4 slices ginger*

*2 dried black mushrooms, soaked in warm water for 1 hour, drained, stems discarded, and shredded*

*1 tablespoon oyster sauce*

*1 tablespoon light soy sauce*

*1 teaspoon dark soy sauce*

*½ teaspoon sesame oil*

*3 cups (24 fl oz/750 ml) chicken broth (stock)*

*1 oz (30 g) pork fillet, finely shredded*

*1 teaspoon Chinese rice wine*

*SERVES 4–6*

❡ For the seasoning: Combine all of the ingredients in a bowl.

❡ Coat the bass with the seasoning ingredients and set aside for 30 minutes.

❡ Heat the oil in a wok or skillet (frying pan), and fry the garlic until lightly browned. Remove the garlic from the pan and set aside.

❡ Add the bass to the wok and fry until lightly browned on both sides. Remove the bass from the wok, drain, and set aside.

❡ Drain all but 2–3 tablespoons of oil from the wok and reheat. Return the garlic to the pan. Add the scallions, ginger, and mushrooms, and sauté over medium heat for 30 seconds.

❡ Mix the oyster sauce, soy sauces, sesame oil, and broth in a bowl. Return the bass to the wok and add the oyster sauce mixture. Cover and cook over medium–low heat for 12 minutes. Add the pork and cook for 3 minutes. Add the wine and serve.

## JO LIU YU

*FILLET OF SOLE IN WINE SAUCE*

*This is a Beijing dish and is very mild, with just enough wine to stimulate the taste buds.*

For the marinade:

*1 teaspoon salt*

*1 teaspoon sugar*

*½ teaspoon sesame oil*

*1 tablespoon cornstarch (cornflour)*

For the fish:

*1 lb (500 g) sole, flounder, or groper fillets, cut into 1½- × 1-inch (3- × 2.5-cm) thick slices*

*2 cups (16 fl oz/500 ml) groundnut (peanut) oil*

*1 teaspoon chopped ginger*

*1 teaspoon chopped garlic*

*1 tablespoon light soy sauce*

*2 teaspoons sugar*

*1–2 tablespoons Chinese rice wine*

*1 teaspoon cornstarch (cornflour)*

*1½ cups (12 fl oz/375 ml) chicken broth (stock)*

*2 tablespoons shredded scallion (spring onion)*

*SERVES 4–6*

❡ For the marinade: Combine all of the ingredients in a bowl.

❡ Marinate the sole for 15 minutes.

❡ Heat the oil in a wok or skillet (frying pan) and add the sole piece by piece. Once the sole turns white, remove it from the pan, drain, and set aside.

❡ Drain all but 2–3 tablespoons of oil from the wok and reheat. Add the ginger and garlic. Mix the soy sauce, sugar, wine, cornstarch, and broth in a bowl.

❡ Return the sole to the wok and add the soy sauce mixture. Bring the mixture to a boil and cook over medium heat for 3 minutes. Transfer to a serving platter, sprinkle with the scallion, and serve.

*Left: Sang Mun Yu; right: Jo Liu Yu*

*Left: Mui Tze Dou Cheung Jing Yu; right: Lo Pak Chu Yu*

## MUI TZE DOU CHEUNG JING YU

*STEAMED TURBOT WITH PICKLED PLUMS AND SOYBEAN PASTE*

*Turbot is as meaty and fine-textured a fish as you can buy, and this recipe gives it an entirely new flavor, with its wonderful sweet-and-sour sauce.*

For the marinade:
*1 teaspoon salt*
*1 teaspoon sugar*
*1 teaspoon sesame oil*
*1 teaspoon cornstarch (cornflour)*
For the fish:
*1 lb (500 g) turbot, flounder, or groper steak, about ³/₄-inch (1.75-cm) thick*
*3 scallions (spring onions), 3 whole, 1 finely chopped*
*2 pickled plums, pitted*
*2 teaspoons sugar*
*2 tablespoons soybean paste*
*2–3 garlic cloves, finely chopped*
*1 chili, seeded and shredded*
*1 tablespoon light soy sauce*
*1 teaspoon cornstarch (cornflour)*
*1 teaspoon Chinese rice wine*
*2–3 tablespoons groundnut (peanut) oil*

*SERVES 4–6*

❡ For the marinade: Combine all the ingredients in a bowl. Marinate the turbot for 15 minutes.
❡ Place the whole scallions on a platter and place the turbot on top.
❡ In a bowl, mash together the pickled plums, sugar, soybean paste, garlic, chili, soy sauce, cornstarch

and wine, and spread evenly over the fish.
❡ Place a steaming rack in a wok or round-bottomed pan and add enough water to reach nearly to the top of the rack. Bring to a rapid boil. Place the platter with the turbot on the rack, cover, and steam over high heat for 12 minutes.
❡ Remove the turbot from the wok and drain the liquid. Sprinkle the chopped scallion over the turbot.
❡ Heat the oil in the wok until very hot, pour over the turbot, and serve.

## LO PAK CHU YU

*YELLOW CROAKER AND TURNIP STEW*

*Turnip blends beautifully with fish in a stew, gradually neutralizing the fishy smell.*

For the seasoning:
*1¹/₂ teaspoons salt*
*1 teaspoon sugar*
*1 tablespoon cornstarch (cornflour)*
For the fish:
*1 lb (500 g) yellow croaker, river carp, or rock cod, cleaned, and patted dry*
*1 lb (500 g) turnips, peeled and cut into 2 × 1 × ¹/₄-inch (5 × 2.5 × 0.5-cm) pieces*
*4 cups (1 qt/1 l) boiling water*
*1 cup (8 fl oz/250 ml) groundnut (peanut) oil*
*2 garlic cloves, crushed*
*2 tablespoons soybean paste*
*1 teaspoon salt*
*1 teaspoon pepper*
*4 cups (1 qt/1 l) chicken broth (stock)*
*2 scallions (spring onions), chopped*

*SERVES 4–6*

❡ For the seasoning: Combine all the ingredients in a bowl. Coat the fish with the seasoning, and set aside for 30 minutes.
❡ Blanch the turnips in the boiling water. Drain and set aside.
❡ Heat the oil in a wok or skillet (frying pan) and fry the fish until lightly browned on both sides. Remove the fish from the pan, drain, and set aside.
❡ Drain all but 2–3 tablespoons of oil from the wok and reheat. Add the garlic and fry until golden brown. Add the soybean paste, salt, and pepper. Add the turnips and cook over high heat for 1 minute.
❡ Return the fish to the wok and add the broth. Bring to a boil and cook over medium–low heat for 10 minutes. Sprinkle the scallions on top, remove to a dish and serve.

## CHOW HEUNG HAI

### STEAMED CRAB WITH WINE SAUCE

*Crab has never been inexpensive in China, but on special occasions people are ready to make a financial sacrifice. To make sure they get their money's worth, though, the Chinese are selective about when they buy their crabs and where the crabs come from. Traditionally, crabs are best during their mating season in the first, fifth, and ninth months of the lunar calendar (around February, July, and October). And the most flavorful crabs are caught around the estuaries of rivers.*

1½ lb (750 g) live hard-shelled sea crab
1 tablespoon chopped ginger
2 tablespoons Chinese rice wine
3–4 cups (24 fl oz–1 qt/750 ml–1 l) water

SERVES 4–6

❡ Place the crab, belly up, on a cutting board and make a deep slit down the middle to kill it. Turn over and remove the top shell and claws. Crack the claw shells. Remove and discard the lung (the feathery substance). Remove the crab meat completely from the shell, wash the meat, cut into six pieces, and pat dry.
❡ Place the crab pieces on a platter. Add the ginger and wine.
❡ Bring the water to a rapid boil in pan. Place a steaming rack in the middle and put the platter on top.
❡ Cover and steam over high heat for 12 minutes.
❡ Serve immediately.

## CHING DOU HAR YAN

### STIR-FRIED SHRIMP WITH GREEN PEAS

*Use small sea shrimp (prawns) for this recipe: They are especially rich in flavor. Be sure to coat every piece completely with the marinade, so that the juices will be sealed in during cooking. Keep the marinating shrimp (prawns) in the refrigerator for a firmer texture.*

For the marinade:
½ egg white
2 teaspoons cornstarch (cornflour)
1 teaspoon salt
½ teaspoon pepper
½ teaspoon sesame oil
For the sauce:
1 tablespoon light soy sauce
2 teaspoons oyster sauce

*Left: Chow Heung Hai; right: Ching Dou Har Yan*

1 teaspoon sugar
2 teaspoons Chinese rice wine
1 teaspoon cornstarch (cornflour)
6 tablespoons chicken broth (stock)
For the shrimp:
12 oz (375 g) uncooked shrimp (green prawns), peeled, deveined, and washed
¾ cup (4 oz /125 g) green peas
1 cup (8 fl oz/250 ml) groundnut (peanut) oil
1 teaspoon chopped ginger
1 teaspoon chopped garlic

SERVES 4–6

❡ For the marinade: Combine all of the ingredients in a bowl.
❡ For the sauce: In a separate bowl, mix all the ingredients well.
❡ Place the shrimp in the marinade and refrigerate for 30 minutes.
❡ In a small pan, bring 1 cup (8 fl oz/250 ml) of water to a boil. Add the peas, and boil for 1 minute. Drain and set aside.
❡ Heat the oil in a wok or skillet (frying pan). Add the shrimp, stirring to separate, and fry for 15 seconds. Remove the shrimp, drain, and set aside.
❡ Drain all but 1–2 tablespoons of the oil from the wok and reheat. Add the ginger and garlic. Return the shrimp and add the peas to the wok. Stir-fry for 1 minute.
❡ Add the sauce to the wok and stir-fry for 20 seconds. Serve.

## HEUNG CHAU LUNG HAR

### FRIED LOBSTER IN PIQUANT SAUCE

The word "lobster" is applied to many types of shellfish. In China, it means the spiny (rock) lobster, which is really closer to the crayfish; there is nothing comparable to the Maine (North Atlantic) lobster. Still, this recipe can be used for any kind of lobster. The Chinese cut the lobster up in little chunks, so that the juices are released in cooking and the table is kept free of shell-crackers and all the other paraphernalia.

For the sauce:
1 tablespoon light soy sauce
1 teaspoon dark soy sauce
1 tablespoon oyster sauce
1 teaspoon sugar
2 teaspoons cornstarch (cornflour)
1 cup (8 fl oz/250 ml) chicken broth (stock)
For the lobster:
3 cups (24 fl oz/750 ml) groundnut (peanut) oil
2 lobster tails, split lengthwise in half, chopped into bite-size pieces, and patted dry
1 tablespoon chopped garlic
1 tablespoon chopped ginger

SERVES 4–6

¶ For the sauce: In a bowl, mix all of the ingredients well.
¶ Heat the oil in a wok or pan until smoking. Add the lobster, and fry for 1 minute. Remove the lobster from the wok, drain, and set aside.
¶ Drain all but 2–3 tablespoons of oil from the wok and reheat. Add the garlic and ginger. Return the lobster to the pan and stir-fry for 30 seconds.
¶ Add the sauce and stir. Cover and cook over medium heat for 1½ –2 minutes. Serve.

## LING JUP TAI HAR

### STIR-FRIED JUMBO SHRIMP IN LEMON SAUCE

If you are tired of the gooey artificially sweet lemon sauce you sometimes find in restaurants, then this recipe will come as a pleasant change. It is important to use fresh lemons that will contrast well with the taste of the seafood.

For the marinade:
½ egg white
1 teaspoon salt
1 teaspoon cornstarch

For the shrimp:
1 lb (500 g) jumbo shrimp (king prawns)
3 lemons
3–4 tablespoons oil
1 teaspoon chopped garlic
1 teaspoon chopped ginger
1 teaspoon Chinese rice wine
1 tablespoon chopped scallion (spring onion)
For the sauce:
juice of 2 fresh lemons
1 teaspoon white vinegar
3 teaspoons sugar
1 teaspoon salt
⅓ cup (3 fl oz/90 ml) chicken broth (stock)
1 teaspoon cornstarch (cornflour)

SERVES 4–6

¶ For the marinade: Mix together all of the ingredients in a bowl.
¶ Remove the shrimp heads but leave the tail attached. Shell, devein, wash, and pat dry.
¶ Marinate the shrimp in the refrigerator for 30 minutes.
¶ Cut the lemons into thin slices, then cut the slices in half. Arrange around a serving platter.
¶ For the sauce: Mix all the ingredients in a bowl, adjusting the sugar to taste.
¶ Heat the oil in a wok or skillet (frying pan) and add the garlic and ginger. Add the shrimp, and stir-fry over high heat for 45 seconds.
¶ Add the sauce, and stir-fry for 20 seconds. Add the wine. Transfer to the serving platter, sprinkle with the scallions, and serve.

*Top: Ling Jup Tai Har; bottom: Heung Chau Lung Har*

# FISH AND SEAFOOD CURIOSITIES

Fish are an important food to the Chinese, who often prize what might be considered by others to be "undesirable" parts. They have a fondness for soft, almost gelatinous textures, which fish provide from several unconventional sources. The head of any fish from the groper family, for instance, is considered a delicacy and is cooked into a rich soup. An even rarer treat are the fleshy lips taken from larger types of fish, and fish "maw" the swim bladder within a conger pike which helps it adjust to water pressure. Flattened, sun-dried octopus, cuttlefish, and squid are also prized for their ability to add intense flavor to dishes in which they are cooked. They are useful in stock for steamboats and hot-pots.

**Fish lips:** Sold dried, usually with the bones attached, fish lips must be soaked in cold water for several days until softened, the water changed every few hours. Then they are boiled until soft enough to remove the bones and to cut the flesh into cubes. They are then marinated in rice wine with ginger and pepper to draw off the fishy odor before being washed again, when they are finally ready for cooking. They are simmered in wine and chicken broth (stock) with ham and soy sauce.

**Fish maw** (*yu to*): These gelatinous bladders with a unique bubbly texture, are sun-dried in large sheets or squares. They are soaked until spongy and soft, and squeezed occasionally to expel air bubbles. Fish maw is boiled for about 30 minutes when it is ready to add, cut into strips or small squares, to soups or other simmered seafood dishes. It is bland tasting, its texture soft and unique.

**Dried cuttlefish:** Cuttlefish, which like small octopus, are caught throughout Chinese and Hong Kong waters, are often confused with squid. They have shorter, wider bodies with a pale brown speckled skin. Cuttlefish are sun-dried on racks near the beach, then packaged for sale. They are also used to make a snack food unique to the Chinese. Dried cuttlefish are flattened by passing through rollers, then are roasted over little charcoal grills until they are crisp. In Chinese movie theaters, strips of chewy roasted cuttlefish are often munched. The flavor is rich and smoky.

**Dried squid:** Squid are somewhat smaller and softer in texture than cuttlefish. This sun-dried sea creature is used, rather like a stock cube, to add concentrated "seafood" flavor to soups and simmered dishes.

**Octopus:** This is dried, flattened and used as a flavor enhancer.

*1. large bubbly sheet of fish maw (yu to); 2. flattened dried squid; 3. strips of dried fish lips; 4. dried cuttlefish*

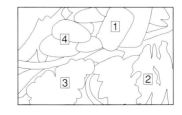

## CHAU HAR KAU

### STIR-FRIED SHRIMP WITH CUCUMBER AND BLACK WOOD FUNGUS

The texture of this fungus is so crispy that it gives a nice, notable contrast to the shrimp. To ensure freshness and crunch, never overcook it.

For the marinade:
½ egg white
1 teaspoon salt

½ teaspoon pepper
2 teaspoons cornstarch (cornflour)
For the shrimp:
8 oz (250 g) uncooked shrimp (green prawns), heads removed, peeled, deveined, washed, and patted dry
1 cup (8 fl oz/250 ml) plus 2 teaspoons groundnut (peanut) oil
6 oz (185 g) cucumber, split, seeded, and cut into slices
1 teaspoon chopped ginger
1 teaspoon chopped garlic
10 pieces dried black wood fungus, soaked in water for 30 minutes and drained

Left: Chau Har Kau; right: Jin Har Pan

For the sauce:
*1 tablespoon light soy sauce*
*2 teaspoons oyster sauce*
*2 teaspoons Chinese rice wine*
*2 teaspoons cornstarch (cornflour)*
*⅓ cup (3 fl oz/90 ml) chicken broth (stock)*

*SERVES 4–6*

❡ For the marinade: Mix together all of the ingredients in a bowl.
❡ Marinate the shrimp in the refrigerator for 30 minutes.

❡ For the sauce: Mix all the ingredients in a bowl and set aside.
❡ Heat the oil in a wok or skillet (frying pan) and stir-fry the shrimp for 20 seconds. Remove, drain, and set aside. Reserve the leftover oil.
❡ Heat 1–2 tablespoons of the reserved oil in the wok and stir-fry the cucumber for 30 seconds. Remove, drain, and set aside.
❡ Heat 1–2 tablespoons of the reserved oil in the wok and add the ginger and garlic. Add the shrimp, cucumber, and fungus to the wok. Add the sauce, and stir-fry for 15 seconds. Serve.

## JIN HAR PAN

*PAN-FRIED SHRIMP AND EGG*

*A simple, delicious dish with some interesting aromas. While some people feel that cornstarch (cornflour) is a merely a filler, the Chinese have used it for generations in marinades, where it acts like a coat that protects an ingredient's juices.*

For the marinade:
*½ egg white*
*1 teaspoon cornstarch (cornflour)*
*½ teaspoon salt*
For the shrimp:
*6 oz (185 g) uncooked shrimp (green prawns), shelled,*
   *deveined, cleaned, and patted dry*
*½ teaspoon salt*
*½ teaspoon pepper*
*1 tablespoon shredded scallion (spring onion)*
*1 teaspoon shredded ginger*
*1 tablespoon chopped cilantro (fresh coriander)*
*4 eggs, beaten*
*2 cups (16 fl oz/500 ml) groundnut (peanut) oil*

*SERVES 4–6*

❡ For the marinade: Mix together all of the ingredients in a bowl.
❡ Marinate the shrimp in the refrigerator for 30 minutes.
❡ Mix the salt, pepper, scallion, ginger, and cilantro with the eggs and stir well.
❡ Heat the oil in a wok or skillet (frying pan) and add the shrimp, stirring to separate. Once the shrimp turn pink, remove them from the pan and add them to the egg mixture.
❡ Drain all but 2 tablespoons of oil from the wok and reheat. Pour in the egg and shrimp mixture. Spread evenly to form a pancake and fry over medium heat until golden brown on both sides. Serve.

## SZE CHIU HAR

*STIR-FRIED JUMBO SHRIMP IN BLACK BEAN AND CHILI SAUCE*

*Jumbo shrimp (king prawns) are relatively expensive, but they have a good deal of meat. You can either cut off the head and tail of the shrimp, or leave the head on, as is often done in China. The head is considered particularly delicious and healthy. If you do keep the head, cut off the pointed tip, which is inedible.*

For the marinade:
1/2 egg white
1 teaspoon cornstarch (cornflour)
1/2 teaspoon salt
For the shrimp:
6 raw jumbo shrimp (green king prawns), shelled, deveined, washed, patted dry, and halved
2 cups (16 fl oz/500 ml) groundnut (peanut) oil
6 slices ginger, finely chopped
1 chili, finely shredded
2 scallions (spring onions), white part only, cut into 1-inch (2.5-cm) lengths
2 tablespoons fermented black beans
2 garlic cloves, finely chopped
1/2 cup (4 fl oz/125 ml) chicken broth (stock)
1 teaspoon sugar
1 teaspoon cornstarch (cornflour)
1 teaspoon Chinese rice wine

*SERVES 4–6*

❡ For the marinade: Mix all the ingredients in a bowl.
❡ Marinate the shrimp in the refrigerator for 30 minutes.
❡ Heat the oil in a wok or skillet (frying pan) and add the shrimp, stirring to separate. Once the shrimp turn pink, remove them from the pan, drain, and set aside.
❡ Drain all but 2–3 tablespoons of oil from the wok and reheat. Mash together the ginger, chili, scallions, black beans, and garlic, and add to the wok. Mix the broth, sugar, and cornstarch in a bowl. When the aroma rises from the wok, add the broth mixture.
❡ Return the shrimp to the wok and stir-fry over high heat for 1 minute. Add the wine and serve.

## CHAU NGAU LIE

*STIR-FRIED MILK WITH CRAB MEAT AND MUSHROOMS*

*This is an unusual dish, but just wait until you taste the combination. Think of it as a kind of soufflé—light and fluffy and tasty. This recipe is from my home region of Shunde.*

*Left: Sze Chiu Har; right: Chau Ngau Lie*

For the marinade:
1 teaspoon light soy sauce
1/2 teaspoon sugar
1/4 teaspoon pepper
1 teaspoon Chinese rice wine
1/4 teaspoon sesame oil
For the crab meat:
4 oz (125 g) cooked crab meat
3 cups (8 oz/250 g) finely shredded lettuce
3–4 tablespoons groundnut (peanut) oil
2 oz (60 g) button mushrooms (champignons), sliced
1 teaspoon finely chopped garlic
1 teaspoon finely chopped ginger
1 cup (8 fl oz/250 ml) milk
1 cup (8 fl oz/250 ml) egg whites (about 6–8 eggs)
1 teaspoon salt
1 teaspoon Chinese rice wine
1 tablespoon very finely chopped ham
1 tablespoon roasted pine nuts
1 tablespoon chopped cilantro (fresh coriander)

*SERVES 4–6*

❡ For the marinade: Mix all the ingredients in a bowl.
❡ Marinate the crab meat for 15 minutes.
❡ Arrange the lettuce on a serving platter and set aside.
❡ Heat 2 tablespoons of the oil in a wok or skillet (frying pan) and sauté the crab meat and mushrooms for 30 seconds. Add the garlic and ginger.
❡ Mix the milk, egg whites, and salt in a bowl. When the aroma arises from the wok, add the milk mixture, and stir-fry over high heat for 5 seconds. Add 2 tablespoons of oil and stir for 10 seconds. Add another 2 teaspoons of oil and stir until just set. Add the wine.
❡ Transfer to the serving platter and sprinkle with the ham, pine nuts, and cilantro. Serve.

# PAK CHERK HAR

### POACHED SHRIMP WITH GINGER, SCALLION, AND CHILI SAUCE

*The dip in this recipe brings out all the flavor of the shrimp, and the shrimp have a smooth and crispy texture.*

For the dip:
2 tablespoons groundnut (peanut) oil
2 tablespoons finely shredded ginger
2 tablespoons finely shredded scallion (spring onion)
1 tablespoon finely shredded red chili
2 tablespoons dark soy sauce
2 tablespoons light soy sauce
1 teaspoon salt
1 teaspoon sugar
1 teaspoon sesame oil
1–2 teaspoons chili oil (optional)
1/4 cup (2 fl oz/60 ml) chicken broth (stock)
For the shrimp:
6 cups (1 1/2 qt/1.5 l) water
2 scallions (spring onions)
6 slices ginger
1 lb (500 g) uncooked shrimp (green prawns), heads
    removed, peeled, deveined, cleaned, and patted dry
2 tablespoons Chinese rice wine

*SERVES 4*

❡ For the dip: Heat the oil in a wok or skillet (frying pan) and add the ginger, scallion, and chili. Sauté over medium heat for 15 seconds. Mix all the remaining ingredients in a bowl and add to the wok. Bring to a boil. Pour into saucers to serve.
❡ Place the water in a large pan and add the scallions and ginger. Bring to a rapid boil. Add the shrimp and wine, and return to a boil. Lower the heat and poach for 2 minutes. Remove the shrimp and drain. Serve with the dip.

# HAR SUNG SANG CHOI BOU

### STIR-FRIED SHRIMP AND WATER CHESTNUTS WITH LETTUCE LEAVES

*Lettuce is used as a wrapper in this dish, but you can substitute Chinese pancakes, with no loss of taste.*

For the marinade:
1/4 egg white
1/2 teaspoon salt
1 teaspoon cornstarch (cornflour)
For the shrimp:
8 oz (250 g) uncooked shrimp (green prawns), heads

removed, peeled, deveined, cleaned, and patted dry
3–4 tablespoons groundnut (peanut) oil
1 teaspoon finely chopped ginger
1 teaspoon finely chopped garlic
2 oz (60 g) button mushrooms (champignons), finely chopped
2 oz (60 g) water chestnuts, finely chopped
1/4 cup (2 fl oz/60 ml) chicken broth (stock)
1 tablespoon light soy sauce
1/2 teaspoon salt
1/2 teaspoon sugar
1 teaspoon cornstarch (cornflour)
1 tablespoon chopped scallion (spring onion)
2 tablespoons chopped cilantro (fresh coriander)
1 tablespoon Chinese rice wine
2 tablespoons pine nuts, roasted
1 lb (500 g) lettuce, washed and dried
For the dip:
2 tablespoons finely shredded ginger
1/4 cup (2 fl oz/60 ml) aromatic or cider vinegar
2 tablespoons hoisin sauce

*SERVES 4–6*

❡ For the marinade: Mix all the ingredients in a bowl.
❡ Cut the shrimp into 1/4-inch (0.5-cm) cubes and marinate in the refrigerator for 30 minutes.
❡ For the dip: Mix all the ingredients in a bowl.
❡ Heat the oil in a wok or skillet (frying pan) and add the ginger and garlic. When the aroma rises, add the shrimp, mushrooms, and water chestnuts. Stir-fry over high heat for 45 seconds.
❡ Mix the broth, soy sauce, salt, sugar, and cornstarch. Add to the wok and stir-fry for 15 seconds. Add the scallion and cilantro. Add the wine, stir well, and transfer to a serving platter. Sprinkle with the pine nuts. Serve with the lettuce leaves as wrappers and the dip.

*Top: Har Sung Sang Choi Bou; bottom: Pak Cherk Har*

*Left: Ma Ti Chau Har; right: Chuen Mai Har*

## MA TI CHAU HAR

*STIR-FRIED SHRIMP, WATER CHESTNUTS, AND BUTTON MUSHROOMS*

*This dish is like an encyclopedia of textures, with its soft shrimp (prawns), chewy button mushrooms, and crunchy water chestnuts.*

For the marinade:
½ egg white
1 teaspoon cornstarch (cornflour)
½ teaspoon salt

For the shrimp and vegetables:
8 oz (250 g) raw shrimp (green prawns), shelled, deveined, cleaned, and patted dry
2 cups (16 fl oz/500 ml) groundnut (peanut) oil
1 teaspoon finely chopped garlic
1 teaspoon finely chopped ginger
2 oz (60 g) water chestnuts, thinly sliced
4 oz (125 g) button mushrooms (champignons)
2 scallions (spring onions), white part only, cut into 1-inch (2.5-cm) lengths
¼ cup (2 fl oz/60 ml) chicken broth (stock)

add the shrimp, stirring to separate. Once they turn pink, remove them and set aside.

¶ Drain all but 2–3 tablespoons of oil from the wok and reheat. Add the garlic and ginger. When the aroma rises, add the water chestnuts and mushrooms. Stir-fry over high heat for 45 seconds.

¶ Add the scallions. Mix the broth, oyster sauce, soy sauce, sugar, and cornstarch in a bowl and add to the wok. Return the shrimp to the wok and stir-fry over high heat for 30 seconds. Add the wine, sprinkle with the cilantro, and serve.

## CHUEN MAI HAR

### *STIR-FRIED SHRIMP SICHUAN-STYLE*

*When you see the words "Sichuan-style," you know that the dish is going to be spicy. The chili, garlic, chili oil, and ginger give it the right zest that is so popular in the region.*

For the marinade:
1/2 egg white
1 teaspoon cornstarch (cornflour)
1/2 teaspoon salt
For the shrimp:
12 oz (375 g) raw shrimp (green prawns), shelled, deveined, cleaned, and patted dry
2 cups (16 fl oz/500 ml) groundnut (peanut) oil
1 teaspoon finely chopped garlic
1 teaspoon finely chopped ginger
1 tablespoon finely chopped red chilis
3 tablespoons chicken broth (stock)
1 tablespoon light soy sauce
1/2 teaspoon sugar
1/2 teaspoon vinegar
1 teaspoon chili oil
1 teaspoon cornstarch (cornflour)
1 teaspoon Chinese rice wine

*SERVES 4–6*

¶ For the marinade: Mix all of the ingredients in a bowl. Marinate the shrimp in the refrigerator for 30 minutes.

¶ Heat the oil in a wok or skillet (frying pan) and add the shrimp, stirring to separate. Once the shrimp turn pink, remove them from the wok, drain, and set aside.

¶ Drain all but 1–2 tablespoons of oil from the wok and reheat. Add the garlic, ginger, and chilis. Return the shrimp to the wok. Mix the broth, soy sauce, sugar, vinegar, chili oil, and cornstarch in a bowl, and add to the wok. Stir-fry over very high heat for 20 seconds. Add the wine and serve.

1 tablespoon oyster sauce
1 teaspoon light soy sauce
1/2 teaspoon sugar
1 teaspoon cornstarch (cornflour)
1 teaspoon Chinese rice wine
1 tablespoon chopped cilantro (fresh coriander)

*SERVES 4–6*

¶ For the marinade: Mix all the ingredients in a bowl and marinate the shrimp in the refrigerator for 30 minutes.

¶ Heat the oil in a wok or skillet (frying pan) and

# DRIED SEAFOOD

Dried seafood has been used in Chinese cooking for centuries. Originally used as a form of preservation, it was discovered that the drying process accentuated the natural flavor of the seafood. Drying acquired, then, a two-fold purpose. Sometimes the process involves drying alone, in other cases the seafood is heavily salted.

Dried seafoods make an invaluable contribution to the table in all parts of China, even along the coast where fresh seafood is plentiful. In land-locked regions like Sichuan province, dried seafood is used as often as is affordable, even though the giant rivers that transgress the area yield an abundance of not only fresh fish, but freshwater shellfish and turtles. So fond are the Sichuanese of seafood tastes, that they even emulate seafood flavors in certain popular meat and vegetable dishes. Some seafoods dry to rock hardness, that require lengthy soaking to reconstitute, others need to be soaked in several lots of water to draw off excess salt. Mostly, they are softened by soaking, before being added to a dish.

**Dried and salted fish:** All kinds of Chinese fish, from 1 inch (2 cm) tiny anchovies to any fish that is not too meaty and plump, are sun-dried whole or in strips, or are salted. Generally, they are cleaned, the stomach cavity opened, and they are pinned out on woven straw mats, between layers of salt, or hung on racks to dry in the sun. The Chinese rarely pack their salt fish in brine, preferring the dried product for both taste and convenience.

Experience will tell a cook just which type of dried fish will give the required depth of flavor in a particular dish. One appreciative sniff, in fact, is usually all that is needed to tell the cook that this fish will give his broth (stock) a deep and instense flavor of the sea, or that fish will add an elusive and mysterious hint of flavor to his sauce.

Dried seafood is often crisp-fried in vegetable oil to make a chewy, crunchy, pungent snack crumbled over noodles or rice, and a sprinkle of it over vegetables heightens their natural flavors. With all dried seafood, moisture is the enemy. It should be hung, if possible, in a dry, airy, or sunny position, otherwise packed in airtight jars and stored away from light.

Various crustaceans and shellfish, too, are preserved and intensified in flavor by drying, and/or salting. Abalone, sea cucumbers (*bêche de mer* or trepang), and jellyfish all have their prescribed roles to play in producing flavors or textures for special Chinese dishes.

**Dried shrimp (prawns):** Bright pink, tiny dried shrimp are a common ingredient in stuffings, vegetable dishes, and soups. They are also ground into a fluffy pink-gold mass called shrimp floss to use primarily as a garnish.

***Conpoy:*** These are hard, amber disks of a type of rare scallop. One of their most expensive ingredients, which makes an appearance usually only in very special banquet meals, the Chinese revere it for its supreme flavor. One of the most revered dishes using this unique dried mollusk is known as "mermaid's tresses." Finely shredded leaves of young Chinese greens are deep-fried until rustling crisp, then dressed with a sprinkle of sugar and fragments of *conpoy*, which has been softened by soaking, then fried and shredded.

**Dried scallops, mussels, and oysters:** These are also expensive ingredients which are used sparingly to enhance the flavor of broths (stocks), or added to stews. They are also slow-cooked, often with mushrooms, to serve in a brown sauce of magically intense flavor, as a feature dish in a banquet menu. The Chinese also endorse the powerful medicinal properties of dried mollusks.

*1. dried shrimp (prawns);*
*2. dried fish; 3. dried oysters;*
*4. dried miniature anchovies;*
*5. dried conpoy*

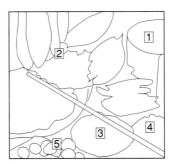

*Left: Har Yeung Dong Ku; center: Jar Har Yuen; right: Chiu Yim Har*

## JAR HAR YUEN

### *FRIED SHRIMP BALLS WITH SPICY SAUCE*

*This dish is a very popular, with its crispy texture and delicious sweet-and-sour sauce.*

1 lb (500 g) uncooked shrimp (green prawns), heads
   removed, peeled, deveined, washed, and patted dry
2 oz (60 g) cooked pork fat, ground (minced)
1 tablespoon chopped cilantro (fresh coriander)
³/4 teaspoon salt
2 teaspoons cornstarch (cornflour)
1 egg white, beaten
2 cups (4 oz/125 g) fresh white breadcrumbs
4 cups (1 qt/1 l) groundnut (peanut) oil
1 teaspoon finely chopped garlic
1 teaspoon finely chopped ginger
1 tablespoon finely chopped red chili
¹/2 cup (4 fl oz/125 g) Sweet-and-sour Sauce (see recipe for
   Sweet-and-sour Pork Chiuchow-style, page 150)

*SERVES 6–8*

❡ In a bowl, mash the shrimp into a smooth paste.
Add the pork fat, cilantro, salt, and cornstarch, and
mix well. Stir in the egg white and mix until sticky.
Form the mixture into balls, about 1 inch (2.5 cm)
in diameter. Coat with the breadcrumbs. Set aside.
❡ Heat the oil in a wok or skillet (frying pan) until
very hot. Reduce the heat slightly and fry the shrimp
balls, a few at a time, until golden brown. Turn the

heat to high and fry for 30 seconds. Remove and
drain. Repeat with the remaining shrimp balls.
❡ Drain all but 1–2 tablespoons oil from the wok
and reheat. Add the garlic, ginger, and chili. When
the aroma rises, add the Sweet-and-sour Sauce.
Bring to a boil. Pour into saucers and serve as a dip.

## HAR YEUNG DONG KU

### *MUSHROOMS STUFFED WITH SHRIMP PASTE*

*You can get shrimp (prawn) paste anywhere, but it's just
as easy to make your own for this recipe.*

For the mushrooms and shrimp:
1¹/2 teaspoons salt
1 teaspoon sugar
2 tablespoons groundnut (peanut) oil
24 dried black mushrooms, soaked, drained, and
   stems discarded
10 cups (2¹/2 qt/2.5 l) water
1 lb (500 g) uncooked shrimp (green prawns), heads
   removed, peeled, deveined, and patted dry
2 teaspoons cornstarch (cornflour)
1 tablespoon chopped cilantro (fresh coriander)
1 teaspoon finely chopped ginger
1 cup (8 fl oz/250 ml) chicken broth (stock)
1 tablespoon light soy sauce
1 teaspoon Chinese rice wine

❡ Place ¾ teaspoon of the salt, sugar, 1 tablespoon of the oil, and the mushrooms in a bowl. Add 4 cups (1 qt/1 l) of the water to a wok or large pan and set a steaming rack on top. Place the bowl with the mushrooms on the rack and bring the water to a boil. Cover and steam for 20 minutes. Remove, drain, and set aside to cool.

❡ Mash the shrimp into a paste, add the remaining salt and 1 teaspoon of the cornstarch, and stir until sticky. Refrigerate for 30 minutes.

❡ Place about 1 tablespoon of the shrimp mixture on the white side of a mushroom and spread evenly. Repeat until all the mushrooms are stuffed. Arrange on a serving platter.

❡ Bring the remaining water to a boil in a wok or large pan. Place a steaming rack in the wok and set the platter with the mushrooms on top. Cover and steam over high heat for 10 minutes. Remove, and drain all liquid. Sprinkle the cilantro on top.

❡ Mix all the remaining ingredients in a bowl. Heat the remaining 1 tablespoon oil in the wok. When the aroma rises, add the broth mixture and bring to a boil. Pour over the mushrooms and serve.

# CHIU YIM HAR

### FRIED SHRIMP WITH CHILI AND SALT

*This is one of the most popular dishes anywhere. You can use frozen shrimp (prawns) here, since the batter, chili, and garlic will make up for any loss of taste.*

*3 cups (24 fl oz/750 ml) groundnut (peanut) oil*
*1 lb (500 g) uncooked shrimp (green prawns), heads removed, peeled, deveined, and patted dry*
*2 teaspoons salt*
*1 tablespoon finely chopped red chilli*
*1 teaspoon finely chopped garlic*
*1 teaspoon Chinese rice wine*
*SERVES 4–6*

❡ Heat the oil in a wok or skillet (frying pan). Add the shrimp and fry for 3 minutes. Remove, drain, and set aside.

❡ Heat a clean wok. Add the salt and sauté over medium heat until lightly browned. Add the shrimp, chili, and garlic, and stir-fry over very high heat for 30 seconds. Add the wine. Transfer to a platter and serve.

*Lower right: "superior grade" canned abalone;*
*lower left: dried abalone; upper left: fresh abalone*

# ABALONE

The abalone resembles a clam, but the mollusk is actually part of the snail family, with an oval black-green shell lined with green-tinged mother-of-pearl. They are harvested from deep waters in various parts of the world, including China. But the Chinese abalone is small and too tough for eating, so their abalone mainly comes from Mexico, Japan, South Korea, and Australia.

Abalone has a taste that is difficult to describe, an indefinable sea flavor, with a texture that is chewy and firm, yet slippery. It is the most expensive seafood used in Chinese cooking and is therefore regarded as a "special" dish. It is cooked in many ways, most often in soup, and at very formal banquets will be served by itself, sliced over a few greens with a simple dressing of oyster sauce.

Fresh abalone must be removed from the shell, trimmed of the little ruffle that surrounds it, and sliced thinly before being simmered slowly until tender. Dried abalone is handled in much the same way, but must be first soaked in cold water for 4–5 days, changing the water every 5 to 6 hours. It should be cleaned to scrape away any slimy residue clinging to the surface, then cooked slowly for about 5 hours in a Chinese clay double-saucepan with hot water or chicken broth (stock), a piece of chicken fat, a little oil and wine. When it is completely tender, slice and serve with sauce.

Canned abalone is pre-cooked, pre-sliced, tender, and ready to use. It, too, can be expensive. Unused abalone can be kept in the refrigerator for a week or so, if the water is changed daily.

*Left: Har Yeung Care Tze; right: Hai Pa Dou Miu*

## HAR YEUNG CARE TZE

### PAN-FRIED EGGPLANT STUFFED WITH SHRIMP PASTE

*Take a Chinese long eggplant (aubergine), and make a slit toward the bottom end. Then make another slit all the way through the vegetable near this. Between these two, you can put the shrimp paste and fry the mixture. I have added wine to the recipe just to give more vigor to the eggplant.*

2 eggplants (aubergines)
6 oz (185 g) uncooked shrimp (green prawns), heads
    removed, peeled, deveined, washed, and patted dry
1 oz (30 g) cooked pork fat, ground (minced)
³/₄ teaspoon salt
2 tablespoons plus 2 teaspoons cornstarch (cornflour)
¹/₂ teaspoon pepper
¹/₂ cup (4 fl oz/125 ml) groundnut (peanut) oil
1 teaspoon minced garlic
1 cup (8 fl oz/250 ml) chicken broth (stock)
1 tablespoon oyster sauce
1 tablespoon light soy sauce
1 teaspoon Chinese rice wine

*SERVES 4–6*

❡ Make a deep incision diagonally in each eggplant, about ¹/₄ inch (0.5 cm) across. Make a second cut, cutting through to make a ¹/₂-inch (1-cm) thick deep slit in the middle. Cut each eggplant in the same way and set aside.

❡ In a bowl, mash the shrimp into a smooth paste. Add the pork fat, salt, 1 teaspoon of the cornstarch, and pepper, and mix until sticky.

❡ Rub a bit of cornstarch in the slit of a piece of eggplant and fill with 2 teaspoons of the shrimp paste. Smooth the edge with a wet finger. Repeat with the remaining eggplant.

❡ Heat the oil in a wok or skillet (frying pan) and fry the eggplants until golden brown on both sides. Remove the eggplants from the wok, drain, and set aside.

❡ Mix the broth, oyster sauce, soy sauce, and 2 tablespoons of the cornstarch in a bowl.

❡ Drain all but 1–2 tablespoons oil from the wok and reheat.

❡ Add the garlic and the broth mixture. Return the eggplant to the wok and reduce the sauce by half. Add the wine.

❡ Serve immediately.

## HAI PA DOU MIU

### *PAN-FRIED SNOW PEAS WITH CRAB SAUCE*

*This recipe can also be made with pea tendrils. The Cantonese thrive on pea tendrils during winter, but since freshness is important, they will use snow peas (mange-tout) at other times of the year.*

For the marinade:
1 teaspoon light soy sauce
1 teaspoon oyster sauce
½ teaspoon Chinese rice wine
½ teaspoon pepper
For the crab and snow peas:
4 oz (125 g) cooked crab meat
½ cup (4 fl oz/125 ml) groundnut (peanut) oil
2 teaspoons finely chopped ginger
2 teaspoons finely chopped garlic
1 teaspoon salt
8 oz (250 g) snow peas (mange-tout)
2 teaspoons Chinese rice wine
1 cup (8 fl oz/250 ml) chicken broth (stock)
1 tablespoon light soy sauce
1 teaspoon cornstarch (cornflour)
1 egg white, beaten

SERVES 4–6

❡ For the marinade: Mix the marinade ingredients and marinate the crab meat in the marinade for 30 minutes.
❡ Heat 4–5 tablespoons of the oil in a wok or skillet (frying pan). Add 1 teaspoon of the ginger, 1 teaspoon of the garlic, and the salt. Add the snow peas and stir-fry over very high heat for 1 minute. Add 1 teaspoon of the wine. Transfer to a serving platter and cover to keep warm.
❡ Heat 3 tablespoons of the oil in the wok. Add the remaining ginger and garlic, and the crab meat. Mix the broth, soy sauce, cornstarch, and the remaining wine, and add to the wok. Bring to a boil and stir in the egg white. Pour over the snow peas and serve.

*Sze Jup Chau Ching Hau*

## SZE JUP CHAU CHING HAU

### *MUSSELS WITH BLACK BEANS AND GARLIC*

*In Fujian province the people love all kinds of seafood. Usually I would recommend smaller mussels for the best taste. But here, where they are covered with a heavy sauce, large mussels are fine.*

6 cups (1½ qt/1.5 l) water
1½ lb (750 g) mussels, cleaned
3–4 tablespoons groundnut (peanut) oil
1 tablespoon fermented black beans, washed and chopped
1 tablespoon finely chopped garlic
1 red bell pepper (capsicum), cut into 1-inch (2.5-cm) squares
1 green bell pepper (capsicum), cut into 1-inch (2.5-cm) squares
1 cup (8 fl oz/250 ml) chicken broth (stock)
1 tablespoon oyster sauce
1 teaspoon sugar
1 teaspoon chili oil (optional)
1 cup cornstarch (cornflour)
1 teaspoon Chinese rice wine

SERVES 4–6

❡ Bring the water to a boil in a large pan. Add the mussels and cook until the shells open. Remove and drain. Rinse under tap water, and shell. Set aside.
❡ Heat the oil in a wok or skillet (frying pan). Add the black beans and garlic. When the aroma rises, add the mussels and peppers, and stir-fry over high heat for 1 minute.
❡ Mix the broth, oyster sauce, sugar, chili oil, and cornstarch in a bowl and add to the wok. Stir-fry over high heat for 1 minute. Add the wine and serve.

# POULTRY

# POULTRY

IN RURAL, AND EVEN SUBURBAN, CHINA VIRTUALLY EVERY HOUSEHOLD RAISED ITS OWN CHICKENS. DUCKS, TOO, IF SPACE AND WATER allowed. The chickens were scrawny, though their meat was sweet, and they required little care, happy to pick on scraps and needing only the most basic habitation. They were economical birds to raise.

¶ Muddy ponds on the outskirts of town are the habitat of noisy, brown-feathered ducks. These are bred as nature intended, by contrast with the rigid breeding methods and forced feeding program used on the famous white-plumed Peking ducks.

¶ A cage of live chickens, or a brace of ducks tied to the back of a bicycle, en route to the market, was a common sight on Chinese roads. Less so now, but village markets still have live poultry for sale. And the poultry section of the food markets in all major cities is a busy and noisy one.

¶ Chinese cooks know countless ways to prepare chicken, which is, next to pork, the most commonly eaten meat throughout China. Every part of the bird, except perhaps the beak, is used. The tender meat is cooked in innumerable ways, from simple roast or barbecue to complex court dishes to please an emperor's palate. The blood is congealed to add to soups, the feet are considered a delicacy and most children adore the wings. The whole bird, slow-cooked for hours, is used to make Superior Broth (stock), which is the basis of many great dishes.

¶ Duck does not enjoy the reverence given to chicken, perhaps, but it has produced the most esteemed dish (Peking Duck), as well as some of the most aromatic recipes. Duck "webs" are enjoyed, like chicken's feet, for their particularly crunchy texture, but also appreciated for the gelatin protein which is thought to keep aging bones supple.

¶ As soup, duck is attributed with extraordinary powers: "When married couples quarrel," said an ancient Chinese sage, "they should immediately make duck soup and eat it together. The soup is so beneficial that even the most argumentative man and wife will be reunited." It helps that the Mandarin duck, which mates for life, is a symbol of felicity and constancy.

¶ The Teochiu Chinese love the fat, rich flavor of goose, finding that it complements the thick soy sauce that is exclusive to this southeastern region of China. They serve goose, with its own liver and blood, sliced as a cold appetizer, accompanied by rice vinegar with garlic for dipping.

¶ Pigeon is also used frequently in China. It is invariably served with its head which, when the plate is served, faces the most-honored guest.

¶ Most poultry markets have live quail for sale, to be fresh-killed and plucked on the spot for the purchaser. Smaller even than these small speckled birds are the tiny sparrows known as "rice birds."

*Previous pages: Duck "herding" is a common sight in China. This foodstuff is often dried and preserved as pressed duck, which requires long steaming before it can be eaten. Duck is also braised and roasted and used in soups; it is the essential ingredient of Peking Duck — in which the meat is eaten inside spicily sauced pancakes.*
ROBERT HARDING PICTURE LIBRARY

*Opposite: A Shaanxi farmer with his chickens. Almost everyone in rural China keeps a few chickens which, along with pork, form the basis of many dishes.* CHINA TOURISM PHOTO LIBRARY/WANG MIAO

*Left: Dou Sze Gai; right: Pak Chit Gai*

## PAK CHIT GAI

*STEAMED CHICKEN WITH GINGER AND SCALLION DIP*

*Timing is fundamental for this dish: Don't ever overcook the chicken. A 2 lb (1 kg) chicken needs about 20 minutes over high heat; for a bigger chicken, add a few minutes more.*

For the dip:
*3 tablespoons finely chopped ginger*
*2 tablespoons finely chopped scallions (spring onions)*
*2 tablespoons light soy sauce*
*1 tablespoon oyster sauce*
*1 teaspoon sesame oil*
For the chicken:
*1 whole chicken, about 2 lb (1 kg)*
*1 tablespoon salt*
*2 scallions (spring onions)*
*2 tablespoons shredded ginger*
*1 tablespoon Chinese rice wine*

*SERVES 4–6*

❧ For the dip: Mix all of the ingredients together in a bowl.

❧ Wash the chicken and pat dry. Rub the salt over the inside and outside of the chicken. Put the scallions and ginger into the cavity of the chicken. Pour in the wine and place the chicken in a deep dish.

❧ Place 4–5 cups (1–1¼ qt/1–1.25 l) of water in a large pan and bring to a boil. Place a steaming rack in the middle and put the dish with the chicken on top. Cover and steam over high heat for 20 minutes. (The chicken can be cooked for 5–10 minutes longer, according to taste.) Remove and set aside to cool.

❧ When cool, chop the chicken into bite-size pieces and transfer to a serving dish. Serve with the dip.

## DOU SZE GAI

*BRAISED CHICKEN LEG WITH BLACK BEAN SAUCE*

*A great recipe with a great sauce. Just as the French and Italians soak up their delicious sauces with pieces of good bread, you'll want to have extra rice on hand so none of this sauce goes to waste.*

For the marinade:
*2 tablespoons light soy sauce*
*1 teaspoon dark soy sauce*
*1½ teaspoons sugar*
*1 teaspoon Chinese rice wine*
*1 tablespoon cornstarch (cornflour)*
For the sauce:
*1 tablespoon oyster sauce*
*1 tablespoon dark soy sauce*
*1 cup (8 fl oz/250 ml) chicken broth (stock)*
*½ cup (4 fl oz/125 ml) water*
For the chicken:
*3 chicken legs, cut into bite-size pieces*
*3–4 tablespoons groundnut (peanut) oil*
*6 slices ginger*
*2 garlic cloves, crushed*
*6 shallot cloves, crushed*
*2 tablespoons fermented black beans*
*1 green bell pepper (capsicum), chopped*
*1 red chili, seeded and chopped*

*SERVES 4–6*

❧ For the marinade: Combine all the ingredients in a bowl. Marinate the chicken for 30 minutes.

❧ For the sauce: In a separate bowl, mix all the ingredients well.

❧ Heat the oil in a wok or skillet (frying pan). Add

the ginger, garlic, shallots, and fermented black beans. Stir-fry for 10 seconds. Add the bell pepper, chili, and chicken. Stir-fry for 1 minute.

❡ Pour the sauce into the wok, cover, and cook over low to medium–low heat for 4 minutes. Serve.

# FAUN KAIR GAI DING

## DICED CHICKEN BREAST IN TOMATO SAUCE

*Don't be put off by the ketchup in this recipe — the Chinese have been using it for more than a century.*

For the marinade:
*1 tablespoon light soy sauce*
*1 teaspoon salt*
*1 teaspoon sugar*
*1 teaspoon sesame oil*
*2 teaspoons cornstarch (cornflour)*
For the sauce:
*1 tablespoon light soy sauce*
*1 tablespoon ketchup*
*2 teaspoons sugar*
*2 teaspoons cornstarch (cornflour)*
*1 cup (8 fl oz/250 ml) chicken broth (stock)*
*1/2 cup (4 fl oz/125 ml) water*
For the chicken:
*2 chicken breasts, cut into 1/2-inch (1.5-cm) dice*
*4 tomatoes, quartered*
*4–5 tablespoons (groundnut) peanut oil*
*1 cup (8 oz/250 g) button mushrooms (champignons)*
*1 teaspoon chopped ginger*
*1 teaspoon chopped garlic*
*1 tablespoon chopped scallions (spring onions)*

*SERVES 4–6*

❡ For the marinade: Combine all the ingredients in a bowl. Marinate the chicken for 15 minutes.

❡ For the sauce: In a separate bowl, mix all the ingredients well.

❡ Blanch the tomatoes in boiling water. Remove and peel. Set aside.

❡ Heat 3–4 tablespoons of oil in a wok or skillet (frying pan). Stir-fry the chicken for 45 seconds. Remove, drain, and set aside. Clean the wok.

❡ In a separate pan, cook the tomatoes and mushrooms with the sauce over medium heat for 3 minutes. Remove from the heat and set aside.

❡ Heat the remaining oil in the wok over medium heat. Add the ginger, garlic, and scallions. Return the chicken to the wok and stir-fry for 15 seconds. Add the tomato and mushroom sauce, and bring to a boil. Transfer to a deep dish and serve.

# MA CHEUNG GAI SZE

## SHREDDED CHICKEN WITH SESAME SAUCE

*This is my original recipe, in which fresh chicken breast is marinated, then steamed.*

For the marinade:
*1 tablespoon light soy sauce*
*1 teaspoon salt*
*1/2 teaspoon pepper*
*1 teaspoon sugar*
*1 teaspoon sesame oil*
*2 teaspoons cornstarch (cornflour)*
For the chicken:
*2 chicken breasts*
*6 oz (185 g) cucumber, cut into 2-inch (5-cm) shreds*
*1 red bell pepper (capsicum), cut into 2-inch (5-cm) shreds*
For the sauce:
*2 tablespoons sesame paste*
*2 tablespoons light soy sauce*
*1 tablespoon aromatic or apple vinegar*
*2 teaspoons sugar*
*2 teaspoons Chinese rice wine*
*2 tablespoons chicken broth (stock)*

*SERVES 4–6*

❡ For the marinade: Combine all the ingredients in a bowl. Marinate the chicken breasts for 30 minutes.

❡ For the sauce: In a separate bowl, mix all the ingredients well.

❡ Place the chicken in a shallow dish and set aside.

❡ Bring 3–4 cups (24 fl oz–1 qt/750 ml–1 l) water to a boil in a large pan. Place a steaming rack in the middle. Put the dish with the chicken on top. Cover and steam for 12 minutes (or 3–5 minutes longer, according to taste). Remove and set aside to cool.

❡ When cool, cut the chicken into thin shreds. Put the cucumber and bell pepper on a serving platter with the chicken on top. Cover with the sauce. Serve cold.

*Top: Faun Kair Gai Ding; bottom: Ma Cheung Gai Sze*

*Top: Chuen Mai Gai; bottom: Dou Cheung Gai*

## DOU CHEUNG GAI

*CHICKEN IN SOYBEAN PASTE SAUCE*

*The people of Teochiu love soybean paste, because it's so rich in flavor. Even the simplest chicken dish has a luscious taste with this sauce.*

For the marinade:
*2 tablespoons light soy sauce*
*2 teaspoons salt*
*1 teaspoon sugar*
*1 tablespoon Chinese rice wine*
*1 tablespoon cornstarch (cornflour)*
For the chicken:
*1 chicken, about 3 lb (1.5 kg), chopped into bite-size pieces*
*1 cup (8 fl oz/250 ml) groundnut (peanut) oil*
*6 slices ginger*
*1 tablespoon chopped garlic*
*2 scallions (spring onions), cut into 2-inch (5-cm) lengths*
For the sauce:

*2 tablespoons soybean paste*
*1 teaspoon sugar*
*1 tablespoon dark soy sauce*
*1 tablespoon Chinese rice wine*
SERVES 6–8

❡ For the marinade: Mix all the ingredients together in a bowl.
❡ Marinate the chicken for 30 minutes.
❡ For the sauce: Combine all the ingredients in a bowl and mix well.
❡ Heat the oil in a wok or skillet (frying pan) and stir-fry the chicken until lightly browned. Remove the chicken from the wok, drain, and set aside.
❡ Drain all but 1–2 tablespoons oil from the wok and reheat. Add the ginger, garlic, and sauce. Return the chicken to the wok and stir-fry over medium heat for 2 minutes.
❡ Transfer the ingredients to a pan and add water to cover by about ½ inch (1.5 cm). Cook over medium–low heat for 10 minutes.
❡ Add the scallions and serve.

## CHUEN MAI GAI

### SICHUAN CHICKEN

*Contrary to popular belief, not all Sichuan dishes are spicy-hot. The real secret to Sichuan cooking is not pungency, but balance. That's why, in this recipe, I've cut down on the chilis; you should taste the meat and the spices. Yes, your lips and tongue might tingle a bit, but the spiciness should never be painful.*

For the marinade:
*1 tablespoon light soy sauce*
*1 teaspoon dark soy sauce*
*2 teaspoons cornstarch (cornflour)*
*1 teaspoon sugar*
*2 teaspoons Chinese rice wine*
For the chicken:
*2 chicken legs, cut into bite-size pieces*
*1 cup (8 fl oz/250 ml) groundnut (peanut) oil*
*2 fresh red chilis, seeded and finely chopped*
*1 dried red chili, finely chopped*
*2 garlic cloves, crushed*
*1 tablespoon hot fava (broad) bean paste*
*1 cup (8 fl oz/250 ml) chicken broth (stock)*

*SERVES 4–6*

❡ For the marinade: Combine all of the ingredients in a bowl.
❡ Marinate the chicken for 30 minutes.
❡ Heat the oil in a wok or skilllet (frying pan) and fry the chicken until lightly browned. Remove the chicken from the wok, and drain.
❡ Drain all but 1–2 tablespoons of oil from the wok and reheat. Fry the fresh chili, dried chili, and garlic for 30 seconds. Add the hot fava bean paste and stir to mix.
❡ Return the chicken to the wok. Add the chicken broth and bring to a boil. Lower heat and simmer for 8–10 minutes. Serve.

## KUNG-PO GAI DING

### KUNG-PO CHICKEN

*During the Qing dynasty, Beijing's finest kitchens were peopled with chefs from various parts of China. So, while this is a Sichuan recipe, it was developed in the home of a Mandarin noble, Ting Kung-po. The chicken is stir-fried quickly, then mixed with crispy groundnuts (peanuts) and a spicy sauce for contrast.*

For the marinade:
*1 tablespoon light soy sauce*
*1 teaspoon dark soy sauce*

*1 teaspoon sugar*
*1 teaspoon Chinese rice wine*
*2 teaspoons cornstarch (cornflour)*
For the chicken:
*2 chicken breast fillets, cut into 1/2-inch (1-cm) cubes*
*1 cup (8 fl oz/250 ml) groundnut (peanut) oil*
*1 fresh red chili, seeded and chopped*
*2 dried red chilis, chopped*
*2 garlic cloves, crushed*
*1 tablespoon hot fava (broad) bean paste*
*1 teaspoon sugar*
*1 teaspoon Sichuan peppercorns, ground*
*1/3 cup (3 fl oz/90 ml) chicken broth (stock)*
*2 scallions (spring onions), cut into 1-inch (2.5-cm) lengths*
*2–3 tablespoons roasted groundnuts (peanuts)*
*1 teaspoon Chinese rice wine*

*SERVES 4–6*

❡ For the marinade: Combine all of the ingredients in a bowl.
❡ Marinate the chicken pieces for 30 minutes.
❡ Heat the oil in a wok or skillet (frying pan) and add the chicken, stirring to avoid sticking. When the chicken turns white, remove it from the wok, drain, and set aside.
❡ Drain all but 1–2 tablespoons of oil from the wok and reheat. Fry the fresh chili, dried chili, and garlic over medium heat for 30 seconds. Add the hot fava bean paste, sugar, and peppercorns, and stir to mix.
❡ Return the chicken to the wok, stirring vigorously over high heat for 30 seconds. Add the chicken broth and stir.
❡ Add the scallions and groundnuts, stirring well to mix. Add the wine and serve.

*Kung Po Gai Ding*

# POULTRY TYPES

**Chicken:** Most chicken is sold live, for cleaning at home, or by an obliging butcher at point of purchase. Free-range chickens in China are small and rather scrawny. Battery-feeding may produce larger birds with plump, tender flesh, but gain in size is usually at the expense of flavor.

The bland flavor and tender texture of chicken make it receptive to most of the Chinese seasoning ingredients. It is sliced, diced, and shredded for stir-fries; cubed and portioned for braised and simmered dishes; and ground (minced) for dumplings and stuffings. Steaming and poaching render it meltingly succulent, roasting crisps the skin to a golden crunch, braising and simmering absorb the surrounding flavors.

Chicken is well represented in each regional cuisine in China. In Sichuan their famous dishes are "*gai kung pao*," chicken breast stir-fried with chili and peanuts, and "*pon pon*," a cold dish of shredded chicken bathed in a nutty sesame dressing. In southern Hainan Island, they poach a whole chicken and serve it sliced with a ginger and scallion (spring onion) sauce, steamed rice, and Chinese greens, plus a thin soup of the poaching liquids. The Cantonese preference is for shredded chicken stir-fried in clear, delicately flavored sauces. In the North, chicken is served "drunken," marinated in yellow rice wine or smoked

to serve sliced, or to crisp-fry with sweet bean paste. One classic dish that appears frequently on banquet tables comprises tender sliced chicken breast layered with the best ham, and steamed to serve under a clear sauce. Braised chickens' feet, usually cooked with garlic, black beans, and chili, are a popular feature on the *dim sum* menu.

**Black chicken:** This is a special Chinese treat. These small birds, with their fluffy feathers and blue-black skin, are cooked into a soup of rich flavor which is said to be an excellent tonic and aphrodisiac.

**Duck:** Duck has a fat meat of rich flavor and dark color, so goes best with strong seasonings and accompanying ingredients. In Sichuan province, camphor wood and black tea leaves are used as the fuel for smoked duck. Duck has a natural affinity with aromatic black mushrooms, as it does with potent bean sauces and seasoning pastes. It is often casserole-cooked, to serve in its pot direct to the table. Duckling simmered in a citrus flavored broth is a south coast specialty. Duck is often featured as a banquet dish, sometimes stuffed with "eight treasures," a combination of glutinous rice, lotus seeds, and black mushrooms, with ingredients that can include ham, dried shrimp (prawns), barley, onions, and bamboo shoots. Or it may be marinated with aromatic brown

peppercorns, ginger, and anise, and cooked by a complex method of slow steaming then deep-frying, until the surface is deeply browned and crisp, the meat within still moist and pink. This is served with the thin pancakes associated with Peking Duck and a fragrant salty dip of roasted salt with five spices.

**Pigeons:** Several species of pigeons are sold at Chinese poultry market. The best have tender flesh which roasts crisp and succulent, others are better suited to stewing or boiling into intensely flavored broths, often with medicinal herbs.

**Quail eggs:** Brown and faun speckled quail eggs are sold fresh at the market, or canned at the grocer's. Hardly a mouthful, these tiny eggs are used as an appealing decoration on many dishes. They are poached to float on soups, or boiled and peeled to include in the filling of tasty dumplings.

*1. Duck; 2. free-range chicken; 3. battery-fed chicken; 4. quail eggs; 5. pigeons (boilers and roasters); 6. black chicken; 7. chicken wings; 8. chicken's feet*

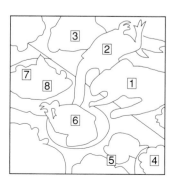

Top: Ho Yau Gai Tu; bottom: Cho Ku Mung Gai

# HO YAU GAI TU

*BRAISED CHICKEN LEGS IN OYSTER SAUCE*

*In this recipe, the natural flavor and aroma of the chicken is enhanced by the flavor of mushrooms—very Cantonese. Cholesterol-conscious cooks can substitute another oil for groundnut (peanut) oil, although groundnut oil is essential to the Cantonese, who enjoy the nutty taste that comes out in the cooking.*

For the marinade:
*1 tablespoon light soy sauce*
*1 teaspoon dark soy sauce*
*1 teaspoon sugar*
*1 teaspoon Chinese rice wine*
*2 teaspoons cornstarch (cornflour)*
For the chicken:
*2 chicken legs, cut into bite-size pieces*
*1 cup (8 fl oz/250 ml) groundnut (peanut) oil*
*3–4 slices ginger*
*1 garlic clove, crushed*
*6 dried black mushrooms, soaked in warm water to cover for*
*    1 hour, stems removed, and drained*
*1 tablespoon oyster sauce*
*1 tablespoon light soy sauce*
*1 teaspoon dark soy sauce*
*2 teaspoons Chinese rice wine*
*1 teaspoon sugar*
*1 1/2 cups (12 fl oz/375 ml) chicken broth (stock)*

*SERVES 4–6*

❡ For the marinade: Combine all of the ingredients in a bowl.
❡ Marinate the chicken for 30 minutes.
❡ Heat the oil in a wok or skillet (frying pan) and

fry the chicken until lightly browned. Remove the chicken from the wok, drain, and set aside.
❡ Drain all but 1–2 tablespoons of oil from the wok and reheat. Fry the ginger and garlic for 30 seconds. Return the chicken to the wok, add the mushrooms, and stir-fry for 30 seconds.
❡ Add all the remaining ingredients, cover, and simmer for 8–10 minutes. Serve.

# CHO KU MUNG GAI

*CHICKEN IN STRAW MUSHROOM SAUCE*

*The secret of this dish is in the mushrooms. Straw mushrooms are raised in northern Guangdong province, and are among the most fragrant of all mushrooms. The fragrance is further enhanced when they are dried, as a special chemical reaction occurs that makes them even tastier. These mushrooms are available in any Chinese grocery shop.*

For the marinade:
*1 tablespoon light soy sauce*
*1 teaspoon dark soy sauce*
*1 teaspoon sugar*
For the chicken:
*2 chicken breasts, cut into finger-size strips*
*1 cup (8 fl oz/250 ml) groundnut (peanut) oil*
*3–4 slices ginger*
*12 dried straw mushrooms, soaked in warm water for 1*
*    hour to soften, drained, and cleaned*
*1 cup (8 oz/250 g) cauliflower florets, blanched*
*2 scallions (spring onions), cut into 1-inch*
*    (2.5-cm) lengths*
*1 1/2 teaspoons salt*
*1 teaspoon sugar*
*1/2 cup (4 fl oz/125 ml) chicken broth (stock)*
*1 teaspoon Chinese rice wine*

*SERVES 4–6*

❡ For the marinade: Mix together all of the ingredients in a bowl.
❡ Marinate the chicken for 30 minutes.
❡ Heat the oil in a wok or skillet (frying pan) and fry the chicken, stirring to separate. When the chicken turns white, remove it from the wok, drain, and set aside.
❡ Drain all but 1–2 tablespoons oil from the wok and reheat. Fry the ginger and mushrooms for 30 seconds over high heat. Add the cauliflower and stir well. Return the chicken to the wok and stir-fry for 30 seconds.
❡ Add the scallions, salt, sugar, and broth, and stir to mix well. Add the wine and serve.

*Ingredients for preparing Peking Duck*

The duck meat was, in those times, offered to less-honored guests, and the bones were brewed into a soup for those farther down the social scale.

The type of duck used for this dish is similar to Long Island duckling, with white feathers and a wide, long back. Today in the North of China, Peking ducks have a short lifespan of just six weeks, and during the latter two they are force-fed on feeding machines to quickly advance their growth to the optimum weight (5–6 pounds/2.5–3 kg) required by the restaurants.

Several different methods are used for roasting Peking duck. The Bianyifang restaurant in Beijing, which has been serving duck for five hundred years, uses a "closed oven." The brick oven walls are heated to the right temperature, then the fire extinguished and the ducks are hung in the oven to cook indirectly by the heat emitted from the walls. Other restaurants use an open fire, heated with wood.

A difficult-to-master method of carving is used in the specialist roast duck restaurants in Beijing. Within 5 minutes of bringing the bird, sizzling, from the oven it must be carved into 100 slices, each slice of meat must have some skin, each piece of skin some meat. It is eaten wrapped in small soft, chewy crêpes, with a sliver of scallion (spring onion) and perhaps one of cucumber for crunch, with a sweet-salt sauce or white sugar for dipping.

# PEKING DUCK

For centuries before the twelfth-century warrior Genghis Khan conquered northern China and assumed power over the whole of China, Mongolians traveled over the mountains, catching wild duck in their traps to roast slowly over a fire. This early precursor to Peking Duck had none of the refinements that were to be introduced during the subsequent Ming Dynasty when the highest forms of imperial cooking were reintroduced to the palace kitchens.

The dish that was to become known the world over as Peking Duck, required birds bred with an especially meaty breast and a fat layer beneath the skin. It is the preparation— whereby air is forced under the skin to help it separate, then the duck is glazed and hung to dry before being roasted in a brick oven— that turns it into an emperor's dream.

The duck skin, prized as much for its glazed amber color, as for its taste and texture, was reserved for the aristocracy. So revered was this dish that imperial scribes recorded its preparation in a 15,000-word "official" recipe.

# MUD JUP TZE KEUNG GAI

### CHICKEN AND YOUNG GINGER IN HONEY SAUCE

*This is one of my favorite dishes. While it is available in many restaurants, I think it tastes best at home, where you can be sure of getting freshly marinated young ginger—which is astonishingly superior to commercially pickled ginger. The pickling takes only half an hour, and doing it yourself makes all the difference. Young ginger is recognizable by its ivory color; it tastes lighter and fresher than old ginger.*

For the chicken marinade:
1 tablespoon light soy sauce
1 teaspoon dark soy sauce
1 teaspoon Chinese rice wine
½ teaspoon salt
1 tablespoon cornstarch (cornflour)
For the ginger marinade:
1 tablespoon sugar
1 teaspoon salt
1 tablespoon white vinegar
For the chicken:
1 lb (500 g) chicken legs, chopped into bite-size pieces
2 cups (16 fl oz/500 ml) groundnut (peanut) oil
4 oz (125 g) young ginger stem, chopped into bite-size pieces and lightly crushed
1 red bell pepper (capsicum), cut into small squares
1 green bell pepper (capsicum), cut into small squares
1 tablespoon honey
1 teaspoon dark soy sauce
1 teaspoon salt
1 teaspoon Chinese rice wine
1 cup (8 fl oz/250 ml) chicken broth (stock)

*SERVES 4–6*

❡ For the chicken marinade: Combine all the ingredients in a bowl.
❡ For the ginger marinade: Combine all the ingredients in a separate bowl.
❡ Marinate the chicken for 30 minutes.
❡ Marinate the ginger for 30 minutes.
❡ Heat the oil in a wok or skillet (frying pan), and fry the ginger until lightly browned. Remove the ginger from the wok, drain, and set aside, but do not drain the oil.
❡ In the same wok, fry the chicken for 45 seconds. Remove the chicken from the wok, drain, and set aside.
❡ Drain all but 2–3 tablespoons of oil from the wok and reheat. Stir-fry the peppers for 30 seconds. Return the chicken and ginger to the wok. Mix all remaining ingredients in a bowl and add to the wok. Cover and cook over medium–low heat for 3 minutes. Serve.

*Top: Mud Jup Tze Keung Gai; bottom: Jar Gai Tu*

# JAR GAI TU

### FRIED CHICKEN DRUMSTICKS

*The Cantonese give an interesting twist to fried chicken, as they generally do not like deep-fried meat. So first they simmer the chicken in flavored broth (stock) to get the spices inside the meat, then they fry it. It comes out crispy on the outside, tender and spicy on the inside.*

*4 cups (1 qt/1 l) water*
*6 chicken drumsticks*
*3–4 slices ginger*
*2 scallions (spring onions)*
*1 tablespoon light soy sauce*
*1 tablespoon dark soy sauce*
*2 teaspoons sugar*
*2 teaspoons five-spice powder*
*1 egg white, lightly beaten*
*2 tablespoons cornstarch (cornflour)*
*3 cups (24 fl oz/750 ml) groundnut (peanut) oil*
*1 tablespoon cilantro (fresh coriander), chopped*

*SERVES 4–6*

❡ Bring the water to a boil in a large pan. Add the chicken, ginger, scallions, soy sauces, sugar, and five-spice powder. When the water returns to a boil, reduce the heat and simmer for 30 minutes.
❡ Remove the chicken from the pan. Strain the broth, return it to the pan and boil rapidly to reduce to 1 cup (8 fl oz/250 ml). Set aside.
❡ Coat the chicken with the egg white and then the cornstarch.
❡ Heat the oil in another large pan and fry the chicken until lightly browned. Remove from the heat, drain, and put the chicken on a serving platter.
❡ Return the broth to a boil and remove from the heat. Stir in the cilantro and serve with the chicken as a dip.

# CHUEN CHIU GAI

### PEPPERY CHICKEN CHIUCHOW-STYLE

*While this dish uses Sichuan peppers, the leaves show that this is a real Teochiu dish. I have used mint leaves in the recipe, because the original (*chin jiu *leaves) are difficult to find outside Asia. Chin jiu means "pearl leaf," and it is one of the most delectable Teochiu vegetables. The taste is not important, since it soaks up most of the oil, but the leaves literally melt in the mouth. If you cannot find them under their Chinese name, try in Thai supermarkets and ask for*

*Chuen Chiu Gai*

bai horaphaa. *Mint leaves are a pretty good substitute, since the minty taste disappears when deep-fried.*

For the marinade:
*1 teaspoon salt*
*1 teaspoon sugar*
*1 teaspoon Chinese rice wine*
*2 teaspoons cornstarch (cornflour)*
*1 tablespoon water*
For the chicken:
*8 oz (250 g) chicken breast, cut into ³⁄₄-inch (2-cm) cubes*
*2 cups (16 fl oz/500 ml) groundnut (peanut) oil*
*12 fresh mint leaves*
*¹⁄₂ teaspoon ground Sichuan peppercorns*
*¹⁄₂ teaspoon black pepper*
*2 teaspoons salted fish sauce*
*1 teaspoon dark soy sauce*
*1 teaspoon Chinese rice wine*
*2 tablespoons chicken broth (stock)*

*SERVES 4–6*

❡ For the marinade: Combine all of the ingredients in a bowl.
❡ Marinate the chicken for 15 minutes.
❡ Heat the oil in a wok or skillet (frying pan), and fry the mint leaves over medium heat until crisp. Remove the mint leaves from the wok, drain, and set aside, but do not drain the oil.
❡ In the same wok, fry the chicken over medium heat for 45 seconds. Remove the chicken from the pan, drain, and set aside.
❡ Drain all but 1–2 tablespoons of oil from the wok and reheat. Return the chicken to the wok and add all remaining ingredients. Stir-fry over high heat until most of the liquid has evaporated. Place on a serving platter, garnish with the mint leaves, and serve.

# BON-BON GAI

### BON-BON CHICKEN

*While the name of this dish sounds French, it is derived from the Chinese word for "stick," because, originally, the chef would use a wooden stick to pound the meat. This is a mild Sichuan dish that makes an excellent appetizer.*

For the sauce:
1 1/2 tablespoons sesame paste
1 tablespoon chili oil
3/4 teaspoon sugar
1 tablespoon light soy sauce
1 teaspoon aromatic or apple vinegar
2 tablespoons chicken broth (stock)
For the chicken:
1/2 chicken, about 1 1/2 lb (750 g)
2 teaspoons salt
1 tablespoon Chinese rice wine
1 teaspoon sesame oil
1 tablespoon sesame seeds
8 oz (250 g) cucumber, shredded
1 red bell pepper (capsicum), shredded

*SERVES 4–6*

❡ For the sauce: Combine all the ingredients in a bowl.
❡ Clean and dry the chicken, and rub with the salt, wine and sesame oil. Bring a large pan of water to a boil, place the chicken on a steaming rack, and steam over medium heat for 18–20 minutes. Remove and drain. When the chicken has cooled, bone, and shred the meat. Set aside.
❡ Sauté the sesame seeds in a wok or skillet (frying pan) over low heat until lightly browned. Remove and set aside.
❡ Place the cucumber on a platter. Arrange the chicken on top and sprinkle with the pepper and sesame seeds. Pour the sauce on top and serve.

# DONG ON GAI

### HUNAN CHICKEN

*Hunan cooking is a provincial style that has not yet really caught on in the West, so it is difficult to find a good Hunan restaurant. But you can still enjoy the cuisine at home with this simple dish, which has such hallmarks of the style as vinegar and ginger—which also give the dish a wonderful aroma.*

For the marinade:
1 tablespoon dark soy sauce
1 teaspoon Chinese rice wine

1 tablespoon cornstarch (cornflour)
For the chicken:
1/2 chicken (about 1 1/2 lb/750 g), cut into 1 1/2-inch (3-cm) squares
2 cups (16 fl oz/500 ml) groundnut (peanut) oil
1 red chili, seeded and cut into rings
2 scallions (spring onions), cut into 1 1/2-inch (3-cm) lengths
1 tablespoon chopped garlic
1 tablespoon chopped ginger
1 tablespoon light soy sauce

*1 teaspoon dark soy sauce*
*1 teaspoon chili oil*
*1 tablespoon aromatic vinegar*
*1 tablespoon sugar*
*1 teaspoon Chinese rice wine*
*1 cup (8 fl oz/250 ml) chicken broth (stock)*

*SERVES 4–6*

❡ For the marinade: Combine all of the ingredients in a bowl.

❡ Marinate the chicken for 15 minutes.

❡ Heat the oil in a wok or skillet (frying pan) over medium heat. Add the chicken and fry for 1½ minutes. Remove the chicken from the wok, drain, and set aside.

❡ Drain all but 2–3 tablespoons of oil from the wok and reheat. Add the chili and stir-fry for 30 seconds. Add the scallions, garlic, and ginger. Return chicken to the wok and stir-fry over high heat for 1 minute.

❡ Mix all the remaining ingredients in a bowl and add to the wok. Cover and cook over medium heat for 3 minutes. Serve.

*Top: Bon-Bon Gai; bottom: Dong On Gai*

## KOU FAR GAI

*BEGGAR'S CHICKEN*

*This is one of the most famous banquet dishes in all of China. For an extra-special touch when serving the dish, crack open the crust in a closed room, so that everyone can enjoy the aroma that pours out.*

1 chicken, about 3 lb (1.5 kg)
2 tablespoons Chinese rice wine
1 teaspoon salt
1 tablespoon dark soy sauce
1 teaspoon sesame oil
For the dough:
1 1/2 lb (750 g) all-purpose (plain) flour
1 3/4 cups (14 fl oz/440 ml) warm water
1/2 cup (4 fl oz/125 ml) Chinese rice wine
For the filling:
1/2 cup (4 fl oz/125 ml) groundnut (peanut) oil
2 oz (60 g) lean pork, shredded
2 oz (60 g) fat pork, shredded
2–3 dried black mushrooms, soaked in warm water for
    1 hour, drained, stems discarded, and shredded
4 oz (125 g) Sichuan pickled vegetables, shredded
1 teaspoon sugar
2 tablespoons water
1 large piece caul fat
2 dried lotus leaves, soaked in boiling water

*SERVES 8–10*

❡ Clean and dry the chicken, and rub with 1 tablespoon wine, the salt, soy sauce, and sesame oil. Let rest for 30 minutes.
❡ For the dough: Place the flour on a flat surface and make a well in the middle. Mix the water and wine in a bowl. Add the liquid to the flour a little at a time, working with the fingers to make a dough. Knead lightly and set aside.
❡ Heat 1–2 tablespoons of oil in a wok or skillet (frying pan). Add the pork, mushrooms, and Sichuan vegetables. Stir-fry over medium heat for 1 minute. Add the remaining 1 tablespoon wine, the sugar, and water, and stir-fry for 1 minute.
❡ Stuff the chicken cavity with the pork mixture, skewer the opening closed, and wrap the whole chicken with the caul fat. Then wrap the chicken with the lotus leaves and tie with string.
❡ Shape the dough into a circle large enough to wrap the chicken. Brush the chicken with oil and wrap with the dough, sealing the edges with cold water. Brush the dough all over with oil. Wrap the chicken in baking foil and place in a roasting pan.
❡ Bake the chicken in the oven at 475°F (240°C/Gas 9) for 1 hour. Reduce the heat to 450°F

*Left: Kou Far Gai; right: Ng Heung Gai*

(230°C/Gas 8) and bake for 1 hour more.
❡ Remove the chicken from the oven, and crack and discard the dough. Place the chicken on a serving platter, untie the string, remove the lotus leaves, and serve.

## NG HEUNG GAI

*SPICY CHICKEN*

*A Cantonese dish, and certainly not too spicy, despite its name. The aroma of the poultry is more important than the pungency of the mild peppers.*

1 chicken, about 3 lb (1.5 kg)
2 tablespoons salt
1 oz (60 g) crushed ginger stems
3 scallions (spring onions)
3 cilantro (fresh coriander) stems
1 tablespoon Sichuan peppercorns
2 tablespoons Chinese rice wine
1 cup (8 fl oz/250 ml) dark soy sauce
1/2 cup (4 oz/125 g) sugar
4 cups (1 qt/1 l) water

*SERVES 8–10*

❡ Clean and dry the chicken, and rub all over with 1 tablespoon salt. Set aside for 30 minutes.
❡ Place all the remaining ingredients in a large pan and bring to a boil. Add the chicken and reduce the heat to medium–low. Cook for 25–30 minutes, turning the chicken several times. Remove the chicken from the pan and reserve the cooking liquid. When cool, chop the chicken into bite-size pieces and arrange on a serving platter.
❡ Pour the cooking liquid into a pan. Boil rapidly to reduce by half, and serve with the chicken as a dip.

# JOY GAI

## *DRUNKEN CHICKEN*

*To make sure the chicken is really inebriated, I've changed around the traditional recipe a bit: Not only does the chicken rest in a wine marinade, but I've added wine to the cavity of the chicken as well. The result is a "spirited" dish — inside and out.*

1 chicken, about 3 lb (1.5 kg)
1 tablespoon salt
1 oz (30 g) crushed ginger
2 scallions (spring onions)
2 tablespoons Chinese rice wine
For the marinade:
½ cup (4 fl oz/125 ml) Chinese rice wine
½ teaspoon sugar
1 teaspoon salt

*SERVES 8–10*

❡ Clean and dry the chicken. Rub the surface with the salt and stuff the cavity with the ginger, scallions, and wine. Bring a large pan of water to a boil, place a steaming rack in the middle, and steam the chicken over medium heat for 20 minutes or more to taste.
❡ Remove the chicken from the pan. When it has cooled, chop it into bite-size pieces and arrange on a serving platter.
❡ For the marinade: Mix all the ingredients in a bowl. Pour over the chicken, cover with plastic wrap, and marinate for 16 hours in the refrigerator.
❡ Serve cold.

# KA HEUNG GAI

## *BRAISED CHICKEN GRANDMA–STYLE*

*I would like to say that it was my grandmother who made this dish, but most Cantonese families have a grandma who makes a variation of this traditional home-cooked recipe. A number of "exotic" flavorings are used, which give the dish fragrance and interest.*

For the marinade :
1 tablespoon light soy sauce
1 teaspoon dark soy sauce
1 teaspoon Chinese rice wine
1 teaspoon sesame oil
2 teaspoons cornstarch (cornflour)
For the chicken:

½ chicken, about 1½ lb (750 g), chopped into bite-size pieces
1 cup (8 fl oz/250 ml) groundnut (peanut) oil
4–5 slices ginger
3 dried black mushrooms, soaked in warm water for 1 hour, drained, stems discarded, and sliced
½ oz (15 g) dried tiger lily buds, soaked in warm water for 1 hour and drained
½ oz (15 g) cloud ear fungus, soaked in warm water for 1 hour and drained
3–4 red dates, pitted
1 scallion (spring onion)
1 tablespoon oyster sauce
1 teaspoon Chinese rice wine
1½ cups (12 fl oz/375 ml) chicken broth (stock)

*SERVES 4–6*

❡ For the marinade: Combine all of the ingredients in a bowl.
❡ Marinate the chicken for 30 minutes.
❡ Heat the oil in a wok or skillet (frying pan). Add the chicken pieces and fry over high heat for 1 minute. Remove the chicken from the wok, drain, and set aside.
❡ Drain all but 1–2 tablespoons of oil from the wok and reheat. Add the ginger, mushrooms, lily buds, fungus, dates, and scallion, and stir-fry for 30 seconds. Return the chicken to the wok and add the oyster sauce, wine, and broth. Bring to a boil, lower the heat, cover, and cook over medium–low heat for 15 minutes. Transfer to a serving platter and serve.

*Left: Ka Heung Gai; right: Joy Gai*

*Top: Bo Ngap Chuen Lin; bottom: Sheung Dong Pa Ngarp*

## BO NGAP CHUEN LIN

### BRAISED LOTUS SEED DUCK

*This is a relatively complicated dish, but any Cantonese household could make it. The recipe, though, was probably reserved for the Mid-autumn (fall) festival. Chinese duck-lings hatch in the spring, and about 4 months later they are tender enough for cooking. After steaming for almost 3 hours the meat is tender enough to fall off the bone and the lotus seeds provide a special festival fragrance.*

For the duck:
*1 tablespoon salt*
*1 teaspoon pepper*
*4 lb (2kg) whole duck, washed, cleaned and patted dry*
*2 tablespoons dark soy sauce*
*4 cups (1 qt/1 l) groundnut (peanut) oil*
*3 scallions (spring onions), cut into 2-inch (5-cm) lengths*
*5 slices ginger*
*4 oz (125 g) dried lotus seeds, soaked in warm water for*
   *3 hours, drained*
*4 dried black mushrooms, soaked in warm water for 1 hour,*
   *drained, stems discarded, caps shredded*
*2 oz (60 g) pork fillet, cut into ¼-inch (0.5-cm) cubes,*
   *soaked in water for 1 hour, drained*
For the sauce:
*2 tablespoons oyster sauce*

*2 teaspoons dark soy sauce*
*1 teaspoon sugar*
*2 teaspoons Chinese rice wine*
*1 tablespoon cornstarch (cornflour)*

*SERVES 6–8*

¶ Rub the salt and pepper inside the cavity of the duck. Rub the soy sauce on the outside. Leave to dry in an airy place for 2 hours.

¶ Heat the oil in a large wok or skillet (frying pan). Deep-fry the duck, over medium heat, basting with the oil, until brown, about 10 minutes. Remove the duck, drain, and set aside.

¶ Stuff the cavity of the duck with the scallions, ginger, lotus seeds, mushrooms, and pork, and place the duck in a deep dish.

¶ Bring 3–4 cups (24 fl oz–1 qt/750 ml–1 l) of water to a boil in a large wok or pan. Place a steaming rack in the middle and place the dish with the duck on top. Cover, and steam over medium heat for 2½ hours.

¶ Remove the duck from the pan. Remove the stuffing and place it on a serving platter. Chop the duck into bite-size pieces and place them on top of the stuffing.

¶ In a small pan, mix any liquid from the steamed duck with the sauce ingredients and bring to a boil. Pour over the duck and serve.

## SHEUNG DONG PA NGARP

*BRAISED DUCK BREAST WITH BLACK MUSHROOMS AND BAMBOO SHOOTS*

*Duck breast is readily available at any butcher, so you won't need to struggle with the whole bird. I use shiitake mushrooms — not from Japan, but the Chinese variety called* tung ko *or "black winter mushroom." They are just as flavorful, but cost a fraction of the price.*

For the marinade:
*1 tablespoon light soy sauce*
*1 teaspoon dark soy sauce*
*1 teaspoon sugar*
*1 teaspoon Chinese rice wine*
*2 teaspoons cornstarch (cornflour)*
For the sauce:
*1 tablespoon oyster sauce*
*1 tablespoon light soy sauce*
*1 teaspoon dark soy sauce*
*1 teaspoon Chinese rice wine*
*1 teaspoon sugar*
*2 teaspoons cornstarch (cornflour)*
For the duck:
*2 duck breasts*
*1–2 tablespoons groundnut (peanut) oil*
*3 garlic cloves, chopped*
*5–6 slices ginger*
*2 cups (16 fl oz/500 ml) chicken broth (stock)*
*10 dried black mushrooms, stems removed, soaked in warm water to cover for 1 hour, drained*
*2 cups (4 oz/125 g) bamboo shoots, cut into bite-size pieces*

*SERVES 4–6*

*Choi Pay Ngarp*

❡ For the marinade: Combine all of the ingredients in a bowl.
❡ For the sauce: In a separate bowl, mix all the ingredients well.
❡ Marinate the duck breasts for 15 minutes.
❡ Heat the oil in a pan. Pan-fry the duck over medium heat until brown on both sides. Add the garlic, ginger, and chicken broth, and simmer for 45 minutes.
❡ Add the mushrooms and bamboo shoots, and simmer for 15 minutes.
❡ Remove the duck breast and cut into bite-size pieces. Return the duck to the pan, pour in the sauce, and bring to a boil. Serve immediately.

## CHOI PAY NGARP

*CRISPY DUCK*

*This Sichuan dish makes a wonderful cold appetizer. The most important part is the oyster sauce, which serves two purposes: It enhances the flavor and moistens the meat. As in many regional recipes for relatively tough meat, the duck is steamed first, to soften it, then fried for crispness.*

*1 duck, about 4 lbs (2 kg), cleaned and dried*
*2 tablespoons salt*
*2 teaspoons Sichuan peppercorns, ground*
*5–6 slices ginger*
*2 scallions (spring onions)*
*4–5 cups (1–1¼ qt/1–1.25 l) water*
*8 cups (2 qt/2 l) groundnut (peanut) oil*
*2 tablespoons oyster sauce*

*SERVES 6–8*

❡ Rub the outside and inside of the duck with salt, and the rub the inside with peppercorns. Put the ginger and scallions in the cavity and place the duck in a deep dish.
❡ Bring the water to a boil in a large pan. Place a steaming rack in the middle and put the dish with the duck on top. Cover and steam for 1 hour. Remove the duck from the pan and reserve any juices that have collected in the dish.
❡ Heat the oil in a large wok or skillet (frying pan) and deep-fry the duck until golden, turning the duck every minute and basting with the hot oil. Remove from the heat and drain.
❡ When cool, chop the duck into bite-size pieces and arrange on a serving platter.
❡ Mix the reserved cooking juices with the oyster sauce and serve with the duck as a dip.

## JOU CHING NGARP

*STEAMED DUCK IN WINE SAUCE*

*When the Cantonese cook with wine, the result isn't quite like coq au vin. Cantonese feel that duck is too strong in flavor and wine is needed to offset the taste. Because the alcohol burns off in cooking, I add a little extra wine at the end, after reducing the sauce. Dry sherry or port makes an excellent substitute for rice wine.*

*1 duck, about 4 lb (2 kg), cleaned and dried*
*10 cups (2 ½ qt/2.5 l) water*
*2 tablespoons dark soy sauce*
*1 tablespoon salt*
*2 teaspoons Sichuan peppercorns, ground*
*3 tablespoons Chinese rice wine*
*5–6 slices ginger*
*2 scallions (spring onions)*

*SERVES 6–8*

❡ Soak the duck in water to cover for 1 hour.
❡ After soaking, drain completely.
❡ In a large pan, bring 5 cups (1¼ qt/1.25 l) of the water to a boil. Add the duck and cook, boiling for 15 minutes. Remove from the heat and drain.
❡ Rub the soy sauce on the skin of the duck. Rub the inside with the salt, peppercorns, and 1½ tablespoons of wine. Put the ginger and scallions into the cavity and place the duck in a deep dish.
❡ Bring 5 cups (1¼ qt/1.25 l) of the water to a boil in a large pan. Place a steaming rack in the middle and put the dish with the duck on top. Cover and steam for 2 hours.
❡ Remove the duck from the pan and reserve any juices that have collected in the dish. When cool, discard the ginger and scallions, cut the duck into bite-size pieces and arrange on a serving platter.
❡ Place the reserved cooking juices in a small pan and reduce to one half. Mix with the remaining Chinese wine, pour over the duck, and serve.

## CHUEN MAI NGARP

*BRAISED DUCK LEG SICHUAN-STYLE*

*I love the pungency of this dish. The bite of ginger, vinegar, and Sichuan peppercorns makes for a rich and memorable dish.*

For the marinade:
*1 tablespoon light soy sauce*
*1 teaspoon dark soy sauce*

*1 teaspoon sugar*
*1 teaspoon Chinese rice wine*
*2 teaspoons cornstarch (cornflour)*
For the duck:
*2 duck legs, cut into bite-size pieces*
*1 cup (8 fl oz/250 ml) groundnut (peanut) oil*
*1 tablespoon chopped ginger*
*2 garlic cloves, crushed*
*4–5 shallots, crushed*
*1 tablespoon hot fava (broad) bean sauce*
*2 teaspoons sugar*
*1 teaspoon Sichuan peppercorns, ground*
*2½ cups (20 fl oz/600 ml) chicken broth (stock)*
*2 teaspoons aromatic or apple vinegar*
*1 teaspoon Chinese rice wine*
*1 tablespoon cilantro (fresh coriander), chopped*

*SERVES 4–6*

❡ For the marinade: Combine all of the ingredients in a bowl.
❡ Marinate the duck for 30 minutes.
❡ Heat the oil in a wok or skillet (frying pan) and fry the duck until lightly browned. Remove the duck from the wok, drain, and set aside.
❡ Drain all but 1–2 tablespoons of oil from the wok and reheat. Fry the ginger, garlic, and shallots for 30 seconds. Add the hot fava bean paste, sugar, and peppercorns, and stir to mix. Return the duck to the wok and stir well.
❡ Add the chicken broth and vinegar, and bring to a boil. Cover and simmer for 30 minutes. Add the wine, sprinkle with cilantro, and serve.

*Top: Jou Ching Ngarp; bottom: Chuen Mai Ngarp*

# SMALL BIRDS

Walk past any roast meat restaurant in Hong Kong or Guangzhou and you'll see rows of tiny birds glazed a glistening red-brown, hanging in the window. These are "rice birds," a type of Javanese sparrow which descends in huge flocks to feed in the rice fields of southern China. A pest in the fields, but a treat on the table, these tiny birds, less than half the size of a quail, are caught in nets in the rice paddies of Guangdong (Canton) and brought live to market.

**Speckled quail:** In these same paddies, drained as the crop ripens ready for harvest, run speckled quail which are trapped for the market where they are sold live in woven bamboo cages.

Both quail and rice birds are marinated in a seasoning similar to that used to make *cha siu*, the glazed, red-roasted Cantonese pork, for sale in roast meat shops. The rice birds are speared onto skewers, six or so at a time, and broiled (grilled) or oven-roasted, their

bones cooking so soft they can be eaten whole.

**Pigeon:** Even more appreciated by the Chinese palate is pigeon meat. Several species are bred for the tables, and there are a number of specialty restaurants, particularly in southern China and Hong Kong, where these prized birds are prepared in hundreds of ways.

**Pigeon eggs:** Generally, pigeon eggs are retained for breeding, but occasionally will be used — steamed or boiled — usually in a dish with pigeon meat.

*1. stewed pigeon; 2. dressed pigeons (larger birds); 3. dressed quail; 4. pigeon's eggs; 5. quail eggs; 6. Quail with pepper-salt*

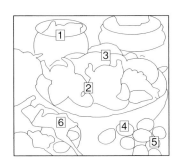

# CHOW NGARP GON

### STIR-FRIED DUCK LIVER SHANGHAI-STYLE

*You don't need French foie gras for this dish; any duck liver will do. The firm texture of the fungus gives a nice contrast to the soft texture of the liver.*

For the sauce:
1 tablespoon light soy sauce
1 tablespoon Chinese rice wine
2 teaspoons aromatic or apple vinegar
2 teaspoons sugar
1 teaspoon salt
2 teaspoons cornstarch (cornflour)
1 cup (8 fl oz/250 ml) chicken broth (stock)
For the marinade:
1 1/2 teaspoons salt
1 1/2 teaspoons sugar
1 1/2 teaspoons Chinese rice wine
3 teaspoons cornstarch (cornflour)
For the duck liver:
6 oz (185 g) duck liver, cut into 1/2-inch (1.5-cm) slices
1 cup (8 fl oz/250 ml) groundnut (peanut) oil
2 teaspoons finely chopped garlic
2 scallions (spring onions), cut into 2-inch (5-cm) lengths, finely shredded
6 dried black fungus, soaked in water to cover for 30 minutes, drained, torn into small pieces

*SERVES 4–6*

❡ For the sauce: Combine all the ingredients in a bowl, mix well.
❡ For the marinade: In a separate bowl, mix all the ingredients well.
❡ Marinate the duck liver for 15 minutes.
❡ Heat the oil in a wok or skillet (frying pan) and fry the duck liver. When the liver turns white, remove it from the wok, and drain.
❡ Drain all but 1–2 tablespoons of oil from the wok and reheat. Add the garlic, scallions, and black fungus. Return the duck liver to the wok and add the sauce. Bring to a boil, stir well, and serve.

# NG HEUNG NGARP

### SPICY DUCK

*While this is a Teochiu recipe, you won't find it in any Teochiu restaurant. That is because Teochiu people are famous for their goose, and this recipe is adapted for duck. If you do have some goose left over from a holiday dinner, you can use it to make this cold appetizer exactly the same way.*

1 duck, about 4 lb (2 kg), cleaned and dried
1 cup (8 fl oz/250 ml) dark soy sauce
2 tablespoons sugar
1 tablespoon salt
5–6 slices ginger
2 garlic cloves, crushed
2 tablespoons Chinese rice wine
3 star anise
1 tablespoon Sichuan peppercorns, ground

*Left: Chow Ngarp Gon; right: Ng Heung Ngarp*

*1 stick cinnamon*
*3 bay leaves*
*SERVES 6–8*

¶ Soak the duck in water to cover for 1 hour.

¶ In a large pan, bring enough water to cover the duck to a boil and cook the duck over medium heat for 15 minutes. Remove from the heat and drain.

¶ Place the duck in a separate pan, add all the remaining ingredients and enough water to cover the duck about 1 inch (2.5 cm) above the surface. Bring to a boil, then reduce heat and simmer for 2 hours.

¶ Remove the duck from the pan. Strain and reserve the cooking liquid.

¶ When cool, chop the duck into bite-size pieces and arrange on a serving platter.

¶ Return the pan with the cooking liquid to the heat and boil briskly to reduce to one half. Serve with the duck as a dip.

*Left: Conpoy Shuen Tze Mun Siu Ngarp; right: Siu Ngarp Sze Chow Ngan Ngar*

## CONPOY SHUEN TZE MUN SIU NGARP

### BRAISED DUCK BREAST WITH CONPOY AND GARLIC

*The idea of making a dish that combines duck and dried scallops may seem novel, but the combination of flavors will melt in your mouth.*

2 cups (16 fl oz/500 ml) groundnut (peanut) oil

20 garlic cloves

1 lb (500 g) roasted duck breast

6 conpoy (dried scallops), soaked in water for 1 hour, and drained

1 cup (8 fl oz/250 ml) chicken broth (stock)

1 tablespoon oyster sauce

1 teaspoon cornstarch (cornflour) dissolved in 1 tablespoon water

1 teaspoon Chinese rice wine

SERVES 4–6

and arrange in the middle of a serving platter with the *conpoy* and garlic around it.

❧ Heat the reserved liquid and reduce by half. Add the oyster sauce and stir in the cornstarch. Add the wine, pour over the duck, and serve.

## SIU NGARP SZE CHOW NGAN NGAR

### *STIR-FRIED ROAST DUCK SHREDS WITH BEAN SPROUTS*

*This dish could be subtitled "The Lazy Person's Guide to Gourmet Food." All you have to do is shred some leftover duck and add this relatively spicy sauce. The result is easy, economical, and tasty.*

For the sauce:
1 tablespoon light soy sauce
1 tablespoon oyster sauce
1 teaspoon Chinese rice wine
2 teaspoons cornstarch (cornflour)
½ cup (4 fl oz/125 ml) chicken broth (stock)
For the duck:
3–4 tablespoons groundnut (peanut) oil
2 garlic cloves, chopped
1 green bell pepper (capsicum), shredded
6 oz (185 g) roasted duck meat, shredded
1 lb (500 g) green bean sprouts, blanched and drained

*SERVES 4–6*

❧ For the sauce: Mix all the ingredients in a bowl.
❧ Heat the oil in a wok or skillet (frying pan). Add the garlic, bell pepper, and duck, and stir-fry for 30 seconds.
❧ Add the sauce and bring to a boil. Add the bean sprouts. Stir well over high heat for 30 seconds and serve.

### *FERMENTED BLACK BEANS*
*Beans are important nutritionally to the Chinese diet, and they are available in many different forms. Among the most commonly used are fermented black beans, which are made from black beans mixed with salt and garlic. With a tart, salty taste, the beans are used in sauces for poultry, red meat, and fish, sometimes also combined with pungent spices, like ginger.*
*To use the beans, simply take the desired amount from the jar, then rinse, drain, and mash them. The beans will keep for a few weeks in the pantry; if they start to dry out, add some groundnut (peanut) or corn oil to moisten. They will last indefinitely in the refrigerator.*

❧ Heat the oil in a wok or skillet (frying pan) and fry the garlic over medium–low heat until golden brown. Remove, drain, and set aside.
❧ Place the duck breast in a bowl and add the conpoy, garlic, and broth. Place the bowl on a rack over boiling water and steam over medium heat for 2 hours. Remove the duck from the bowl. Drain the *conpoy* liquid into a small pan and set aside.
❧ Cut the duck into ½-inch (1.5-cm) wide strips

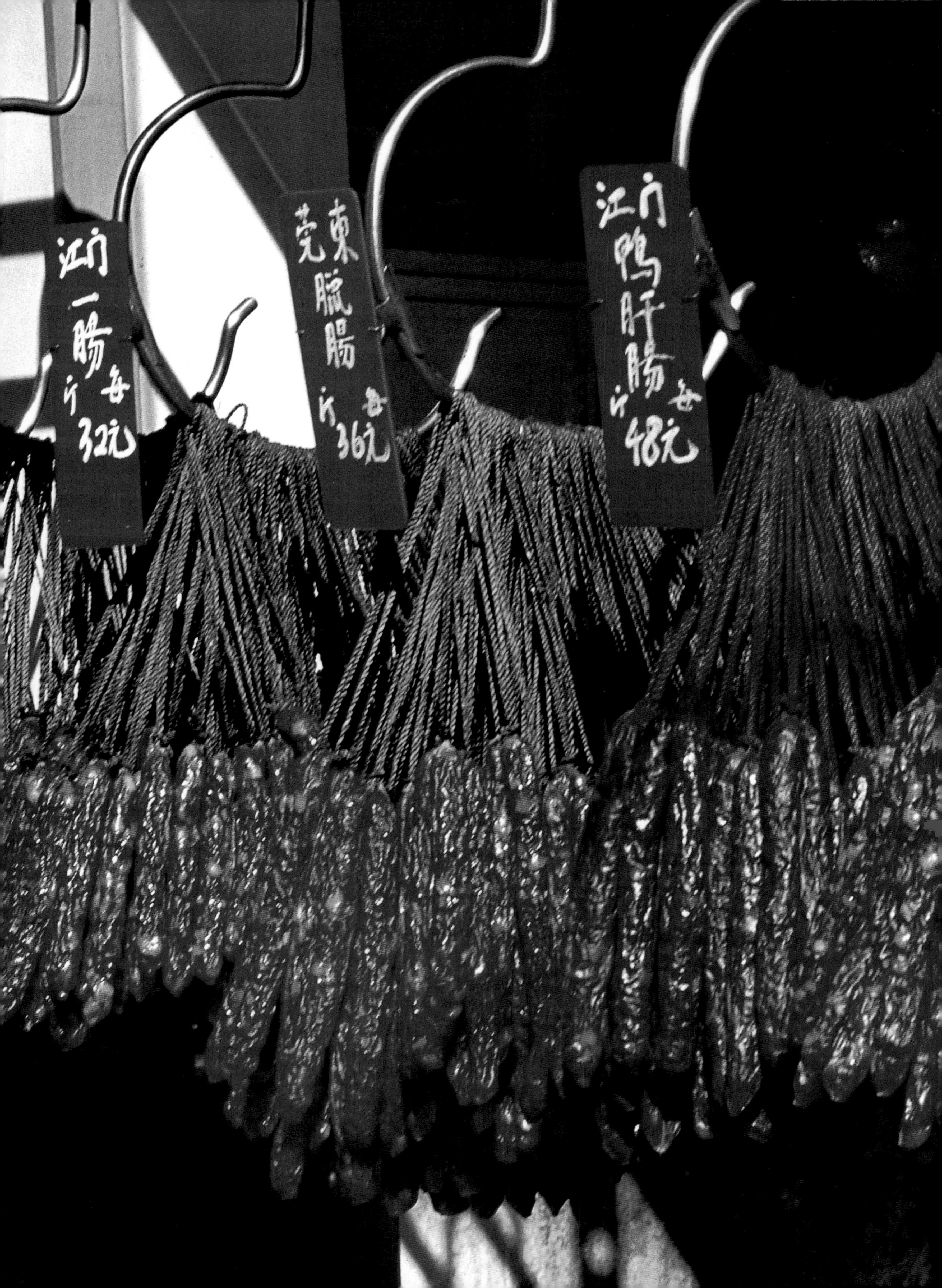
江门一腸
每斤32元
東莞臘腸
每斤36元
江门鴨肝腸
每斤48元

# Pork, Beef and Lamb

# PORK, BEEF AND LAMB

THE CHINESE DIET IN GENERAL, IS MUCH LOWER IN MEAT CONSUMPTION THAN THAT OF THEIR WESTERN COUNTERPARTS. Pork and mutton have been historically the meats of importance, pork for the Chinese in general, mutton in the far North. But in more modern times, beef has become a little more appreciated, and creative chefs in major centers are even experimenting with lamb.

❡ Eating pork goes back to the earliest years of Chinese history. Pickled pork was a delicacy as far back as the fourth century BC. But the earliest known pork recipe comes from the *Lei-chi*, the "Book of Rituals" of the Han Dynasty, around 206 BC. Here were listed the Eight Delicacies, the most prized of which was what would now be called Stuffed Suckling Pig.

❡ Centuries ago, the Emperor would sacrifice pigs along with other offerings, to make a good harvest. Instead of being left to the "gods," the carcasses would be taken to a shop where they would be cooked and distributed free to the poor. One such shop, *Sha guo ju*, is still in Beijing, still cooking up pigs in huge ceramic pots. All-pork banquets

*Previous pages: Like some fish and vegetables, meats are often preserved by smoking or wind-drying. Market stalls like this sell a wide range of products such as pork, or pork and duck liver, sausages, and smoked bacon or beef.*
BRUCE COLEMAN LIMITED/FRASER HALL

*Opposite: Pork is one of the main ingredients of Chinese food, particularly in the southern and eastern regions. Practically nothing is wasted, with the meat, ribs, liver, kidney, trotters, and tripe all used to create a mind-boggling array of inventive dishes.* LEO MEIER/WELDONS

include fried ribs, pork liver, pig tail (the Chinese will sometimes wait in line for this), and pork soup.

❡ Chinese beef dishes are very popular in Hong Kong and among Westerners, but in China, beef has never been at the top of the list. In the South, pork is more popular, and in the North, beef is second to lamb. The reason is largely economic, as beef cattle are expensive to raise and require larger tracts of land than are available. According to murals from the *Ma-wang-tui* tombs, built in the early Han dynasty, around the time of Emperor China (156–141 BC), cows were classified with other wild animals; beef flank was served with dog, bear's paw, and panther breast for special banquets.

❡ By definition, food in China is medicine, but red meat qualifies on the thinnest grounds. The traditional medicine books say that beef and other red meats are good for underweight people and general weakness.

❡ Lamb, along with goat and mutton, is an esoteric taste for the Chinese. It is enjoyed to the full by the Moslems of Manchuria and Mongolia, and was given pride of place in Peking cooking in the Yüan dynasty (1271–1368) when the Mongols ruled. Ibn Batuta, the great Arab traveler, noted in the fourteenth century that banquets consisted mainly of lamb boiled whole, which guests with sharp knives would divide amongst themselves. The Chinese avoided such close encounters with this meat they did not enjoy, and chose to remain loyal to their prized Peking Duck at such state affairs.

❡ The Chinese rarely indulge in more exotic meats, although, undoubtedly, game such as hare and venison is consumed in remote parts of the country, particularly in the mountainous region of Sichuan where game is plentiful.

*Top: Ching Chiu Yuk Sze; bottom: Suen Tim Ko Yuk*

## SUEN TIM KO YUK

### *SWEET-AND-SOUR PORK CHIUCHOW-STYLE*

*While some believe that sweet-and-sour sauce was invented for Chinese restaurants in the West, it is, in fact, a traditional Chinese sauce. You can use this recipe to make extra sauce, which will keep in the refrigerator for up to three months. The people of Teochiu make a sausage unique in all of China: It is made with caul fat, stuffed with water chestnuts, steamed and deep-fried.*

For the marinade:
1 tablespoon light soy sauce
1 teaspoon salt
1 teaspoon sugar
1 teaspoon five-spice powder
2 teaspoons cornstarch (cornflour)
For the sweet-and-sour sauce:
2¹/₂ cups (20 fl oz/625 ml) white vinegar
2 teaspoons salt

2 cups (15 oz/450 g) sugar
1 cup (8 fl oz/250 ml) ketchup
2 tablespoons Worcestershire sauce
2 teaspoons dark soy sauce
For the pork:
6 oz (185 g) pork fillet, finely shredded
2 oz (60 g) water chestnuts, finely shredded
1 large piece pig's caul
1 teaspoon cornstarch (cornflour) mixed with 1 teaspoon
    water to form paste
3 cups (24 fl oz/750 ml) water
cornstarch (cornflour), for coating
3 cups (24 fl oz/750 ml) groundnut (peanut) oil
1 teaspoon finely chopped ginger
1 teaspoon finely chopped garlic
2 oz (60 g) red chili, seeded and cut into 1-inch
    (2.5-cm) slices
2 oz (60 g) pineapple, cut into 1-inch (2.5-cm) cubes
2 oz (60 g) green bell pepper (capsicum), cut into 1-inch
    (2.5-cm) squares

*SERVES 2*

❦ For the marinade: Combine all of the ingredients in a bowl.

❦ For the sauce: In a pan, bring the vinegar to a boil, then lower heat to a simmer. Add the salt and sugar, and stir until dissolved. Add the ketchup, Worcestershire sauce, and dark soy sauce, stirring to mix. Remove from heat and set aside.

❦ Marinate the pork and water chestnuts together for 15 minutes.

❦ Spread the caul on a flat surface. Cut it in half. Place half the pork mixture on top of each half of caul fat and roll into two 1-inch (2.5-cm) diameter sausages. Seal the edges with the cornstarch paste and trim any excess caul. Place the sausages on a long platter.

❦ Bring the water to a rapid boil in a large pan. Place a steaming rack in the middle. Put the platter with the sausages on top and steam for 15 minutes. Remove the sausages from the pan and set aside to cool.

❦ When cool, cut the sausages into 1¼-inch (3-cm) long pieces. Coat each piece with a thin layer of dry cornstarch.

❦ Heat the groundnut oil in a large pan or wok. Deep-fry the sausage pieces over medium heat for 1 minute or until lightly browned. Remove the pieces and set aside.

❦ Drain all but 1–2 tablespoons of oil from the wok and reheat. Add the ginger, garlic, chili, pineapple, and bell pepper. Stir-fry over high heat for 15 seconds. Return the sausages to the wok and add ½ cup (4 fl oz/125 ml) of the sauce. (Reserve the remaining sauce for later use.) Stir-fry for 30 seconds and serve.

---

### GOLDEN NEEDLES

*"Golden needles" is the poetic name for dried lily buds (gum jum), which are the color of burnished gold. The buds can be purchased in bags from any Chinese grocery and will keep indefinitely in a closed container. To use the buds, soak them for 30 minutes in warm water, then rinse them and squeeze out the liquid. When Chinese chefs cook them, they often tie a knot in the center of each bud; the only reason they give for this custom is "tradition."*

*The buds are used to flavor many vegetarian dishes, but are best known in one of Hangzhou's two great pork dishes. In Mu Shu pork Hangzhou-style, mushrooms, fungus, and golden needles are used for a seasoning mixture in which the pork is dipped. As with Peking Duck, the pork slices are put in thin pancakes, then dipped into the mixture, which is sweet and fairly pungent.*

---

# CHING CHIU YUK SZE

*STIR-FRIED PORK SHREDS WITH BELL PEPPERS*

*Easy and tasty, this is one of the most common dishes in China. It is also an economical way to use leftover pork — the peppers will disguise your thriftiness, as well as add balance and a fine aroma.*

For the marinade:
*1 teaspoon light soy sauce*
*¼ teaspoon salt*
*1 teaspoon sugar*
*1 teaspoon sesame oil*
*2 teaspoons cornstarch (cornflour)*
*1 tablespoon water*
For the sauce:
*1 tablespoon light soy sauce*
*1 teaspoon dark soy sauce*
*1 tablespoon oyster sauce*
*1 teaspoon Chinese rice wine*
*¼ cup (2 fl oz/60 ml) water*
For the pork:
*½ lb (8 oz/250 g) pork fillet, cut into 2-inch (5-cm) long thin shreds*
*1 cup (8 fl oz/250 ml) groundnut (peanut) oil*
*1 green bell pepper (capsicum), cut into 2-inch (5-cm) long thin shreds*
*1 red bell pepper (capsicum), cut into 2-inch (5-cm) long thin shreds*
*½ teaspoon salt*
*1 teaspoon finely chopped garlic*
*1 teaspoon finely chopped ginger*
*1 teaspoon chopped shallot*

*SERVES 4–6*

❦ For the marinade: Combine all of the ingredients in a bowl.

❦ For the sauce: In a separate bowl, mix all the ingredients well.

❦ Marinate the pork for 15 minutes.

❦ Heat 1 tablespoon of the oil in a wok or skillet (frying pan). Add the bell peppers and salt. Stir-fry over high heat for 30 seconds. Remove, drain, and set aside.

❦ Heat the remaining oil in a separate wok or pan. Add the pork, stirring to separate. When it turns white, remove the pork, drain, and set aside.

❦ Drain all but 1–2 tablespoons of oil from the wok and reheat. Add the garlic, ginger, and shallot. Return the pork to the wok and stir-fry over high heat for 10 seconds. Add the bell peppers and stir-fry for 10 seconds.

❦ Pour the sauce into the wok, stir-fry for 15 seconds, and serve.

## KAIR TZE YUK SZE

### BRAISED PORK WITH EGGPLANT

*The Chinese have many kinds of eggplant (aubergine), and any type can be used in this dish. The recipe is typical of southern home cooking—convenient and delicious—and is a wonderful accompaniment to rice.*

For the marinade:
*1 teaspoon salt*
*1 teaspoon sugar*
*1 teaspoon sesame oil*
*1 1/2 teaspoons cornstarch (cornflour)*
*1 tablespoon water*
For the pork:
*6 oz (185 g) pork fillet, cut into 2 1/2-inch (7-cm) long*
   *finger-width strips*
*1 cup (8 fl oz/250 ml) groundnut (peanut) oil*
*8 oz (250 g) eggplant (aubergine), cut into 2 1/2-inch (7-cm)*
   *long finger-width strips*
*1 teaspoon chopped garlic*
*1 teaspoon chopped ginger*
*1 tablespoon light soy sauce*
*1 teaspoon dark soy sauce*
*1 teaspoon sugar*
*1 teaspoon Chinese rice wine*
*1 teaspoon aromatic or cider vinegar*

*Left: Kair Tze Yuk Sze; right: Ham Yuk Ching Dou*

*1 cup (8 fl oz/250 ml) chicken broth (stock)*
*1 tablespoon chopped scallions (spring onions)*

SERVES 4–6

❡ For the marinade: Mix the ingredients in a bowl.
❡ Marinate the pork for 30 minutes.
❡ Heat the oil in a wok or skillet (frying pan), and sauté the eggplant until lightly browned. Remove the eggplant from the wok, drain, and set aside, but do not drain the oil.
❡ Reheat the oil and add the pork, stirring to separate. Fry until lightly browned. Remove the pork from the wok, drain, and set aside.
❡ Drain all but 2–3 tablespoons of oil from the wok and reheat. Add the garlic and ginger. Return the eggplant and pork to the wok and stir-fry for 30 seconds.
❡ Mix the soy sauces, sugar, wine, vinegar, and broth in a bowl and add to the wok. Bring to a boil, then lower the heat to medium–low. Cover and cook for 5 minutes. Uncover and cook over high heat until the liquid has almost evaporated.
❡ Transfer to a serving platter, sprinkle with the scallions, and serve.

## HAM YUK CHING DOU

### STIR-FRIED BACON WITH SNOW PEAS

*Although Chinese bacon is different from the kind found in the West, you can use any kind of bacon here. This is a traditional dish among the Teochiu people, and is often eaten with congee, which is a rice gruel.*

*3-4 tablespoons groundnut (peanut) oil*
*1 cup (8 oz/250 g) snow peas (mange-tout), strings removed*
*3–4 tablespoons chicken broth (stock)*
*1/2 teaspoon salt*
*4 oz (125 g) bacon, cut into 2- x 1-inch (5- x 2.5-cm) pieces*
*1 teaspoon chopped garlic*
*1 teaspoon Chinese rice wine*

SERVES 4

❡ Heat 1–2 tablespoons of oil in a wok or skillet (frying pan). Add the snow peas and sauté over medium heat until they turn dark green. Add the broth and salt, cover, and cook for 1 minute. Remove, drain, and set aside. Clean the wok.
❡ Heat the remaining oil in the wok. Add the bacon and garlic, and fry over low heat until lightly browned. Return the peas to the wok and stir-fry over very high heat for 30 seconds.
❡ Add the wine and serve.

*Top: Wui Wor Yuk; bottom: Yuk Sue Por Choi*

## YUK SUE POR CHOI

### GROUND PORK WITH SPINACH

*This is a common dish, obviously devised for housewives who want to use up leftover pork. But with fresh spinach and ginger, it is also very flavorful.*

For the marinade:
*1 tablespoon light soy sauce*
*½ teaspoon sugar*
*½ teaspoon sesame oil*
*1 teaspoon cornstarch (cornflour)*
For the pork:
*4 oz (125 g) ground (minced) pork fillet*
*3–4 tablespoons groundnut (peanut) oil*
*4–5 slices ginger*
*1¼ lb (600 g) spinach (English spinach), cleaned
  and torn into pieces*
*1½ cups (12 fl oz/375 ml) chicken broth (stock)*
*1 teaspoon chopped garlic*
*1 teaspoon salt*
*1 teaspoon Chinese rice wine*

*SERVES 4*

❡ For the marinade: Combine all of the ingredients in a bowl.
❡ Marinate the pork for 15 minutes.
❡ Heat 1–2 tablespoons of oil in a wok or skillet (frying pan). Add the ginger and fry until lightly browned. Add the spinach and stir-fry for 1 minute. Add 1 cup (8 fl oz/250 ml) broth, cover, and cook over medium heat for 7 minutes. Uncover and cook over high heat until the liquid has almost

evaporated. Transfer to a serving platter and set aside. Clean the wok.
❡ Heat the remaining oil in the wok. Add the garlic and pork, and stir-fry over medium heat for 1 minute. Add the remaining broth and stir to mix. Cook over low heat for 1 minute. Add the salt and wine, pour over spinach, and serve.

## WUI WOR YUK

### DOUBLE-COOKED PORK

*If you had to name the most famous Sichuan home-cooked dish, this might qualify. It's especially good for leftover pork, which gets an extra zing from the ingredients. I've decided to add wine, to give it even more excitement.*

*10 oz (315 g) pork fillet*
*6 cups (1½ qt/1.5 l) cold water*
*½ cup (4 fl oz/125 ml) groundnut (peanut) oil*
*4 oz (125 g) firm bean curd, cut into ½-inch (1-cm) pieces*
*4 oz (125 g) leeks, cut into 1-inch (2.5-cm) lengths*
*1 red chili, seeded and cut into rings*
*1 tablespoon chopped garlic*
*1 tablespoon hot fava (broad) bean paste*
*½ cup (4 fl oz/125 ml) chicken broth (stock)*
*½ teaspoon ground Sichuan peppercorns*
*1 teaspoon sugar*
*1 teaspoon salt*
*1 teaspoon aromatic or cider vinegar*
*1 teaspoon chili oil (optional)*
*1 teaspoon cornstarch (cornflour)*
*1 teaspoon Chinese rice wine*

*SERVES 4–6*

❡ Place the pork in a large pan with the cold water. Bring to a boil and cook for 10 minutes. Remove, drain, and cut into ⅛-inch (0.25-cm) thin slices. Set aside.
❡ Heat the oil in a wok or skillet (frying pan) and fry the bean curd until golden brown on both sides. Remove the bean curd from the wok, drain, and set aside.
❡ Drain all but 2–3 tablespoons of oil from the wok and reheat. Sauté the leeks and chili for 30 seconds. Add the garlic and hot fava bean paste. When the aroma rises, return the pork and bean curd to the wok and stir-fry over high heat for 1 minute.
❡ Mix the broth, peppercorns, sugar, salt, vinegar, chili oil, and cornstarch in a bowl and add to the wok. Stir-fry over high heat for 30 seconds. Add the wine and serve.

## YUK YUEN PAI CHOI

### PORK MEATBALLS WITH CABBAGE

*Every region in China boasts its own variety of meatball. In Shanghai, they are called "Lion's Hat" meatballs because of their unique shape. The Cantonese version is a bit smaller and, in this recipe, is served with cabbage.*

For the pork:
*1 tablespoon light soy sauce*
*1 teaspoon salt*
*1 teaspoon sugar*
*1 teaspoon sesame oil*
*2 teaspoons cornstarch (cornflour)*
*3 tablespoons water*
*6 oz (185 g) ground (minced) pork*
*1 cup (8 fl oz/250 ml) groundnut (peanut) oil*
*4–5 slices ginger*
*2–3 garlic cloves*
*10 oz (315 g) cabbage, cut into 3-inch (7.5-cm) long strips*
*2 oz (60 g) button mushrooms (champignons), halved*

*2 cups (16 fl oz/500 ml) water*
For the sauce:
*1 tablespoon light soy sauce*
*2 tablespoons oyster sauce*
*1 tablespoon Chinese rice wine*
*1 teaspoon salt*
SERVES 4

❡ Mix the first six ingredients in a bowl. Add the pork and stir with a fork until the mixture becomes sticky. Shape into balls 1 inch (2.5 cm) in diameter.
❡ Heat the oil in a wok or skillet (frying pan) and add the meatballs. Fry until lightly browned. Remove the meatballs from the wok, drain, and set aside.
❡ Drain all but 2–3 tablespoons of oil from the wok and reheat. Add the ginger and garlic. Add the cabbage, and stir-fry for 1 minute. Add the mushrooms, and stir-fry for 1 minute.
❡ Add the water and return the meatballs to the wok. Cook over medium–low heat for 10 minutes.
❡ Mix the sauce ingredients in a bowl. Add the sauce to the wok, stir, and serve.

*Upper left: leg; center right: strips for stir-fry and Mongolian barbecue; front: lamb ribs*

## LAMB

The Chinese considered the mutton-eating Mongols to be barbarians. Their eating habits, which they brought with them to court during their ruling Yüan dynasty (1271–1368), were never assimilated into the Chinese diet. The Chinese found lamb, mutton, and goat malodorous and unappetizing, and even today eat it with restraint, if at all. In the North, lamb usually comes to the capital from Inner Mongolia in winter, when it is eaten to "heat" the body. Perhaps the only mutton eating habits they did acquire were for the classic Mongolian barbecue in which finely sliced winter mutton is cooked, sizzling, on giant hotplates over roaring fires—the cookers resembling giant iron drums—with scallions (spring onions), fragrant oils, and vegetables. The other famous lamb dish is Mongolian Hot Pot, whereby the leanest possible meat is cut into slivers and dipped in boiling stock to cook it at the table.

Southerners, however, turn up their noses at the "too-strong" taste of lamb and recipes for it are nearly nonexistent, except among creative chefs and the Moslem restaurants of Guangzhou. One popular dish, however, is a casserole made from chunks of lamb shoulder boiled first in water to rid it of some of its smell, then in soy sauce with dried citrus peel and spices, and the saltiness of bean curd "cheese." Finely shredded lime leaves add last-minute fragrance to this delicious dish, which is often sold by street-side food vendors, who serve it in small clay pots. The same dish is also made with goat meat. In central Hunan province, where they like their foods powerfully flavored, lamb shanks are braised with peppercorns, chili, soy, and spices to make an enjoyable and thoroughly warming meal.

*Top: Tze Keung Yuk Pin; bottom: Yuk Yuen Pai Choi*

## TZE KEUNG YUK PIN

### *STIR-FRIED PORK WITH YOUNG GINGER*

*When using ginger with chicken, it is often a good idea to pickle it, because the taste can be very strong. With pork, the meat is stronger, so I use young ginger (which you can recognize by its ivory color), which gives a fresher flavor.*

For the ginger:
*1 tablespoon sugar*
*1 tablespoon white vinegar*
*1 teaspoon salt*
*4 oz (125 g) young ginger, cut into 2- × 1-inch (5- × 2.5-cm) slices*
For the pork marinade:
*1 teaspoon salt*
*1 teaspoon sugar*
*1 teaspoon Chinese rice wine*
*½ teaspoon sesame oil*
*1 teaspoon cornstarch (cornflour)*
*1 tablespoon water*
For the pork:
*6 oz (185 g) pork fillet, cut into 2- × 1-inch (5- × 2.5-cm) slices*
*1 cup (8 fl oz/250 ml) groundnut (peanut) oil*
*1 teaspoon chopped garlic*

*½ red bell pepper (capsicum), cut into 1-inch (2.5-cm) square pieces*
*½ green bell pepper (capsicum), cut into 1-inch (2.5 cm) square pieces*
*1 teaspoon oyster sauce*
*1 teaspoon light soy sauce*
*1 teaspoon Chinese rice wine*
*1 teaspoon cornstarch (cornflour)*
*2–3 tablespoons chicken broth (stock)*

SERVES 4

❡ For the ginger: Combine the sugar, vinegar, and salt in a bowl. Add the ginger, mix well, and marinate for 1 hour.
❡ For the pork marinade: In a separate bowl, mix all of the ingredients well. Marinate the pork for 15 minutes.
❡ Heat the oil in a wok or skillet (frying pan). Add the pork, stirring to separate, and stir-fry for 45 seconds. Remove the pork from the wok, drain, and set aside.
❡ Drain all but 2–3 tablespoons of oil from the wok and reheat. Add the garlic and peppers, and stir-fry over medium heat for 30 seconds. Add the ginger and stir-fry for 45 seconds. Return the pork to the wok and stir-fry over very high heat for 30 seconds.
❡ Mix all the remaining ingredients in a bowl and stir into the wok. Mix well and serve.

# SAUCES, OILS AND VINEGARS

In every Chinese kitchen there will be at least two bottles of soy sauce, the most important flavoring ingredient. Standing with them will be a bottle or two of vinegar distilled from rice wine; three types of oils, two fragrant, one functional, and a couple of jars of intensely flavored seasoning sauces. With this battalion lined up on the kitchen shelf, the Chinese cook can go confidently into battle, creating a wondrous array of flavors and aromas. Depending on his origins or taste propensity, the Chinese chef will aim for the blandness that characterizes southern styles of cooking, where it is paramount to maintain the natural taste of the main ingredients; or if from the Central provinces, he may pile in peppercorns and bean pastes, garlic, and

chilis, to bathe the meats and vegetables in potent sauces where a multitude of harmonious flavors can be detected. In the North he might be more restrained: a hint of saltiness, of vinegar and fermented seasonings, a wisp of chili; and on the North coast he will concoct a rich brown sauce for many of his dishes, and send them to the table doused with pepper.

## SAUCES AND PASTES

**Soy sauce:** One of the oldest condiments known to man, with a documented history that stretches back 3,000 years. Many rural households in China still produce, by time-proven methods, this simple, salty black liquid as a family enterprise. Soy sauce is made, of course, from the soy bean and its method of preparation is simple

fermentation. The soy beans are boiled or steamed until tender, then mixed with a flour made from roasted barley or wheat. The concoction is salted, packed into a crock, covered, and left to ferment. The first liquor drawn off, after about 40 days, is light in color and flavor, but the mash can be left to ferment for up to three years to intensify the flavor. It is filtered before use, and nowadays may have caramel for color, and preservatives added. There are no international standards for consistency, so different companies can label their soy sauce as they wish. Many now even spike the soy with ingredients like mushrooms, chili, sesame, garlic, shrimp (prawn) roe, and spices.

**Light soy sauce:** Usually known as "superior soy"

and the most common type for cooking. It is saltier than its darker counterpart, but thinner in consistency and lighter in color.

**Dark soy sauce:** This has had caramel, and perhaps molasses, added to make the deep coloring that makes it useful in the sort of dishes they call "red-cooked," where meats are slowly cooked with soy in a dark red-brown gravy.

**Heavy soy sauce:** Usually sold under the name "black soy," it is slightly sweeter than dark soy, thick, and glossy. It is usually incorporated into sauces to use as a condiment dip.

**Plum sauce:** This sweet-salty thick sauce is made from plums, native apricots, vinegar, salt, and sugar. Its slight acidity makes it a natural companion for the more fatty types of roast meat such as duck and pork. While more commonly used as a dip, it is sometimes added to a sauce.

**Oyster sauce:** This thick, glossy brown sauce is one of China's most prized seasonings. A good quality oyster sauce—and unfortunately there are many inferior types on the market—has a richness of flavor that is incomparable. Made from dried oysters, it is not too pungent and quite "meaty" in taste. In addition to its use in cooking, to add depth to a sauce, it can be an appealing dip, but more commonly it comes to the table as a dressing for poached green vegetables, abalone, and white rice noodles; its salty intensity transforms them into dishes of outstanding flavor. Oyster sauce should be kept in the refrigerator once opened.

**Shrimp (prawn) sauce:** Walk through any small coastal village of China and you are bound to catch a wisp of a pungent-pleasant "fishiness." Seafood processing is a vital industry to these villages. They might salt and dry the catch of fish, squid, or cuttlefish. There may be rows and rows of flat bamboo trays arrayed on the beach to catch the sun—spread with oysters, mussels, or shrimp—or there might be deep vats from which a particularly pungent odor emanates. This is shrimp sauce in ferment—tiny whole shrimp (prawns), shells and all, are packed with salt and left to ferment until they decompose into a pungent rose-gray mass. This is ground to a paste which

may add an unpleasant aroma to a kitchen, but which adds magic to a dish. It is recognized at the grocers as a bottled smooth thick paste of pale gray-pink color. Store in the refrigerator once opened.

While seasoning pastes made from soy beans are used extensively, there are two others worth mentioning. One is a sweet sauce made from roasted flour, that gives a pleasing "barbecue" style of flavor, the other is made in Sichuan, from fava (broad) beans and can range from mild in flavor to highly pungent depending on its chili content.

**Fermented black beans:** Beans are important nutritionally to the Chinese diet, and they are available in many different forms. Among the most commonly used are fermented black beans. Their distinct, salty taste is one of the most easily recognizable Chinese flavors. The small, wrinkled beans should be rinsed, dried, and chopped for use, and are commonly cooked with garlic and chili. They will keep indefinitely in a sealed container.

## OILS

Chinese cooks use a variety of vegetable oils. Some households appreciate the pervasive taste and aroma of groundnut (peanut) oil, others prefer oils where no flavor element unbalances their selection of spices and seasonings. Most, however, agree that a "cooked oil," one that has been used for frying, gives the very best flavor to a stir-fry. They will, therefore pour fresh oil into the wok for deep-frying, and when it has

acquired food flavors from one or two uses, it will be transferred to the oil pot and placed above the wok they use for stir-frying. Animal fats are not widely used as a cooking medium, although lard is an ingredient much appreciated by the pastry-cook. But they might save chicken or duck fat to splash, piping hot, over a dish just before it goes to the table for extra richness and glossiness. When they want flavor, they add a sprinkle of chili-oil or aromatic sesame oil. Neither of these is used as the main cooking oil, but a dash in a dip or sauce livens up even the blandest dish.

## VINEGARS

Vinegar, usually fermented from rice grains, has been used in Chinese cooking since ancient times. Vinegars are used in sauces, as a condiment and to brighten up any pallid-tasting dish.

**White rice vinegar:** This can actually range in color from clear through yellow to a pale amber, and is the sharpest in taste—though not as sharp as a Western distilled vinegar—with a flavor akin to cider vinegar.

**Dark or aromatic vinegar:** This may be labeled brown or black vinegar on the bottle. It is deep brown in color,

strongly flavored and, like white vinegar, is used more as a seasoning than a dip.

**Red vinegar:** Bright amber in color, the aromatic, mild flavor of red vinegar is appreciated in dips, and it has a natural affinity for seafood. It never overpowers food, but gives a tangy richness.

**Sweet vinegar:** A dark, rich vinegar very sweet in taste, but with a pungency that makes it a useful addition to stewed and braised dishes. It is cooked with ginger in one dish that is said to be highly beneficial to women.

**Rice wine:** This adds flavor to many Chinese dishes. It is added to braised, stewed, and stir-fried dishes. A clear, mild cooking wine is generally sold in Chinese grocers. From the wine-making process they also derive an unusual ingredient called "wine lees" or fermented rice mash (*hongzao*), an ingredient appreciated more in the North.

*1. sesame oil; 2. chili oil; 3. groundnut oil; 4. red vinegar; 5. sweet vinegar; 6. white rice vinegar; 7. brown/black rice vinegar; 8. rice wine; 9. dark soy sauce; 10. light soy sauce; 11. thick soy sauce; 12. mashed chili paste; 13. plum sauce; 14. shrimp sauce; 15. oyster sauce*

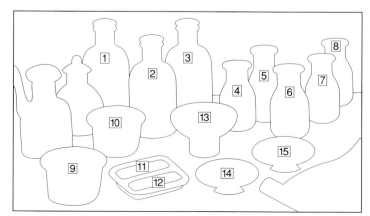

*Left: Chung Yau Yuk Pai; right: Chiu Yim Yuk Lau*

# CHUNG YAU YUK PAI

### FRIED PORK CHOPS WITH SCALLION SAUCE

*This sounds like a Western dish, but whereas Westerners might add the salt and onions to the pork after cooking, the Chinese cook the meat and vegetables together in the sauce. The result is that the taste comes straight from the chop itself.*

For the marinade:
1 tablespoon light soy sauce
1 teaspoon dark soy sauce
1 teaspoon salt
2 teaspoons five-spice powder
2 teaspoons Chinese rice wine
1 tablespoon cornstarch (cornflour)
2 tablespoons water
For the sauce:
2 tablespoons light soy sauce
1 teaspoon salt
1 teaspoon sugar
2 teaspoons cornstarch (cornflour)

For the sauce: In a separate bowl, mix all the ingredients well.

Pound the pork chops lightly to tenderize, and marinate for 30 minutes.

Heat 6 tablespoons of oil in a skillet (frying pan). Pan-fry the pork chops over medium heat for 3 minutes on each side. Remove, drain and set aside.

Heat 2 tablespoons of oil in a separate pan. Fry the scallions and ginger until lightly browned. Add the sauce and stir. Add the pork chops, cover, and cook over medium–low heat for 3 minutes.

Arrange the tomatoes on a serving platter. Transfer the pork chops to the platter and serve.

## CHIU YIM YUK LAU

### *FRIED FILLET OF PORK COATED WITH PEPPERY SALT*

*The secret here is the five-spice powder. The cinnamon taste in the powder blends with the other spices to give the pork a variety of aromas and delicate flavors.*

For the marinade:
*1 tablespoon light soy sauce*
*1 teaspoon dark soy sauce*
*1 teaspoon Chinese rice wine*
*1 teaspoon sugar*
*1 tablespoon cornstarch (cornflour)*
For the pork:
*12 oz (375 g) pork fillet, cut into 1-inch (2.5-cm) cubes*
*3 cups (24 fl oz/750 ml) groundnut (peanut) oil*
*1 1/2 teaspoons salt*
*1/4 teaspoon five-spice powder*
*1 teaspoon pepper*

*SERVES 4*

For the marinade: Combine all of the ingredients in a bowl.

Pound the pork lightly to tenderize and marinate it for 30 minutes.

Heat the oil in a pan. When the oil starts to smoke, add the pork and fry over medium heat for 1 minute. Remove the pan from the heat and leave the pork in the hot oil for 1 minute. Remove the pork from the pan, but do not drain the oil.

Reheat the oil until it starts to smoke. Return the pork to the pan and fry for 30 seconds. Remove, drain, and set aside.

Clean the pan and return it to the heat. Add the salt, five-spice powder, and pepper. Return the pork to the pan and toss to coat the cubes evenly.

Serve immediately.

*1 cup (8 fl oz/250 ml) chicken broth (stock)*
For the pork chops:
*6 rib pork chops, 1/2-inch (1-cm) thick*
*1/2 cup (4 fl oz/125 ml) groundnut (peanut) oil*
*3 scallions (spring onions), cut into 2-inch (5 cm) lengths*
*6 slices ginger*
*2–3 tomatoes, sliced*

*SERVES 4–6*

For the marinade: Mix together all of the ingredients in a bowl.

*Left: Yuk Sown Sang Choi Bou; right: Sze Tze Tou*

## YUK SOWN SANG CHOI BOU

### STIR-FRIED PORK SAUSAGE WITH LETTUCE LEAVES

*Visitors to Hong Kong restaurants may have already eaten this dish—without knowing it. Some restaurateurs use a bit of pork to fill out an order of ground (minced) pigeon or quail on lettuce. But this dish is pure, with savory pork sausages.*

For the marinade:
1 teaspoon light soy sauce
½ teaspoon sugar
½ teaspoon cornstarch (cornflour)
1 teaspoon Chinese rice wine
For the pork sausage:
6 oz (185 g) pork fillet, ground (minced)
1 head lettuce
2–3 tablespoons groundnut (peanut) oil
2 links Cantonese pork sausage, cut into ¼-inch
   (0.5-cm) slices
3 dried black mushrooms, soaked, drained, stems discarded,
   and finely chopped
1 teaspoon finely chopped ginger
1 teaspoon finely chopped garlic
4 oz (125 g) bamboo shoots, finely chopped
½ cup (4 fl oz/125 ml) chicken broth (stock)
1 tablespoon oyster sauce
1 teaspoon light soy sauce
½ teaspoon cornstarch (cornflour)
2 tablespoons chopped cilantro (fresh coriander)

SERVES 4–6

❡ For the marinade: Mix together all of the ingredients in a bowl.
❡ Marinate the pork for 15 minutes.
❡ Wash the lettuce leaves and pat dry. Place on a platter and set aside.
❡ Heat the oil in a wok or skillet (frying pan). Sauté

the sausages and mushrooms for 1 minute over low heat. Add the ginger, garlic, and pork. Sauté over low heat for 1 minute. Add the bamboo shoots, and stir-fry over medium heat for 1 minute.
❡ Turn the heat to high. Mix the broth, oyster sauce, soy sauce, and cornstarch in a bowl and add to the wok, stirring until the liquid has evaporated. Add the cilantro and mix. Transfer to separate serving platter. Serve with the lettuce leaves as wrappers.

## SZE TZE TOU

### PAN-FRIED PORK PATTIES

*Thanks to the crunchy water chestnuts and cilantro (fresh coriander), these are not conventional "burgers." If you are kosher or hallal (Islamic dietary rules), you can substitute beef for the pork.*

8 oz (250 g) pork fillet, finely chopped
2 oz (60 g) cooked pork fat, finely chopped
2 oz (60 g) water chestnuts, finely chopped
2 tablespoons chopped cilantro (fresh coriander)
1 teaspoon salt
1½ teaspoons cornstarch (cornflour)
1½ tablespoons water
½ cup (4 fl oz/125 ml) groundnut (peanut) oil
¾ cup (6 fl oz/185 ml) chicken broth (stock)
1 tablespoon light soy sauce
1 teaspoon ketchup (tomato sauce)
1 teaspoon Worcestershire sauce
1 teaspoon Chinese rice wine
¾ teaspoon cornstarch (cornflour)
1 teaspoon finely chopped garlic
1 teaspoon finely chopped ginger

SERVES 4–6

❡ Put the pork, pork fat, water chestnuts, and cilantro in a bowl. Add the salt, cornstarch, and water. Work with the fingers to mix well. Make 12 patties, ½ inch (1 cm) thick, and set aside.
❡ Heat the oil in a wok or skillet (frying pan). Fry the patties over medium–low heat until lightly browned on each side. Remove the patties from the wok, drain, and set aside.
❡ Mix the broth, soy sauce, ketchup, Worcestershire sauce, cornstarch, and Chinese wine.
❡ Drain all but 1–2 tablespoons oil from the wok and reheat. Add the garlic and ginger. When the aroma rises, add the broth mixture and bring to a boil. Return the patties to the wok and simmer over low heat until the liquid has almost evaporated. Transfer to a serving platter and serve.

## GEUNG CHONG NGAU LAU

### *FILLET OF BEEF WITH GINGER AND SCALLIONS*

*You can get this dish in any chop-suey restuarant in the world. But I've made a special sauce for this recipe, for an altogether different taste.*

For the marinade:
*1 tablespoon light soy sauce*
*2 teaspoons cornstarch (cornflour)*
*1 teaspoon sugar*
*1 tablespoon groundnut (peanut) oil*
For the sauce:
*1 tablespoon light soy sauce*
*1 tablespoon oyster sauce*
*½ cup (4 fl oz/125 ml) chicken broth (stock)*
*2 teaspoons cornstarch (cornflour)*
*1 teaspoon Chinese rice wine*
For the beef:
*6 oz (185 g) beef fillet, thinly sliced*
*1 cup (8 fl oz/250 ml) groundnut (peanut) oil*
*6–8 slices ginger*
*3 scallions (spring onions), cut into 2-inch (5-cm) lengths*

*SERVES 2–4*

❡ For the marinade: Combine all of the ingredients in a bowl.
❡ For the sauce: In a separate bowl, mix all the ingredients well.
❡ Marinate the beef for 15 minutes in the marinade.
❡ Heat the oil in a wok or skillet (frying pan). Add the beef, stirring to separate, and fry for 5 seconds. Remove the beef, drain, and set aside.
❡ Drain all but 1–2 tablespoons of oil from the wok

*Left: Geung Chong Ngau Lau; right: Sze Chiu Ngau Yuk*

and reheat. Add the ginger and scallions, and stir-fry for 10 seconds. Return the beef to the wok and add the sauce. Bring to a boil. Transfer immediately to a platter and serve.

## SZE CHIU NGAU YUK

### *FILLET OF BEEF WITH BELL PEPPERS AND BLACK BEAN SAUCE*

*Black bean sauce makes any dish richer, and blends well with most meats. The sauce itself exemplifies the phrase, "Necessity is the mother of invention." Without refrigeration, housewives had to keep the black beans underground until they fermented. Now these salty, preserved beans are available at any grocer's.*

For the marinade:
*1 tablespoon light soy sauce*
*1 teaspoon sugar*
*2 teaspoons cornstarch (cornflour)*
*1 tablespoon groundnut (peanut) oil*
For the sauce:
*1 tablespoon light soy sauce*
*1 teaspoon dark soy sauce*
*1 teaspoon Chinese rice wine*
*2 teaspoons cornstarch (cornflour)*
*⅓ cup (3 fl oz/90 ml) water*
For the beef:
*6 oz (185 g) beef fillet, thinly sliced*
*1 cup (8 fl oz/250 ml) groundnut (peanut) oil*
*1 red bell pepper (capsicum), cut into 1-inch (2.5-cm) squares*
*1 green bell pepper (capsicum), cut into 1-inch (2.5-cm) squares*
*1 tablespoon chopped garlic*
*2 tablespoons fermented black beans, chopped*

*SERVES 4*

❡ For the marinade: Combine all of the ingredients in a bowl.
❡ For the sauce: In a separate bowl, mix all the ingredients well.
❡ Marinate the beef for 15 minutes in the marinade.
❡ Heat the oil in a wok or skillet (frying pan). Add the beef, stirring to avoid sticking, and fry for 5 seconds. Remove the beef, drain, and set aside.
❡ Drain all but 1–2 tablespoons of oil from the wok and reheat. Add the bell peppers and stir-fry for 10 seconds. Add the garlic and black beans. When the aroma rises, add the sauce, and bring to a boil. Return the beef to the wok and stir-fry for 5 seconds. Transfer to a platter and serve.

## JIN NGAU YUK PAN

### PAN-FRIED BEEF CAKES

*This is, of course, the Chinese hamburger—but such beef cakes were known in China long before the hamburger was "invented." The crispy water chestnuts give this dish extra flavor and texture.*

For the marinade:
*2 tablespoons light soy sauce*
*2 teaspoons sugar*
*1 tablespoon Chinese rice wine*
*½ tablespoon pepper*
*1 tablespoon cornstarch (cornflour)*
For the sauce:
*2 tablespoons light soy sauce*
*1 teaspoon dark soy sauce*
*1 teaspoon salt*
*1 teaspoon sugar*
*1 teaspoon aromatic or cider vinegar*
*1 teaspoon pepper*
*1 tablespoon Chinese rice wine*
*2 teaspoons cornstarch (cornflour)*
*⅓ cup (3 fl oz/90 ml) chicken broth (stock)*
For the beef:
*8 oz (250 g) ground (minced) beef*
*6 water chestnuts, finely chopped*
*2 tablespoons chopped scallion (spring onion)*
*2 tablespoons groundnut (peanut) oil*

*SERVES 4–6*

❡ For the marinade: Mix together all of the ingredients in a bowl.
❡ For the sauce: Mix the ingredients in a bowl.
❡ Mix the beef, water chestnuts, and scallions with the marinade. Stir with a fork until sticky. Divide into 12 portions and flatten to make ½-inch (1-cm) thick patties.
❡ Heat the oil in a wok or skillet (frying pan) and fry the patties over medium heat until browned on both sides. Add the sauce and bring to a boil. Turn the patties and cook for 5 seconds. Serve.

## DUN NGAU NAM

### DOUBLE-BOILED BRISKET OF BEEF WITH RED DATES AND GINGER

*This is a very common Cantonese home-cooking recipe. We serve this dish in winter, since it invigorates the body: The dates help circulation, the ginger gives warmth, and the orange helps in respiration.*

*1½ lb (750 g) beef brisket, off the bone, cut into bite-size pieces*
*12 cups (3 qt/3 l) cold water*
*6 Chinese red dates, pitted*
*6 slices ginger*
*1 piece dried orange peel, about 2 inches (5 cm) square*
*1 tablespoon Chinese rice wine*
*1 teaspoon salt*

*Left: Jin Ngau Yuk Pan; right: Dun Ngau Nam*

*4 cups (1 qt/1 l) boiling water*

*SERVES 4–6*

❧ Place the beef in a large pan with the cold water. Bring to a boil and cook for 8–10 minutes. Remove, drain, and rinse the beef.

❧ Place the beef in a dish together with all of the remaining ingredients. Carefully add the boiling water and cover.

❧ Bring the remaining cold water to a rapid boil in a wok or large pan. Place a steaming rack in the center and place the dish with the beef on top. Cover and steam over medium–low heat for 3 hours. If the water in the wok evaporates, add more boiling water.

❧ Divide among soup bowls and serve.

## CHAU NGAU LAU LUP

### *FILLET OF BEEF WITH ROASTED GROUNDNUTS*

*This is one of my favorites: It is easy to prepare, and the contrast between the juicy beef and crunchy groundnuts (peanuts) is irresistible.*

For the marinade:
*1 teaspoon salt*
*1 teaspoon sugar*
*1 teaspoon ground Sichuan peppercorns*
*1 1/2 teaspoons cornstarch (cornflour)*
*1 tablespoon water*
For the beef:
*10 oz (315 g) beef fillet, cut into 1/2-inch (1-cm) cubes*
*2 cups (16 fl oz/500 ml) groundnut (peanut) oil*
*1 red bell pepper (capsicum), cut into 1/2-inch (1-cm) squares*
*1 green bell pepper (capsicum), cut into 1/2-inch (1-cm) squares*
*1 teaspoon chopped garlic*
*1 teaspoon chopped ginger*
*1 tablespoon hot fava (broad) bean paste*
*1 tablespoon oyster sauce*
*1 teaspoon chili oil (optional)*
*1 teaspoon sugar*
*1 1/2 teaspoons cornstarch (cornflour)*
*1/4 cup (2 fl oz/60 ml) chicken broth (stock)*
*1 teaspoon Chinese rice wine*
*3/4 cup (4 oz/125 g) roasted groundnuts (peanuts) or almonds*

*SERVES 4–6*

❡ For the marinade: Mix all of the ingredients together in a bowl.
❡ Marinate the beef for 15 minutes.
❡ Heat the oil in a wok or skillet (frying pan). Fry the peppers for 1 minute. Remove the peppers from the wok, drain, and set aside.
❡ In the same oil, fry the beef. Once it changes color, remove, drain, and set aside.
❡ Drain all but 2–3 tablespoons of oil from the wok and reheat. Add the garlic and ginger, and return the peppers to the wok. When the aroma rises, add the broad bean paste and stir-fry over medium–low heat for 30 seconds. Return the beef, and stir-fry over high heat for 30 seconds.
❡ Mix the oyster sauce, chili oil, sugar, cornstarch, and broth in a bowl and add to the wok. Stir-fry over high heat for 45 seconds. Add the wine and nuts. Stir well and serve.

## SHEUNG DONG NGAU LAU

### *STIR-FRIED BEEF WITH BAMBOO SHOOTS AND BLACK MUSHROOMS*

*This dish, with tender beef complemented by crisp bamboo, is popular throughout China.*

For the marinade:
*1 teaspoon salt*
*1 teaspoon sugar*
*1/2 teaspoon pepper*

*Left: Chau Ngau Lau Lup; right: Sheung Dong Ngau Lau*

*Snake meat is enjoyed as a warming soup*

## EXOTICA

Over the centuries, gourmandizing at one end of the socio-economic scale, and depravation at the other, have led the Chinese to pursue any avenue in search of possible edibles.

"Exotica" such as frogs, small lizards, and fowl are, however, now restricted to certain rural areas and specialist restaurants.

Bear's paw is still eaten extensively in Manchuria, where black bears are relatively plentiful. But outside of North China, bear is, to say the least, an endangered species.

Being a warming food, snake is eaten mostly during the fall and winter in China, and then for its health-giving properties. But snake meat is so popular in many parts of China, that it is possible to purchase it all year round.

In Hong Kong, it's easy to tell when snake season is about to begin. Giant colorful billboards appear over the entrance to restaurants, to be followed by a stack of wire cages containing a surge of coiling, live snakes. Diners can select the snake of their choice, and an intrepid cook plunges his hand into the seething mass to extract his prey.

Preparation is ritual. First the stomach is slit to release the little bulb that is the bile duct; its jade-green contents are squeezed into a tiny glass of wine to down in a gulp as a cure-all for an endless list of ailments. Then the blood is drained into another glass, if the diner wishes a particularly warming experience. A few long, skilfull slashes of the cleaver and the meat has been stripped from the skeleton to be shredded for "Dragon, Phoenix, Tiger" soup a broth made with snake, chunks of chicken and the meat of an edible wild cat. This is regularly served in Canton (Guangdong) province and in Taiwan. A nutritious soup is made with chicken broth (stock), thin strips of chicken, snake, and *jin hwa* ham, black fungus, fish maw, and bamboo shoots. In Macau, several "millionaire restaurants" serve bowls of soup almost filled with cobra meat, which is accompanied by bowls of white chrysanthemum petals, finely shredded lime leaves and crisp pretzels which are sprinkled into the soup.

1 ½ teaspoons cornstarch (cornflour)
1 tablespoon water
For the beef:
8 oz (250 g) beef fillet, cut into 1-inch (2.5-cm) thick slices
6 dried black mushrooms, soaked in water for 30 minutes, drained, and stems discarded
1 teaspoon sugar
¼ teaspoon salt
1 cup (8 fl oz/250 ml) groundnut (peanut) oil
4 oz (125 g) bamboo shoots, sliced
1 teaspoon finely chopped ginger
1 teaspoon finely chopped garlic
2 scallions (spring onions), cut into long pieces
1 cup (8 fl oz/250 ml) chicken broth (stock)
1 tablespoon oyster sauce
1 tablespoon light soy sauce
½ teaspoon sesame oil
1 ½ teaspoons cornstarch (cornflour)
1 teaspoon Chinese rice wine

*SERVES 4–6*

❡ For the marinade: Mix all of the ingredients together in a bowl.
❡ Marinate the beef for 15 minutes.
❡ Place the mushrooms in a bowl and add the sugar, salt, and 1 tablespoon of the oil. Place the bowl on a rack over boiling water and steam for 15 minutes. Remove and set aside.
❡ Sauté the bamboo shoots with a little of the oil in a pan over medium heat for 1 minute. Remove and set aside.
❡ Heat the remaining oil in a wok or skillet (frying pan) and add the beef, stirring to separate. Once the beef changes color, remove it from the wok and drain.
❡ Drain all but 2–3 tablespoons of the oil from the wok. Add the ginger, garlic, and scallions. When the aroma rises, add the beef, mushrooms (with any accumulated liquid), and bamboo shoots.
❡ Mix the broth, oyster sauce, soy sauces, sesame oil, and cornstarch in a bowl and add to the wok. Stir-fry over high heat for 1 minute. Add the wine and serve.

is the stuffing in many dumplings, and is shaped into the giant meatballs called "lion's head."

Nothing is wasted: **Pig's feet** (trotters) are an essential flavor element in any rich broth, and are also deboned to stuff as a kind of sausage; **noses**, **ears**, and **tails** marinated and boiled or barbecued, make a crunchy snack; kidneys are sliced thin to float in *congee* or soup; the lacy **caul** that lines the stomach is used to wrap tasty morsels for broiling (grilling) or steaming; the blood is congealed to slice into soups.

Not to be overlooked is **roast suckling pig**, which is the highlight of any Cantonese banquet. The bubbly skin, light and crunchy as a crispbread, is eaten first, carved into neat little squares to dip into a thick sweet-spicy brown sauce. Only when the last sliver of skin has been snatched up is the meat carved for eating.

# PORK

When European missionaries examined the eating habits of the Chinese in the nineteenth century, they discovered that the Cantonese ate virtually every portion of the pig. "It was all consumed," said one anonymous aphorist, "except the squeal." Indeed, besides using the meat (and the feet, tongue, **organs, tail, and tripe**) in cooking, the Chinese use the skin for leather, the hair for paintbrushes, and the fat as a lubricant.

Pork is used in some of China's most extravagant recipes, as well as in some of the simplest. Besides being an economical meat to produce, pork has a mild flavor that mixes well with an endless variety of vegetables and spices. Chinese cooks rarely trim the fat from pork, enjoying the richness it brings to a dish. Similarly the skin is retained to add its particular taste and texture. This is most evident in the many braised dishes, such as the famed *so tung po*, in which pork is slow-cooked, usually with soy sauce and often with cabbage, until the meat is melt-in-the-mouth tender.

For stir-fries where the pork is finely shredded, **pork tenderloin** is the choice. But **belly pork**, which they call "five flower" pork for its five alternating layers of meat and fat, is favored for dishes cooked a little longer. A popular way to cook **pork chops** is to fry them and serve with a fragrant "pepper-salt" dip.

**Pork ribs**, steam-braised with black beans, chili, and garlic is one of the delights of the *dim sum* cart.

**Ground (minced) pork**

*1. pork ribs; 2. pork tenderloin; 3. pork hocks; 4. pork tenderloin; 5. ground (minced) pork; 6. pork tripe; 7. caul fat; 8. pork kidneys; 9. shredded pork; 10. pork belly; 11. pork chops; 12. pork shoulder; 13. pork butt*

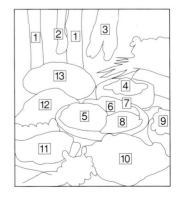

## LO PAK NGAU NAM

### BRAISED BRISKET OF BEEF WITH TURNIPS

*Brisket of beef is popular all over China, and not just because it's an inexpensive cut. When simmered for a few hours, the meat actually melts in the mouth. The garlic, ginger and cilantro (fresh coriander) give this dish a lively flavor that is picked up by the turnips.*

*1 lb (500 g) beef brisket, off the bone, cut into bite-size cubes*
*1 lb (500 g) turnips, cut into bite-size cubes*
*2–3 tablespoons groundnut (peanut) oil*
*3 garlic cloves, crushed*
*6 slices ginger*
*4 oz (125 g) leeks, cut into 1½-inch (4-cm) lengths*
*1 tablespoon soybean paste*
*4 cups (1 qt/1 l) water*
*1 tablespoon oyster sauce*
*1 tablespoon chopped cilantro (fresh coriander)*

*SERVES 4–6*

❡ In a large pan, blanch the brisket of beef in boiling water for 5 minutes. Remove, drain, and set aside.
❡ Blanch the turnips in boiling water for 5 minutes. Remove, drain, and set aside.
❡ Heat a wok or skillet (frying pan) and sauté the beef until lightly browned. Remove and set aside.
❡ Heat the oil in the wok. Add the garlic, ginger, and leeks. When the aroma rises, add the soybean paste. Return the beef to the wok, and stir-fry over medium heat for 2 minutes.
❡ Transfer the beef to a large pan, add the water and the oyster sauce. Bring to a boil. Cover and simmer over low heat for 2 hours. Add the turnips, simmer for 30 minutes. Sprinkle with cilantro and serve.

*Top: Lo Pak Ngau Nam; bottom: Gone Chau Ngau Yuk Sze*

## GONE CHAU NGAU YUK SZE

### CRISP BEEF SHREDS WITH CHILI

*This is a dish from Sichuan, where deep-frying and pungent chilis are common. Take very special note of the last instruction: Put the wine in at the very last moment.*

*10 oz (315 g) beef fillet, shredded*
*1 teaspoon salt*
*1 teaspoon sugar*
*½ beaten egg*
*1½ tablespoons cornstarch (cornflour)*
*3 cups (24 fl oz/750 ml) groundnut (peanut) oil*
*1 red chili, shredded*
*3 garlic cloves, thinly sliced*
*1 teaspoon Chinese rice wine*
*1 tablespoon chopped cilantro (fresh coriander)*
*For the sauce:*
*1 tablespoon light soy sauce*
*1½ teaspoons sugar*
*1 teaspoon aromatic or cider vinegar*
*1–2 teaspoons chili oil*
*6 tablespoons chicken broth (stock)*

*SERVES 4–6*

❡ Mix the beef with the salt, sugar, and egg and let rest for 15 minutes. Mix in the cornstarch just before frying.
❡ Heat the oil in a wok or skillet (frying pan). Deep-fry the chili and garlic for 30 seconds. Remove them from the wok, drain, and set aside.
❡ Add the beef to the wok and deep-fry until lightly browned. Remove the beef from the wok, drain, and set aside.
❡ Drain all but 2–3 tablespoons of oil from the wok. Add the beef, chili, and garlic. Mix the sauce ingredients in a bowl and add to the wok. Stir-fry over a high heat for 30 seconds. Add the wine. Sprinkle with cilantro and serve.

*Left: Ngan Ngar Satay Ngau; right: Kun Choi Ngau Yuk*

## NGAN NGAR SATAY NGAU

### *FILLET OF BEEF IN SATAY SAUCE WITH BEAN SPROUTS*

*Satay sauce is hardly new to Chinese cooking—at least not to the people of Teochiu, where this recipe comes from. Hundreds of years ago, they sailed to Indonesia for trade and brought back the recipe for this savory sauce, which is made with groundnuts (peanuts), chilies, sesame seeds and shallots. Peanuts were already available in China; according to evidence found at an archaeological dig around Xi'an in 1993, groundnuts (peanuts) have been known in China since the second century BC.*

For the marinade:
*1 tablespoon light soy sauce*
*1 teaspoon sugar*
*2 teaspoons cornstarch (cornflour)*
*1 tablespoon groundnut (peanut) oil*
For the sauce:
*2 tablespoons satay sauce*
*1 tablespoon light soy sauce*
*1 teaspoon Chinese rice wine*
*1/3 cup (3 fl oz/90 ml) chicken broth (stock)*
For the beef:
*6 oz (185 g) beef fillet, thinly sliced*
*1 cup (8 fl oz/250 ml) groundnut (peanut) oil*

¶ Bring the water to a rapid boil in a large pan. Add the bean sprouts and cook for 1 minute. Remove from the heat, drain, and place on a serving platter.
¶ Heat the reserved oil in a wok or skillet (frying pan). Add the scallions and chili. Pour in the sauce and bring to a boil. Add the beef and stir-fry for 5 seconds.
¶ Pour over the bean sprouts and serve.

## KUN CHOI NGAU YUK

### STIR-FRIED BEEF WITH CELERY

*These days, the Chinese eat celery because it lowers blood pressure. But originally, it was used as an herb, popular for its pungency. It pairs particularly well with beef, giving this dish extra savor.*

For the marinade:
*1 tablespoon light soy sauce*
*1 teaspoon sugar*
*1 teaspoon salt*
*1/2 teaspoon pepper*
*2 teaspoons Chinese rice wine*
*2 teaspoons cornstarch (cornflour)*
*2 tablespoons water*
*2 tablespoons groundnut (peanut) oil*
For the beef:
*8 oz (250 g) rump steak, cut into 2-inch (5-cm) long strips*
*1 cup (8 fl oz/250 ml) groundnut (peanut) oil*
*6 oz (185 g) celery, cut into 2-inch (5-cm) long strips*
*4–5 slices ginger*
*2 teaspoons chopped garlic*
For the sauce:
*2 tablespoons light soy sauce*
*1 tablespoon oyster sauce*
*1 tablespoon Chinese rice wine*
*2 teaspoons cornstarch (cornflour)*
*1 teaspoon sesame oil*
*1/3 cup (3 fl oz/90 ml) chicken broth (stock)*

*SERVES 4*

¶ For the marinade: Mix all the ingredients in a bowl.
¶ Marinate the beef for 15 minutes.
¶ Heat 1–2 tablespoons of the oil in a wok or skillet (frying pan), and stir-fry the celery for 1 minute. Remove, drain, and set aside.
¶ Heat the remaining oil in the wok. Add the beef, stirring to avoid sticking, and fry for 10 seconds. Remove the beef from the wok, drain, and set aside.
¶ Drain all but 1–2 tablespoons of oil from the wok and reheat. Add the ginger and garlic. Return the beef and celery to the wok, and stir-fry for 15 seconds. Add the sauce ingredients and stir. Serve.

*4 cups (1 qt/1 l) water*
*2 1/2 cups (8 oz/250 g) bean sprouts*
*1 tablespoon chopped scallions (spring onions)*
*1 teaspoon seeded and chopped red chili*

*SERVES 2*

¶ For the marinade: Combine all of the ingredients in a bowl.
¶ For the sauce: In a separate bowl, mix all the ingredients well.
¶ Marinate the beef for 15 minutes in the marinade.
¶ Reserve 2 tablespoons of oil. Heat the remaining oil in a pan. Add the beef, stirring to separate, and fry for 5 seconds. Remove, drain and set aside.

# GAR LAI YEUNG YUK

### STIR-FRIED LAMB AND ONION IN A LIGHT CURRY SAUCE

*Curry is an East Indian invention, but the Chinese have been using a kind of curry sauce for almost 200 years. Chinese curry is not very hot, but it gives an uncommon flavor to the dish.*

For the marinade:
1 tablespoon light soy sauce
1 teaspoon salt
1 teaspoon sugar
1 teaspoon Chinese rice wine
2 teaspoons cornstarch (cornflour)
For the lamb:
6 oz (185 g) lamb fillet, cut into strips
1 tablespoon light soy sauce
1 teaspoon salt
2 teaspoons sugar
1 cup (8 fl oz/250 ml) chicken broth (stock)
2 teaspoons cornstarch (cornflour)
1 cup (8 fl oz/250 ml) groundnut (peanut) oil
2 onions, halved then shredded
1 tablespoon chopped garlic
1 red chili, seeded and shredded
2 tablespoons curry paste
1 teaspoon Chinese rice wine
1 tablespoon cilantro (fresh coriander), chopped

*SERVES 4*

Top: Chiu Yim Yeung Lau; bottom: Gar Lai Yeung Yuk

¶ For the marinade: Combine all of the ingredients in a bowl.
¶ Marinate the lamb for 15 minutes.
¶ Mix the soy sauce, salt, sugar, chicken broth, and cornstarch in a bowl.
¶ Heat the oil in a wok or skillet (frying pan). Add the lamb, stirring to avoid sticking. When the lamb turns white, remove it from the wok, and drain.
¶ Drain all but 2–3 tablespoons of oil from the wok and reheat. Stir-fry the onion until translucent. Add the garlic, chili, and curry paste, stirring well to mix. Stir in the soy sauce mixture and bring to a boil. Return the lamb to the wok and cook over high heat for 30 seconds, stirring constantly. Add the wine, sprinkle with cilantro, and serve.

# CHIU YIM YEUNG LAU

### FRIED FILLET OF LAMB WITH PEPPERY SALT

*No thrifty Chinese household would sacrifice a lamb just for fillet when they could have a full mutton dish instead. But I think lamb is the most delicious meat and worth the sacrifice.*

For the marinade:
1 teaspoon salt
1 teaspoon sugar
1 teaspoon pepper
1 teaspoon sesame oil
1 teaspoon Chinese rice wine
1 tablespoon cornstarch (cornflour)
1 tablespoon water
For the lamb:
1 lb (500 g) lamb fillet, cut into 1-inch (2.5-cm) cubes
3 cups (24 fl oz/750 ml) groundnut (peanut) oil
For the peppery salt:
2 tablespoons salt
1 tablespoon Sichuan peppercorns

*SERVES 4–6*

¶ For the marinade: Combine all of the ingredients in a bowl.
¶ Marinate the lamb for 30 minutes.
¶ Heat the oil in a wok or skillet (frying pan) until very hot. Add the lamb and reduce the heat to medium. Fry for 1–2 minutes. Remove and drain. Transfer to a serving dish and serve with peppery salt.
¶ For the peppery salt: Heat a wok or skillet (frying pan), add the salt, and sauté over low heat for 30 seconds. Add the peppercorns and sauté for 1 minute. Sieve the salt to remove the peppercorns.
¶ Serve immediately.

somewhat unpleasant odor.

The Chinese also have a penchant for crisp, dry textures, and cook beef in this way for two highly regarded dishes. In Sichuan, thinly sliced beef is cooked to crisp with fragrant peppercorns, dried citrus peel, and chilis; a classic imperial dish comprises fine shreds of beef which are fried, marinated, then fried again with honey and strips of carrot until each strand is toffee-glazed, crisp to bite, but somehow still supremely tender. As a more everyday dish, slivers of beef are stir-fried with broccoli to serve over flat rice ribbon noodles in a dressing of oyster sauce. It is in this kind of dish that skill with the cleaver to carve the slices tissue-thin helps to ensure tenderness. And tenderness is paramount when it comes to beef. The Chinese cook will marinate the meat for many hours, with wine, sugar, soy, and selected natural meat tenderizers to ensure that the beef will melt on the tongue.

## Beef

In China, beef is something of a paradox: It is considered a relative luxury, but it is also not as highly regarded as other types of meat. Indeed, cattle were known traditionally as work animals—the value of their muscles was in their strength, not their taste. Consequently, cattle were slaughtered for food only when they were too old to work, so the meat was tough. The resourceful Chinese counteracted this problem by marinating beef to make it more tender and flavorful, or by shredding it finely for quick cooking. They also used slow-simmering or "red-cooking" (braising with soy sauce) methods for such cuts as **shin**, **skirt**, and **chuck**. In northern China, in Xinjiang province, beef brisket slow-cooked with spices and soy is widely appreciated. Fine-textured **meatballs**, flavored with lime or cilantro (fresh coriander), are a favorite steamed *dim sum*. The economical Chinese chef can find something deliciously edible from the most unexpected sources. Thus **spinal cord** and **beef tendons** are both prized for their part yielding, part chewy texture. They are slow cooked, in much the same way as tripe, which enjoys such widespread popularity in *yum cha* restaurants, with a number of spices and ginger to overcome their

*1. tripe; 2. beef tendons; 3. beef tenderloin; 4. skirt; 5. shin (shank); 6. steak for stir-fries; 7. stewing (braising) steak*

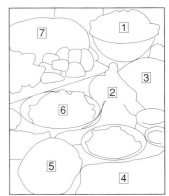

*Left: Chung Bou Yeung Yuk; right: Chee Chuk Yeung Tui*

## CHUNG BOU YEUNG YUK

### EXPLOSIVE-FRY LAMB SLIVERS WITH LEEK

*"Explosive-fry" is a Beijing expression that has basically the same meaning as "quick stir-frying" in Canton. You cut the lamb into slivers, make the fire as hot as possible and, before you know it, the lamb is cooked. Now that's fast food.*

For the marinade:
*1 tablespoon light soy sauce*
*1 teaspoon dark soy sauce*
*1 teaspoon salt*
*3–4 tablespoons water*
*1 teaspoon sugar*
*¹/₂ teaspoon sesame oil*
*¹/₂ teaspoon black pepper*

<sup></sup>¼ cup (2 fl oz/60 ml) water
2 teaspoons chopped garlic

*SERVES 4–6*

❡ For the marinade: Combine all of the ingredients in a bowl.
❡ Marinate the lamb for 15 minutes.
❡ Heat 1 tablespoon of oil in a wok or skillet (frying pan). Stir-fry the leek with the salt and the water for 1½ minutes. Set aside. Clean the wok.
❡ Heat the remaining oil in the wok until very hot. Add the lamb and garlic, stirring quickly over high heat for 5 seconds.
❡ Add the leek to the wok, stir well, and serve.

## CHEE CHUK YEUNG TUI

*BRAISED LEG OF MUTTON WITH BEAN CURD STICKS*

*Mutton is relatively rare in southern China. But during winter, it makes a warming stew. In this recipe, the dried bean curd sticks serve two purposes: They pick up the flavor of the sauce and add a crunchy texture.*

For the sauce:
*2 tablespoons soybean paste*
*1 tablespoon oyster sauce*
*1 teaspoon salt*
*1 teaspoon sugar*
*2 teaspoons Chinese rice wine*
For the mutton:
*1½ lb (750 g) mutton leg steak, cut into bite-size pieces*
*3–4 tablespoons groundnut (peanut) oil*
*1 tablespoon chopped garlic*
*6 slices ginger*
*3 dried bean curd sticks*
*6 dried black mushrooms, stems discarded, soaked in water to cover for 1 hour, and drained*

*SERVES 4–6*

❡ For the sauce: In a bowl, mix all of the ingredients together well.
❡ Place the mutton in a pan, adding water to cover. Bring to a boil and cook for 2 minutes. Remove mutton from the water, rinse, and set aside.
❡ Heat the oil in a wok or skillet (frying pan). Add the garlic, ginger, sauce, bean curd sticks, and mutton. Stir-fry for 1 minute. Add enough water to cover 1 inch (2.5 cm) above the surface, and simmer for 1 hour. Add the mushrooms and cook for 15 minutes. Serve.

*2 teaspoons Chinese rice wine*
*2 teaspoons cornstarch (cornflour)*
For the lamb:
*6 oz (185 g) lamb fillet, cut into ¼-inch (0.5-cm) thin slivers*
*4–5 tablespoons groundnut (peanut) oil*
*2 medium leeks, thinly sliced*
*1 teaspoon salt*

*Hanging: pork and liver* lap cheong *sausages,* cha siu *red barbecued pork strips; dried pork strips; lying to front right: flattened sweet dried pork and seasoned beef "jerky"*

# THE CHINESE DELICATESSEN

### CHINESE HAM

The Chinese enjoy cured pork. Ham from the Yunnan province is considered by many to be the finest in China, but *jin hwa*, from a country district north of Shanghai, rivals it with a ham of exceptional quality. Chinese ham is firm and dryish, in the tradition of an Italian Parma or Spanish *jamon*. It is used as a flavor enhancer, chopped for soups, sliced for stews, or finely shredded as a garnish for vegetables. The best broth (stock) would be the poorer without a piece of Chinese ham. Two of China's most famous dishes are based on ham: *Chin hwa yu shu chi* is sliced chicken, layered with sliced ham, interspersed with Chinese green cabbage and bathed in a clear sauce. Yunnan ham is steamed in a piece, glazed with sugar syrup and rice wine to counteract the saltiness, to serve thinly sliced and succulent with plump, white, folded crescents of steamed bread.

### CHINESE SAUSAGES

Chinese pork sausages are sold at most Chinese butcher shops, where they are usually seen hanging, linked together, outdoors to catch the winds and complete their drying process. *Lap cheong*, as they are known, come in several types: The most common is a red-brown, slightly wrinkled and dry-looking thin sausage made of ground (minced) pork, pork fat, and spices. It has a distinct sweetness which makes it excellent, sliced into rice dishes, *congee*, stuffings, and as a filling for buns. Another type contains liver, making it darker and more savory in taste. Duck meat and duck liver are also used to make a sausage of intense flavor, which is excellent in soups.

Chinese sausages are generally inexpensive and will keep indefinitely in the freezer, or for several weeks hung in an airy place. Rich and flavorful, they are used in everyday cooking, are essential on the Chinese New Year table, and can be steamed or broiled (grilled) to eat plain or with a mustard dip.

### CHA SIU

Strips of pork tenderloin, marinated in a mixture of soy sauce, sugar, and spices, are oven roasted on high heat, or barbecued to make the characteristic brown-flecked, glistening "*cha siu*" or Cantonese roast pork. Sweet, tender, *cha siu* is indispensable to slice over rice for a quick meal, to float in soups, to pile on pickled vegetables, or as the sweet filling for the popular *cha siu bao*.

### DRIED AND PROCESSED PORK

Strips of pork belly are sometimes cured and air-dried to use as a flavoring in soups and braised dishes. Marinated, sweetened, flattened with rollers and then dried into large wafer-thin squares, pork "jerky" is a tasty snack to buy from the roast meat shop. Beef is processed in the same way, its sticky surface sprinkled with sesame seeds or chili flakes.

## CHUEN JUP YEUNG PAI

### *PAN-FRIED LAMB MEDALLIONS WITH SICHUAN SAUCE*

*I must make a confession here: I'm originally Cantonese and Cantonese are not supposed to like lamb, but I love lamb, and see no reason to use it only in recipes from northern China. So I've developed some original lamb recipes that you would never find in South China. In fact, if you tried to tell a Cantonese chef that you had a South China lamb recipe, he would think you were trying to pull the wool over his eyes!*

For the marinade:
1 ½ teaspoons light soy sauce
1 ½ teaspoons dark soy sauce
1 ½ teaspoons sugar
1 ½ teaspoons Sichuan peppercorns, ground
2 teaspoons cornstarch (cornflour)
For the lamb:
12 oz (375 g) lamb fillet, cut ½ inch (1 cm) thick and
   pounded lightly to tenderize
3–4 tablespoons groundnut (peanut) oil
2 garlic cloves, chopped
1 red chili, seeded and chopped
1 tablespoon hot fava (broad) bean paste
1 tablespoon light soy sauce
2 teaspoons sugar

*Left: Chuen Jup Yeung Pai; right: Mun Yeung Yuk*

1 teaspoon aromatic or cider vinegar
2 teaspoons Chinese rice wine
2 teaspoons cornstarch (cornflour)
1 cup (8 fl oz/250 ml) chicken broth (stock)

*SERVES 4*

❡ For the marinade: Combine all of the ingredients in a bowl.
❡ Marinate the lamb for 30 minutes.
❡ Heat the oil in a wok or skillet (frying pan) and fry the lamb over medium heat until lightly browned on both sides. Remove the lamb from the wok, drain, and set aside.
❡ Return the wok with the oil to the heat and add the garlic, chili, and hot fava bean paste. Stir to mix well.
❡ Add all the remaining ingredients and bring to a boil, stirring. Return the lamb to the wok, turning quickly to make sure each piece is well coated with the sauce. Serve.

## MUN YEUNG YUK

### *LAMB STEW*

*The Cantonese may joke that a master chef is someone who cooks lamb so well that it does not taste like lamb any more, but this stew proves how tasty it can be—especially with such "exotic" ingredients as tangerine (mandarin) peel.*

1 lb (500 g) leg of lamb, chopped into 1-inch (2.5-cm) cubes
3 onions, quartered
6 red dates, pitted
1 piece dried tangerine (mandarin) peel, soaked in water to
   cover for 1 hour, and drained
5–6 slices ginger
5–6 garlic cloves
1 star anise
1 tablespoon light soy sauce
1 tablespoon dark soy sauce
1 tablespoon Chinese rice wine
4 cups (1 qt/1 l) water
salt

*SERVES 4–6*

❡ Put the lamb in a large pan and add enough water to cover. Bring to a boil slowly and cook for 10 minutes. Remove from the heat and drain.
❡ Put the lamb and all the remaining ingredients except the salt in a separate pan. Bring to a boil, then lower heat, cover, and simmer for 1½ hours. Adjust taste with salt and serve.

*Top: Ma Tai Yeung Yuk Ding; bottom: Dong Suen Yeung Yuk Sze*

¶ For the sauce: In a separate bowl, mix all the ingredients well.

¶ Marinate the lamb for 15 minutes in the marinade.

¶ Heat 1 tablespoon of oil in a wok or skillet (frying pan). Stir-fry the bell peppers and water chestnuts for 1 minute. Remove, drain and set aside.

¶ Heat the remaining oil in a separate wok or skillet (frying pan). Add the lamb, stirring to avoid sticking, and fry for 10 seconds. Remove the lamb from the wok and set aside.

¶ Drain all but 1–2 tablespoons of oil from the wok and reheat. Add the ginger, garlic, and sauce. Return the lamb and add the bell peppers and water chestnuts to the wok. Stir-fry for 30 seconds and serve.

## MA TAI YEUNG YUK DING

### *STIR-FRIED LAMB WITH BELL PEPPERS AND WATER CHESTNUTS*

*This is a rich combination of lamb, bell peppers (capsicum), crunchy water chestnuts, and hoisin sauce. Hoisin sauce is often served with Peking duck. Hoisin means "sea flavor" and the sauce is a complex mixture of beans, ginger, garlic, spices, and sugar.*

For the marinade:
*1 tablespoon light soy sauce*
*1 teaspoon sugar*
*2 teaspoons Chinese rice wine*
*1/2 teaspoon sesame oil*
*1/2 teaspoon pepper*
*2 teaspoons cornstarch (cornflour)*
For the sauce:
*2 teaspoons chili bean paste*
*3 teaspoons hoisin sauce*
*1 tablespoon light soy sauce*
*1 teaspoon aromatic or cider vinegar*
*2 teaspoons Chinese rice wine*
*2 teaspoons cornstarch (cornflour)*
*6 tablespoons chicken broth (stock)*
For the lamb:
*12 oz (375 g) lamb fillet, cut into 1/2-inch (1-cm) cubes*
*1 cup (8 fl oz/250 ml) groundnut (peanut) oil*
*1 red bell pepper (capsicum), chopped*
*1 green bell pepper (capsicum), chopped*
*4–5 water chestnuts*
*1 teaspoon chopped ginger*
*1 teaspoon chopped garlic*

*SERVES 4–6*

¶ For the marinade: Mix together all of the ingredients in a bowl.

## DONG SUEN YEUNG YUK SZE

### *STIR-FRIED LAMB WITH BAMBOO SHOOTS*

*This dish has to be done quickly for success—like "explosive-fry." Cut the lamb into slivers and don't overcook it; the results will be warming and delicious.*

For the marinade:
*1 tablespoon light soy sauce*
*1 teaspoon sugar*
*2 teaspoons Chinese rice wine*
*1/2 teaspoon sesame oil*
*1/2 teaspoon pepper*
*2 teaspoons cornstarch (cornflour)*
For the sauce:
*1 tablespoon light soy sauce*
*1 teaspoon dark soy sauce*
*1 teaspoon salt*
*1 teaspoon aromatic or cider vinegar*
*2 teaspoons Chinese rice wine*
*1 teaspoon cornstarch (cornflour)*
*1/3 cup (3 fl oz/90 ml) chicken broth (stock)*
For the lamb:
*8 oz (250 g) lamb fillet, finely shredded*
*1 cup (8 fl oz/250 ml) groundnut (peanut) oil*
*3 cups (6 oz/185 g) bamboo shoots, finely shredded*
*1 teaspoon chopped ginger*
*1 teaspoon chopped garlic*
*2 tablespoons chopped cilantro (fresh coriander)*

*SERVES 4*

¶ For the marinade: Combine all of the ingredients in a bowl.

¶ For the sauce: In a separate bowl, mix all the ingredients well.

¶ Marinate the lamb for 15 minutes in the marinade.

¶ Reserve 3 tablespoons of oil. Heat the remaining

oil in a wok or skillet (frying pan). Add the lamb, stirring to separate, and fry for 5 seconds. Remove, drain and set aside. Clean the wok.

❡ Heat 1 tablespoon of the reserved oil in a separate wok or skillet (frying pan). Stir-fry the bamboo shoots for 30 seconds. Remove, drain, and set aside.

❡ Heat the remaining 2 tablespoons of oil in the first wok or skillet (frying pan). Add the ginger, garlic, lamb, and bamboo shoots to the wok, stir-fry for 15 seconds. Add the sauce, stirring well to mix.

❡ Transfer to a serving platter, sprinkle the cilantro on top, and serve.

*Top: Sze Jup Yeung Yuk; bottom: Heung Suen Yeung Lau*

## SZE JUP YEUNG YUK

*STIR-FRIED FILLET OF LAMB IN SHALLOT AND BLACK BEAN SAUCE*

*The taste of black bean sauce can be overpowering, so in this dish I make it lighter, letting it add just a hint of flavor to the lamb and shallots.*

For the marinade:
*1 tablespoon light soy sauce*
*1 teaspoon sugar*
*2 teaspoons cornstarch (cornflour)*
*1 teaspoon Chinese rice wine*
For the lamb:
*6 oz (185 g) lamb fillet, thinly sliced*
*1 tablespoon salted black beans*
*2 garlic cloves*
*1 tablespoon light soy sauce*
*1 teaspoon sugar*
*2 teaspoons cornstarch (cornflour)*
*½ cup (4 fl oz/125 ml) chicken broth (stock)*
*1 cup (8 fl oz/250 ml) groundnut (peanut) oil*
*1 red bell pepper (capsicum), finely diced*
*1 green bell pepper (capsicum), finely diced*
*4 shallots, coarsely chopped*
*1 teaspoon Chinese rice wine*

*SERVES 4–6*

❡ For the marinade: Combine all of the ingredients in a bowl.

❡ Marinate the lamb for 15 minutes.

❡ With a pestle and mortar, pound the black beans and garlic to a paste.

❡ Mix the soy sauce, sugar, cornstarch, and chicken broth in a bowl.

❡ Heat the oil in a wok or skillet (frying pan). Add the lamb, stirring to avoid sticking. When the lamb turns white, remove it from the pan, drain, and set aside.

❡ Drain all but 2–3 tablespoons of oil from the wok and reheat. Add the bell peppers and stir-fry over medium heat for 30 seconds. Add the shallots and the black bean and garlic paste, stirring well to mix. Stir in the soy sauce mixture and return the lamb to the wok. Add the wine and serve.

## HEUNG SUEN YEUNG LAU

*FRIED FILLET OF LAMB WITH GARLIC SAUCE*

*The sauce in this recipe is what makes the dish. I use it not only for lamb, but also with duck. It is pungent and aromatic, and adds real interest to meat and fowl.*

For the marinade:
*1½ teaspoons salt*
*1½ teaspoons sugar*
*2 teaspoons Chinese rice wine*
*2 teaspoons cornstarch (cornflour)*
For the lamb:
*12 oz (375 g) lamb fillet, cut into 1-inch (2.5-cm) cubes*
*1 cup (8 fl oz/250 ml) groundnut (peanut) oil*
*4 garlic cloves, chopped*
*2 tablespoons hoisin sauce*
*1 tablespoon soybean paste*
*1 tablespoon Chinese rice wine*

*SERVES 4*

❡ For the marinade: Combine all of the ingredients in a bowl.

❡ Marinate the lamb for 30 minutes.

❡ Heat the oil in a wok or skillet (frying pan) and fry the lamb until lightly browned. Remove the lamb from the wok, drain, and place on a serving platter.

❡ Drain all but 1–2 tablespoons of oil from the wok and reheat. Fry the garlic over low heat until golden. Add the *hoisin* sauce, soybean paste, and wine, and stir to mix well. Serve with the lamb as a dip.

## KUM NGAN NGAU YUK SZE

### STIR-FRIED BEEF WITH PICKLED KALE AND BEAN SPROUTS

*This dish takes many steps to prepare, but it is still good home-cooking. The women in Guangzhou would tradition-ally cook each ingredient separately, but the method described here is acceptable. The flavor is rich and varied, including a slightly sour taste from the preserved kale.*

For the marinade:
1 teaspoon salt
1 teaspoon sugar
½ teaspoon pepper
1½ teaspoons cornstarch (cornflour)
1 tablespoon water

For the beef:
8 oz (250 g) beef fillet, cut into ¼-inch (0.5-cm) thick slices
4 oz (125 g) pickled kale or mustard greens, soaked in water for 1 hour and cut into ¼-inch (0.5-cm) wide strips
1½ teaspoons sugar
¾ cup (6 fl oz/185 ml) chicken broth (stock)
1 lb (500 g) bean sprouts
1 cup (8 fl oz/250 ml) groundnut (peanut) oil
1 tablespoon finely chopped ginger
1 tablespoon finely chopped garlic
1 red chili, shredded
2 teaspoons cornstarch (cornflour)
1 tablespoon light soy sauce
1 teaspoon Chinese rice wine

SERVES 4–6

❡ For the marinade: Mix all the ingredients in a bowl.
❡ Marinate the beef for 15 minutes.

*Left: Kum Ngan Ngau Yuk Sze; right: Lai Woo Ngau Yuk Bo*

❡ Heat a pan and sauté the kale over medium heat until lightly browned. Add the sugar and 2 tablespoons of broth, and cook until all the liquid has evaporated. Remove and set aside.

❡ Blanch the bean sprouts in rapidly boiling water for 1 minute. Remove and drain. Arrange on a serving platter, cover, and set aside.

❡ Heat the oil in a wok or skillet (frying pan) and add the beef, stirring to separate. Once the beef changes color, remove it from the wok, drain, and set aside.

❡ Drain all but 2–3 tablespoons of oil from the wok. Add the ginger, garlic, and chili. Stir-fry over medium heat until the aroma rises. Add the beef and kale.

❡ Mix the remaining broth with the cornstarch and soy sauces in a bowl and add to the wok. Stir-fry over high heat for 1 minute. Add the wine. Pour over the bean sprouts and serve.

# LAI WOO NGAU YUK BO

### BEEF AND TARO IN A CLAY POT

*This is one of the more unusual dishes in China, as it contains milk. Chinese generally get their "milk" nutrients from soybeans and other vegetables, because buffalo are scarce (buffalo milk, rather than cow's milk, being the norm). But in my home town of Shunde, in southern China, we did have buffalo, and a few interesting milk dishes like this one.*

For the marinade:
1 teaspoon salt
1 teaspoon sugar
1 1/2 teaspoons cornstarch (cornflour)
1/2 teaspoon pepper
1 tablespoon water
For the beef:
10 oz (315 g) beef fillet, shredded
2 cups (16 fl oz/500 ml) plus 2–3 tablespoons groundnut (peanut) oil
1 lb (500 g) taro, peeled and cut into bite-size wedges
6–8 small dried black mushrooms, soaked in water for 30 minutes, drained, stems discarded
2–3 slices ginger
1 teaspoon finely chopped garlic
2 scallions (spring onions)
1 teaspoon salt
1 teaspoon sugar
3 cups (24 fl oz/750 ml) chicken broth (stock)
1/2 cup (4 fl oz/125 ml) milk
1 teaspoon Chinese rice wine
1 tablespoon chopped cilantro (fresh coriander)

*SERVES 4–6*

❡ For the marinade: Mix all of the ingredients together in a bowl.

❡ Marinate the beef for 15 minutes.

❡ Heat the 2 cups (16 fl oz/500 ml) of oil in a wok or skillet (frying pan) and fry the taro until lightly browned. Remove the taro, drain, and set aside, but leave the oil in the wok and set aside.

❡ Heat the remaining 2–3 tablespoons of oil in a clay pot or large pan and add the mushrooms, ginger, garlic, and scallions. When the aroma rises, add the taro, salt, sugar, and broth. Bring to a boil and cook, covered, over medium heat for 20 minutes. Stir in the milk and cook over very low heat for 5 minutes.

❡ Reheat the oil in the wok and add the beef, stirring to separate. When it changes color, remove and drain. Add the beef to the taro mixture and stir. Add the wine, sprinkle with the cilantro, and serve.

# VEGETABLES

# VEGETABLES

LONG BEFORE THE INFLUENCE OF THE DOCTRINES OF BUDDHISM, THE CHINESE HAD BELIEVED THAT VEGETABLES WERE the healthiest food. As far back as 2780 BC, Emperor Shen Nung would go to the countryside with a red whip, searching for vegetables. When he came upon a plant new to him, he would beat it with his whip to release its juices, then he would mash it, taste it, and study it. The beginnings of Chinese medicine emerged with the new herbs and vegetables discovered around this time.

❡ Eating vegetables was not only considered religiously and medicinally favorable, in the south of China it was also an economic necessity. Meat was usually reserved for festive occasions.

❡ During the Tang dynasty, around the eighth century, the country's boundaries extended southward, taking in land with tropical and sub-tropical climates, adding many new vegetables to the Chinese diet. Traders from Europe and the Middle East brought yet more varieties of vegetables including spinach and peppers of both sweet and hot varieties (capsicum and chilies). Bean curd became a vital protein ingredient in the Chinese diet.

❡ During the Mongol invasion of China, in the thirteenth and fourteenth centuries, culinary innovations reached an all-time low and vegetarianism became necessity rather than choice. One writer, Li Yu, enjoyed meat, but rationalized the starvation sweeping the country when he wrote in 1650, "Vegetarians are closer to nature. The ancients had clothes made from reeds and rushes, and ate from plants." The country learnt to economize by pickling vegetables for the long, hard winters.

❡ The twentieth century has also been a time of hardships, but today in China vegetables are again readily available and valued for their unique textures and flavors. Vegetable markets in the bigger towns are scenes of color and activity, with a profusion of fresh greens.

❡ In the North, vegetables are the hardier variety— turnips, giant radishes, melons, and gourds of many kinds, and of course the tightly packed long heads of Tientsin cabbage. Central China is a prolific vegetable growing region, producing eggplant (aubergine), peppers (capsicums), and chilis of all kinds, beans, and various members of the yam and onion families.

❡ In the South, where temperatures range from tropical to temperate, the vegetables are of the more perishable types: spinach, long slender beans, lettuce, and sprouts. Here too, tuber vegetables like lotus, water chestnuts, and caltrops, taro and yam bean (*sar kok*) are important vegetable crops. Raw vegetables eaten as salad, are not a notable part of the Chinese diet, they prefer instead, the tart taste and crunch of pickled vegetables as a before meal snack. Mushrooms, which grow throughout China in many varieties, add their magic to many dishes.

*Previous pages: Green vegetables, particularly cabbage, spinach, and mustard greens, are an important element of Chinese cooking. Vegetables are usually cooked in a wok and are stir-fried quickly in oil, garlic, ginger, and salt to retain their freshness and crunchy quality.* PHOTOGRAPHIC LIBRARY OF AUSTRALIA

*Opposite: Yunnan Province, in China's far South, produces a great variety of ingredients for the table. This farmer carries his wicker basket in the traditional "backpack" manner.* CHINA TOURISM PHOTO LIBRARY/WANG MIAO

## YUK SUI DOU KOK

### *STRING BEANS WITH GROUND PORK*

*Why all the garlic and shallots and chili bean paste? First, because this dish is from Sichuan, a region renowned for its spicy food. Second, because the Chinese consider string beans to be a bland vegetable that definitely needs to be jazzed up a bit.*

For the marinade:
*1 teaspoon light soy sauce*
*1 teaspoon sugar*
*1 teaspoon cornstarch (cornflour)*
For the pork and beans:
*2 oz (60 g) pork, ground (minced)*
*1 cup (8 fl oz/250 ml) groundnut (peanut) oil*
*1 lb (500 g) green string beans, cut into 2-inch (5-cm) lengths*
*3 tablespoons chopped shallots*
*1 tablespoon soybean paste*
*1 teaspoon chili bean paste*
*1 teaspoon sugar*
*¼ cup (2 fl oz/60 ml) water*
*1 teaspoon Chinese rice wine*
*1 teaspoon chopped garlic*

*SERVES 4–6*

❡ For the marinade: Combine all of the ingredients in a bowl.
❡ Marinate the pork for 15 minutes.
❡ Reserve 2 tablespoons of oil. In a wok or skillet (frying pan) heat the remaining oil and fry the beans for 1 minute. Remove the beans, drain, and set aside, but do not drain the oil.

*Top: Sin Ku Care Tze; bottom: Yuk Sui Dou Kok*

❡ Reheat the oil and fry the shallots until golden. Remove, drain, and set aside.
❡ Mix the soybean paste, chili bean paste, sugar, water, and wine in a bowl.
❡ Heat the reserved oil in a separate wok or skillet (frying pan). Add the garlic, pork, and soybean paste mixture. Stir.
❡ Add the beans and stir-fry until the liquid has almost evaporated. Add the shallots and serve.

## SIN KU CARE TZE

### *BRAISED EGGPLANT WITH FRESH MUSHROOMS*

*The French writer Alexandre Dumas once wrote that chefs do not use eggplant (aubergine), because anybody can make it taste good. Perhaps that is true, because this dish is very common throughout China. The recipe is vegetarian, but the result tastes almost meaty, with the mushrooms lending a chunky texture.*

For the sauce:
*1 teaspoon dark soy sauce*
*1 tablespoon oyster sauce*
*1 teaspoon sugar*
*2 teaspoons salt*
*⅔ cup (5 fl oz/155 ml) water*
For the eggplant:
*¼ cup (2 fl oz/60 ml) groundnut (peanut) oil*
*1 lb (500 g) eggplant (aubergine), cut into finger-size pieces*
*6 oz (185 g) button mushrooms (champignons)*
*1 teaspoon chopped garlic*
*1 teaspoon chopped ginger*
*1 tablespoon chopped scallions (spring onions)*

*SERVES 4–6*

❡ For the sauce: In a bowl, mix together all the ingredients well.
❡ Heat 1 tablespoon of the oil in a wok or skillet (frying pan). Stir-fry the eggplant until lightly browned. Remove and set aside.
❡ In a medium pan, bring 2 cups (16 fl oz/500 ml) of water to a boil. Blanch the mushrooms in the water for 1 minute. Remove, drain, and set aside.
❡ Heat 3 tablespoons of the oil in a separate pan and add the garlic, ginger, eggplant, and mushrooms.
❡ Add the sauce, stirring well. Cover and cook over medium to medium–low heat until the sauce is reduced by two-thirds.
❡ Transfer to a serving dish, sprinkle with the scallions, and serve.

*Upper left: bean curd sheets, bean curd sticks; upper right in glass jars: left: pickled "red" bean curd; right: salted bean curd "cheese"; center (long oval shapes): frozen bean curd; all of right corner: various types of fried bean curd; center: soft fresh bean curd; left: firm bean curd; front: dried soy beans*

# BEAN CURD (DO FU OR TOFU)

The soy bean became, after rice, the single most important vegetable plant in China. At first used for the extraction of oil and for fermenting into sauces and seasoning pastes, it was discovered, possibly as long as 2,000 years ago, that a milky liquid, made by mixing the crushed beans with water, could be coagulated into a soft jelly by introducing gypsum as a setting agent.

Fresh bean curd comes in two main types: fragile soft bean curd with a smooth, silken texture and bland taste; and firm bean curd which has been weighted during its preparation to extract water and compress the solids into a cake of firmer texture which also has a notably stronger flavor than soft bean curd.

It is sold cut into squares, and can be kept in a tray of cold water, in the refrigerator for up to three days. It is now available in vacuum-packed plastic containers, which are of quite good quality. Canned bean curd is of lesser quality, generally.

In central and northern China bean curd is frozen to produce a product of different texture, being more rubbery and sponge-like. It is also seasoned in soy and spices giving it a deep brown appearance and distinct taste. Bean curd, cut into cubes or squares, is deep-fried to produce yet another product. This has a bubbly golden exterior, almost hollowed inside. Its chewy texture and distinct flavor make it a delicious addition to soups and braised dishes and to vegetarian cooking, and it can be shredded to

add to stir-fries. Cubes of bean curd, sometimes seasoned with chili, are cured in brine to make a pungent seasoning with a taste similar to a strong blue vein cheese, which has earned it the name "bean curd cheese." Another kind of "cheese" (*tofu kon*) is a compressed bean curd which is used in vegetarian cooking. A firm skin that forms on setting bean curd is lifted off, dried, and used as a vegetarian ingredient and as a food wrapper—it fries lightly crisp. It is sold in sheets and folded "sticks" and must be softened in water before use.

Each province has developed special dishes made from bean curd. In Sichuan province, which prides itself on its quality bean curd, it is possible to eat a meal of over forty courses, each dish with a

unique flavor or texture. In this province the famed dish known as *ma po dofu* or "pock-marked mother's bean curd," a fiery combination of ground (minced) meat, chili, and bean curd was first created. In Beijing "smelly" bean curd is made by curing cubes of soft curd with salted soya beans, mushrooms, and bamboo shoots in rice wine. The bean curd, deep-fried to a crisp crust on the outside while still tender inside, is eaten with great delight throughout northern China. The Cantonese prefer tender soft bean curd with few embellishments, even serving it simply bathed in sesame oil and soy sauce and scattered with scallions (spring onions) or cilantro (fresh coriander) leaves.

*Bottom: Ng Choi Ngan Ngar; top: Ho Yau Sang Choi; right: Cho Liu Pak Choi*

# NG CHOI NGAN NGAR

*STIR-FRIED BEAN SPROUTS WITH SHREDDED MUSHROOMS AND BELL PEPPERS*

*Bean sprouts give this dish a wonderful texture. And the mushrooms (I like to use* shiitake *mushrooms) lend a crispy-crunchy character. That's why this dish should never be overcooked.*

*1 lb (500 g) green bean sprouts
4* shiitake *mushrooms or dried black mushrooms soaked in warm water for 30 minutes and drained
3 tablespoons groundnut (peanut) oil
1 teaspoon chopped garlic
1 teaspoon chopped ginger*

*1 green bell pepper (capsicum), shredded
1 red bell pepper (capsicum), shredded
2 teaspoons salt
1 teaspoon sugar
1½ tablespoons oyster sauce*

*SERVES 4–6*

❡ Wash the bean sprouts, drain, and set aside.
❡ In a small pan, steam the mushrooms for 15 minutes. When cool, cut into shreds and set aside.
❡ Heat the oil in a wok or skillet (frying pan). Add the garlic, ginger, bell peppers, and mushrooms. Stir-fry for 45 seconds.
❡ Add the bean sprouts to the pan. Add the salt, sugar, and oyster sauce, and stir-fry for 1 minute.
❡ Serve immediately.

## HO YAU SANG CHOI

### STIR-FRIED LETTUCE WITH OYSTER SAUCE

*The Chinese love lettuce, and this recipe can be made with any kind of lettuce for a really refreshing dish in any season.*

3 tablespoons groundnut (peanut) oil
1 tablespoon shredded ginger
1½ lb (750 g) lettuce, torn into large pieces
1½ tablespoons oyster sauce
1½ teaspoons salt

SERVES 4–6

❦ Heat the oil in a wok or skillet (frying pan), add the ginger, and fry until lightly browned. Add the lettuce and stir-fry until soft.
❦ Add the oyster sauce and salt. Cook, stirring well, over high heat for 30 seconds. Serve.

## CHO LIU PAK CHOI

### STIR-FRIED CABBAGE WITH AROMATIC VINEGAR

*Cabbage means Tianjin, where the famous Tianjin cabbages are grown. They keep especially well in colder climates, so even in the depths of winter, northerners can keep hale and healthy with enough vegetables to eat.*

For the sauce:
2 tablespoons aromatic or cider vinegar
3 teaspoons sugar
1 teaspoon salt
1 teaspoon Chinese rice wine
⅓ cup (3 fl oz/90 ml) chicken broth (stock)
2 teaspoons cornstarch (cornflour)
For the cabbage:
2 tablespoons groundnut (peanut) oil
12 oz (375 g) Chinese cabbage, cut into 3- × ¼-inch
    (7.5 × 0.5-cm) shreds
1 teaspoon chopped ginger
1 teaspoon chopped garlic
1 tablespoon shredded chili

SERVES 4–6

❦ For the sauce: Mix all the ingredients in a bowl and set aside.
❦ Heat the oil in a wok or skillet (frying pan). Add the cabbage, and stir-fry for 2 minutes. Remove the cabbage from the wok, drain, and set aside.
❦ Reheat the oil and add the ginger, garlic, and chili. Return the cabbage to the wok and add the sauce. Stir-fry for 1 minute and serve.

## SOY BEAN PASTES AND SAUCES

There are two main styles of bean-based seasoning, those made from salt-fermented beans and those made with salted, boiled dried beans.

Salt-fermentation takes several months. The beans are packed in tubs and thickly coated with salt. They slowly absorb the salt, wrinkle up, and turn black, developing a strong salty taste. They are then ground to a paste. This potent purée is bottled as plain soy bean sauce, or combined with select ingredients — Sichuan peppercorns, chili, garlic, soy sauce — to produce several quite different styles of powerfully flavored paste and sauce, each with its own prescribed usage in cooking. It is also sweetened with sugar and spices to use as a condiment. Salted soy beans remain yellow and are used whole as the salty seasoning, yellow bean sauce, or to blend into a pungent sauce with mashed chili, and often garlic, as chili-bean sauce.

Bean pastes and sauces can be used in marinades, added to stir-fries and sauces, give depth of flavor to stewed and braised dishes and add color to roasted meats.

*1. yellow bean sauce; 2. chili-bean sauce; 3. hoisin sauce; 4. black bean paste/sauce; 5. barbecue sauce; 6. soy chili bean paste; 7. chili-soy bean sauce; 8. ground soy bean sauce*

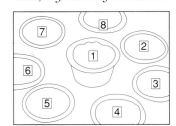

# MUSHROOMS AND FUNGI

Botanically, mushrooms are part of the all-embracing fungi family. But the Chinese differentiate between the two. "Fungi" is *yi* meaning ear, since so many of these seem to resemble an ear. Mushrooms, *gu*, simply mean mushrooms. The gathering of wild mushrooms and fungi has always been a popular family activity, and in the mountainous regions of Central China where some of the finest varieties grow, collecting prized or rare fungi for sale to the food and medical industries is a lucrative business.

## MUSHROOMS

The use of mushrooms in Chinese cooking is noted in manuals that date back to the earliest dynasties. Many types of wild mushrooms have been used over the centuries, and are still in rural areas, including a type of rare mushroom from Inner Mongolia which has a unique aroma and flavor and is used in northern Chinese dishes. But four types of mushroom, gathered from the wild, or cultivated, are prevalent in the vegetable markets.

**Black mushrooms:** *tung gu*, which are almost always sold dried, are related to the Japanese *shiitake*, but the Chinese consider theirs meatier and tastier. *Tung gu* must be reconstituted before use by soaking in warm water for at least 25 minutes and up to 1 hour so the caps swell

to their full size and the rich flavors are fully released. When soft, strain off the liquid (add it to soups and stock for extra flavor) and squeeze the mushrooms to get rid of any excess water. Trim off the hard stem close to the cap. Black mushrooms give a superb flavor to many dishes, and particularly to those cooked long and slow.

Chinese stores sell dried black mushrooms in loose form by weight, enabling one to choose each piece individually, an ideal situation as they can be quite expensive. Look for pieces with a thick, umbrella-like cap covered with "cracks." Prepacked dried black mushrooms may be less costly, but the pack often contains offcuts of inferior quality. Store them in a closed jar in a cool place away from light and moisture and they will keep indefinitely.

**Straw mushrooms:** The name of these mushrooms, *tsin cho gu*, refers to their growing habit: Straw mushrooms are raised in beds of rice straw, which accounts for their earthy taste. Their outer shape, gray-brown in color, is like a slightly elongated globe, but in cross-section they reveal an inner shape of a little stemless umbrella. Though they don't have the meatiness of dried black mushrooms, they release a strong aroma when stir-fried or cooked in soup. Usually sold in cans in Chinese stores, the mushrooms last about a week after opening, in the refrigerator, but the water must be changed daily. Fresh straw mushrooms

can be stored for just a few days in the refrigerator.

**Oyster mushrooms:** *Kwan gu* are known by several names: abalone mushrooms, oyster mushrooms, or bracket mushrooms. They have a flat, cornucopia shape and are of a soft grayish or light ocher color. They are prized for their smooth texture, subtle aroma, and delicate taste. The mushrooms are widely available fresh and can be kept, refrigerated, for about five days. Canned oyster or abalone mushrooms are a substitute in a stewed dish or soup, but would not be suitable for stir-frying.

**Button mushrooms** (champignons): *Lau lap pat kwan* are white, button-shaped cultivated mushrooms sold fresh, or a dull ocher color when canned. They have an enjoyable crunchy texture.

**Golden mushrooms:** Golden-cream in color, these mushrooms have miniature caps on long slender stems. They grow in tiny clumps at the base of certain native Chinese trees. Their flavor is delicately earthy which makes them a useful ingredient in vegetarian cooking, though their appearance in other Chinese dishes, except soups, is rare and generally for aesthetic appeal.

## FUNGI

"The family of fungi are so palatable because they have no roots, yet they spring to life suddenly as if from emptiness. The fungi are the essence of wild nature," so said seventeenth-century

author Li Yu.

Many types of Chinese fungi are indeed wild and exotic in their names, shapes and tastes, but the ones most commonly eaten go by the more homely name of "ears." Their appearance, too, is hardly inspiring: dry, crinkly curls in grays, dusky silver, and rusting black. Most fungi used in Chinese cooking, is sold dried, and will keep indefinitely in a tight-lidded container. It must be soaked before use and will soften and expand to at least three times its volume. Soaked, it can be stored in the refrigerator safely for several days.

**Cloud ear fungus** (*win yi*): This most common Chinese fungus has many names: wood ears, tree fungus, brown fungus, and silver ears. It has little taste or aroma of its own, but readily takes on the flavors of ingredients cooked with it while adding an agreeable, slightly chewy-crunchy texture.

**Black wood fungus** (*mok yi*): Similar to cloud ear fungus, this is a bit thicker and has a crisper texture. Its Chinese name, *mok yi*, is sometimes translated on a restaurant menu as "champignon chinoise," which is misleading.

**Elm fungus** (*yu yi*): This fungus which grows on elm trees is also similar to cloud ear fungus, but, like *mok yi*, it is thicker and has a crisp texture. It is a favored fungi in vegetarian dishes, and also with seafood where its mild taste is appreciated; stir-fried shrimp (prawns) with *yu yi*, for instance, is a prized Cantonese dish.

**Bamboo fungus** (*chok sung*): This lace-like rare fungus grows in the bamboo groves of Sichuan and Yunnan. It is highly aromatic, has a delicate musty-earthy taste and fragile though slightly chewy texture. It is expensive, so is usually reserved for banquet dishes or special vegetarian dishes.

**White fungus** (*aan yi*): These crinkly puffs of fungus resemble something from the sea. The most superior type is snowy white, earning it the name "snow" or "silver" fungus, while others vary from cream to gold in color. It is most valued as a dessert ingredient, boiled with sugar into a sweet soup that is believed to be beneficial to the complexion. Its neutral taste with a hint of sweetness, and its gelatinous, crunchy texture make it an interesting addition to soups and vegetarian dishes.

*1. dried and fresh black mushrooms; 2. cloud ear and black fungus; 3. "silver" fungus; 4. white fungus; 5. golden mushrooms; 6. champignons; 7. straw mushrooms; 8. oyster mushrooms*

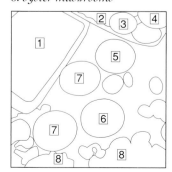

## FO TUI DONG QUA

*WINTER MELON WITH HAM*

*Winter melon is the ideal summer dish—so cooling and smooth, it breaks through any torpor. With the addition of ham, and a few herbs and spices, you have a Chinese picnic dish.*

2 lb (1 kg) winter melon, peeled and cut into
　2- × 1- × ¼-inch (5- × 2.5- × 0.5-cm) pieces
3 oz (90 g) Chinese or Virginia ham, cut into 2- × ¼-inch
　(5- × 0.5-cm) thin slivers
2–3 tablespoons groundnut (peanut) oil
1 garlic clove
2–3 slices ginger
2 cups (16 fl oz/500 ml) chicken broth (stock)
½ teaspoon sugar
1 teaspoon cornstarch (cornflour), diluted in
　1 tablespoon water
1 teaspoon Chinese rice wine

*SERVES 4–6*

❡ Arrange the winter melon and ham on a platter.
❡ Heat the oil in a wok and fry the garlic and ginger until golden brown. Remove and discard. Carefully add the broth and sugar, and boil rapidly to reduce by half. Stir in the cornstarch and cook for 1 minute; add the wine. Pour over the melon and ham, and serve.

## KING SIU SHEUNG DONG

*BRAISED BLACK MUSHROOMS AND BAMBOO SHOOTS PEKING-STYLE*

*It is hard to resist black mushrooms or bamboo shoots, especially when they are cooked with wine and vinegar. A tip when buying canned bamboo: See if the label says "winter shoots." These are always less fibrous and more tender than summer bamboo.*

1 cup (8 fl oz/250 ml) groundnut (peanut) oil
12 oz (375 g) bamboo shoots, cut into wedges
1 garlic clove
2–3 slices ginger
1 scallion (spring onion)
8 dried black mushrooms, soaked in warm water for 1 hour,
　drained, and stems discarded
2 cups (16 fl oz/500 ml) chicken broth (stock)
1 tablespoon light soy sauce
1 teaspoon dark soy sauce
1½ teaspoons sugar
½ teaspoon aromatic or cider vinegar
1 tablespoon Chinese rice wine

*SERVES 4–6*

❡ Heat the oil in a wok or skillet (frying pan) and fry the bamboo shoots until lightly browned. Remove the bamboo shoots from the wok, drain, and set aside.

*Left: Fo Tui Dong Qua; right: King Siu Sheung Dong*

❡ Drain all but 3–4 tablespoons of oil from the wok and reheat. Add the garlic, ginger, and scallion and fry until brown. Remove and discard.
❡ Return the bamboo shoots to the wok, add all the remaining ingredients, and bring to a boil. Cover,

reduce the heat to medium–low, and simmer for 15 minutes. Uncover, increase the heat, and boil rapidly until the liquid has nearly evaporated. Transfer to a serving dish and serve.

# GINGER

Ginger is one of the ingredients that makes Chinese cooking so distinctive. It neutralizes fishy odors, adds a fresh, peppery flavor to dishes, yet remains discreet and subtle. The Chinese also have a high regard for ginger as a medicinal food for ailments associated with the stomach.

The fresh root is what the Chinese use for cooking, never the powdered spice. It is peeled and cut into chunks, slices, or shreds as fine as cotton, or is grated to a pulp which might then be squeezed to extract its fragrant juices. When adding ginger to a stewed or poached dish, chefs on the east coast of China and in Taiwan have their own special method. They hit the root firmly a few times with the top edge of their cleaver, with the right skill and pressure, so that the fibers are broken and the full flavor can be extracted during cooking.

Fresh ginger mixed with soy, scallions (spring onions), and garlic is a distinctive dip for fresh-cooked seafood or poached chicken. Ginger pickled in rice wine is a sharp tasting, aromatic additive to sauces or dips, or flavorsome accompaniment to pungent foods like hundred-year-old eggs. Ginger preserved in a sweet syrup is a useful ingredient in desserts and in some sauces such as sweet and sour, and it is also added to sweet Chinese pickles.

*1. fresh young ginger root;*
*2. bamboo ginger grater;*
*3. pink pickled sliced ginger;*
*4. ginger shreds; 5. red pickled ginger chunks*

## GEUNG CHAU KAI NAN

### STIR-FRIED KALE WITH GINGER AND WINE SAUCE

*The beauty of these greens is that they taste great whether cooked till soft (as when served with bean curd), or when cooked crisp (as in this recipe). This dish has many marvellous flavors—the pungency of ginger juice, the sweet fragrance of wine, and the crispy greens.*

4–5 tablespoons groundnut (peanut) oil
2 lb (1 kg) kale or mustard greens, outer leaves and
    flowers discarded
½ cup (4 fl oz/125 ml) chicken broth (stock)
1 tablespoon finely chopped garlic
1 teaspoon salt
2 teaspoons sugar
1 tablespoon Chinese rice wine
1 knob ginger, about 2 inches (5 cm) long, grated, with
    juice squeezed and reserved

*SERVES 4–6*

❡ Heat 1–2 tablespoons of the oil in a wok or skillet (frying pan) and add the kale and chicken broth. Cover and cook over medium heat for 5 minutes. Remove, drain, and set aside.

❡ Heat the remaining oil in the wok. Add the garlic and return the kale to the wok. Stir-fry over high heat for 30 seconds.

❡ Mix all the remaining ingredients in a bowl and add to the wok. Stir-fry over high heat for 30 seconds and serve.

## SIN KU CHOI SUM

### STIR-FRIED MUSHROOMS WITH FLOWERING CABBAGE

*Dried straw mushrooms are usually very strong and aromatic. But this recipe calls for fresh mushrooms, which are more subtle. This is a simple vegetable dish, but very tasty.*

2 cups (16 fl oz/500 ml) water
½ lb (500 g) fresh straw mushrooms, halved
6 tablespoons groundnut (peanut) oil
1 tablespoon finely chopped ginger
1½ lb (750 g) flowering cabbage, outer leaves and flowers
    discarded, chopped
1 cup (8 fl oz/250 ml) chicken broth (stock)
1 teaspoon finely chopped garlic
1 tablespoon oyster sauce

*Top: Geung Chau Kai Nan; bottom: Sin Ku Choi Sum*

1 tablespoon light soy sauce
1 teaspoon cornstarch (cornflour)
1 teaspoon Chinese rice wine

*SERVES 4–6*

❡ Bring the water to a boil in a large pan and blanch the mushrooms for 2 minutes. Remove, drain, and set aside.

❡ Heat 3 tablespoons of oil in a wok or skillet (frying pan) and add half of the ginger. Add the cabbage, and stir-fry over high heat for 1 minute. Add ½ cup (4 fl oz/125 ml) of the chicken broth. Cover and cook for 1½ minutes over medium heat. Remove and set aside.

❡ Heat the remaining oil in the wok. Add the remaining ginger, the garlic, and mushrooms. Mix the remaining broth, the oyster sauce, soy sauce, and cornstarch in a bowl, add to the wok and cook for 1 minute. Return the cabbage to the wok, add the wine, and serve.

### CAMELLIA OIL

*The mountains of central China are the source of the most perfect cooking oil. It comes not from a vegetable or nut, but from the camellia. Local monks crush the leaves into a paste, filter the juice and make an oil for their most prized dishes. Camellia oil, sometimes called "tea oil" because Chinese tea is also harvested from a species of camellia, is used with fried rice, seaweed, and pine nuts and for stir-frying the smooth leaves of* saan choi. *The monks claim that foods cooked with camellia oil have an airiness and sprightly taste that can lead, naturally, to enlightenment and levitation.*

fresh vegetable tends toward bitterness. It is cured in brine, and packed into large glazed clay pots for maturation, storage, and transport.

***Een choi***: Chinese spinach is grown and eaten only in summer. Medicinally it acts as a "dehumidifier," removing excess moisture from the body. High in protein, it is enjoyed stir-fried with garlic, or in a soup.

***Ong choi***: This is not to be confused with *een choi*, although the leaves have a similar taste and texture and they are virtually interchangeable in recipes. This vegetable is not of the spinach family, but a water vegetable that grows naturally in marshes and swamps or is cultivated under similar situations, often along the muddy banks of rice paddies. The plant has long hollow stems with slender, or arrow head shaped leaves. It is commonly stir-fried with garlic, fermented bean curd or fermented shrimp (prawn) sauce.

## Cabbages and Greens

*Choi* or *cai* is the word for leafy green vegetables, of which the Chinese are inordinately fond. It includes the many Chinese derivatives of the *brassicas* (cabbage) family including:

***Bok choi***: The Chinese white cabbage, which has smooth, plump white stems beneath dark green leafy tops. It has been grown in China since the fifth century and is used fresh, dried, or salted. Baby *bok choi*, small and tender, have a superlative flavor without the slight bitterness associated with many other Chinese greens.

***Choi sum***: The most common of all Chinese greens is this flowering cabbage with slender green stems, sparse leaves and its characteristic yellow flowers. *Choi sum* is particularly popular with the Cantonese, who use it in dozens of recipes — everything from street vendors' simple noodles to restaurant banquet dishes.

***Kai larn choi***: This edible kale is used in the most varied of dishes. It resembles *choi sum* in appearance, but with white flowers and stems that are too thick and hard to be enjoyed. The leaves and more tender flower stalks are eaten, often with a strong rich dressing like oyster sauce, or stir-fried with black beans.

***Tai gu choi***: This is similar to *bok choi* in taste, though tougher in texture with

stems a pale green color. It is often braised with garlic.

***Tientsin cabbage***: The large, tightly packed heads of Tientsin cabbage remain a popular vegetable in China, particularly in the North, where they are used fresh and salted. The flavor is mild, yet distinctive and lacks the stronger odor of a common cabbage.

***Gai choi***: Mustard greens look like heads of escarole. It comes in two varieties: *dai gai choi* are Swatow mustard greens, and *jock gai choi* are bamboo mustard greens. This could be the oldest vegetable in Chinese culinary history. Pickled *gai choi* is considered to have a more agreeable taste, as the

*1. kai larn choi; 2. tai gu choi; 3. bok choi; 4. gai choi; 5 choi sum; 6. kai larn choi; 7. ong choi; 8. Tientsin cabbage; 9. een choi*

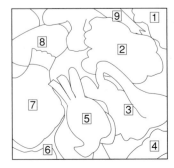

*Top left: winter melon; center left: bottle gourd; center: bitter melon; top right: snake gourd; bottom right: angled luffa*

# MELONS AND GOURDS

Sweet melons are enjoyed as a snack or after a Chinese meal, and are occasionally made into puddings. Candied melon rind is a favorite confection and salted melon seeds are a crunchy challenging snack—shelling the flat pods in the mouth takes years of practice. Melon seeds are enjoyed by Chinese of all ages as a snack. They can be encountered in dark movie theaters where your feet might crunch the discarded shells on the floor. Both watermelon and the huge bland winter melon are used for these. However, it is melons in a savory role that are important to the Chinese. There are many different types of melon used in their cooking. They are considered a cooling food, and are served throughout summer, although certain distinct-tasting melons are added to dishes containing strong-flavored ingredients.

**Angled luffa** (*sze gwa*): This elongated vegetable is not actually of the melon family, but is used in similar ways. They can be up to 25 inches (68 cm) long and are easily recognized by the distinct, hard ridges that run along the length. These must be removed with a sharp knife or vegetable parer before the slightly bitter flesh can be peeled and used in dishes that have a strong flavor.

**Bitter melon** (*fu gwa*): This melon, celebrated throughout Asia for its cooling and blood purifying properties, should be eaten when immature, when its smooth, distinctively knobbly skin is bright or light green. It has firm, bitter flesh with a strong flavor. It can be hollowed, sliced, and stuffed or is braised and steamed with rich ingredients such as eel or eggs. Vegetarians use it with ingredients like deep-fried bean curd. Bitter melon can be bought canned, but the loss of flavor and texture makes it inferior to the fresh vegetable which will keep for several weeks in the refrigerator.

**Bottle gourd** (*mo gwa*): This smooth-skinned gourd has a fine-textured, firm white flesh within a firm rind. It is so named as the dried, hollowed skin was, in times past, a useful water container. The Chinese use the hairy immature fruit as a bland tasting vegetable in soups and simmered dishes, and in vegetarian cooking.

**Chayote** (*faat sau gwa*): Originally grown by Buddhist monks outside temples, the Cantonese name of this perennial vine is similar to that meaning "the hands of Buddha." Not used extensively in China, chayote can be used as a replacement for winter melon in a recipe, and used in soups and stir-fries.

**Hairy or fuzzy melon** (*jit gwa*): These small melons are the size of a plump cucumber, with a mottled to deep green rind covered with tiny dark hairs. A staple throughout summer, this bland vegetable, similar to a zucchini (courgette) in taste and texture, is added to combination vegetable and meat dishes. The fresh melon will keep for about two weeks in the vegetable crisper of the refrigerator.

**Snake gourd:** One of nature's anomalies, these elongated, mid-green gourds come in a variety of interesting shapes as their length and weight causes them to assume curves and angles depending on their position on the vine. Their delicate, bland flesh makes them useful in many dishes.

**Winter melon** (*dung gwa*): One of the largest vegetable melons in the world—growing to reach a weight of up to 100 pounds (about 45 kg)—it is a favorite summer vegetable for its effect of "cooling" the body. The entire melon is edible, including the rind which is pickled or candied, the flesh used in vegetable dishes and soups, and the pits which are dried and salted as a snack. Winter melon can be steamed which turns the flesh a delicate green, braised, or stir-fried. The melon has little taste of its own, but its soft slightly fibrous flesh absorbs the flavors of the meat, other vegetables and mushrooms cooked with it.

As a banquet table centerpiece, the melon skin is hollowed and the outside decoratively carved. The flesh is cooked up as a soup with myriad finely diced ingredients, and served in the shell.

## KUM OU LO PAK

### BRAISED TURNIPS WITH DRIED SHRIMP

*This is a very tasty home-cooked recipe. Prudent cooks always keep dried shrimp (prawns) on hand for recipes like this. The shrimp are sun-dried and should be stored in a cool, dark place.*

1 lb (500 g) turnips, peeled, halved, and cut into slivers
3–4 tablespoons groundnut (peanut) oil
1 tablespoon finely chopped garlic
3 tablespoons dried shrimp (prawns), soaked in warm
    water for 30 minutes, and drained
1 cup (8 fl oz/250 ml) chicken broth (stock)
1 teaspoon cornstarch (cornflour)
1 teaspoon pepper
1/2 teaspoon salt
1 teaspoon Chinese rice wine
1 scallion (spring onion), chopped

SERVES 4–6

❡ Blanch the turnips in boiling water for 5 minutes. Remove, drain, and set aside.
❡ Heat the oil in a wok or skillet (frying pan) and add the garlic and shrimp. Stir-fry for 30 seconds. Add the turnips and stir-fry for 1 minute. Add the broth, cornstarch, pepper, and salt. Cover and cook over medium–low heat for 2 minutes. Add the wine, sprinkle the scallion on top, and serve.

## YU HEUNG CARE TZE

### FISH-FLAVORED EGGPLANT SICHUAN-STYLE

*Eggplant (aubergine) is often used in Sichuan recipes, but it never becomes monotonous because it blends well with other flavors. This dish is typical of Sichuan cooking, with its hot bean paste, vinegar, and Sichuan peppercorns.*

1/4 cup (2 fl oz/60 ml) groundnut (peanut) oil
1 1/2 lb (750 g) eggplant (aubergine), cut into
    finger-size strips
1 teaspoon finely chopped ginger
1 teaspoon finely chopped garlic
1 tablespoon chopped scallion (spring onion)
1 tablespoon hot fava (broad) bean paste, mashed
1 teaspoon sugar
1 teaspoon aromatic or cider vinegar
1 teaspoon ground Sichuan peppercorns
1 teaspoon sesame oil
1 teaspoon chili oil

1 teaspoon dark soy sauce
1 1/2 cups (12 fl oz/375 ml) chicken broth (stock)
2 teaspoons cornstarch (cornflour), diluted in
    1 tablespoon water
1 teaspoon Chinese rice wine

SERVES 4–6

*Top: Yu Heung Care Tze; bottom: Kum Ou Lo Pak*

❡ Heat 2 tablespoons of the oil in a wok or skillet (frying pan) and sauté the eggplant until soft. Remove and set aside.

❡ Heat the remaining oil in the wok and add the ginger, garlic, and scallion. In a bowl, mix together the hot fava bean paste, sugar, vinegar, peppercorns, sesame oil, chili oil, and soy sauce. When the aroma rises from the wok, add the hot fava bean paste mixture and stir-fry over low heat for 30 seconds.

❡ Stir in the broth and return the eggplant. Cook, stirring, over high heat for 15 seconds. Reduce the heat to medium–low, cover, and simmer for 5 minutes.

❡ Stir in the cornstarch and cook for 1 minute, add the wine, and serve.

*Upper left: sesame oil; upper right: white sesame seeds; lower right: black sesame seeds; left: sesame paste/butter*

## SESAME

Take that maligned sea creature, the jellyfish, dry it, shred it, poach it, and bathe it in sesame oil or sesame paste. Sprinkle it with sesame seeds—and it is transformed into a delightful cold appetizer. Add a dash of sesame oil to the pan when stir-frying vegetables, delicious!

Sesame—in the form of oil, seeds, and a buttery paste—is as indispensable to the gourmet Chinese kitchen as are soy sauce and ginger. Sesame grows throughout Asia and has been used for centuries. Evidence of sesame seeds have been found in ancient Chinese tombs, they were used in the emperors' kitchens and are a part of every family's larder as a seasoning for noodles, rice, and vegetables. All sesame ingredients last indefinitely in well-sealed containers without refrigeration.

**White sesame seeds:** These should be toasted to release their fragrance and full nutty flavor before use. Simply put them in a wok or pan over low heat, shaking it so they don't stick, until they turn golden brown and begin to pop. Once toasted, they can be cooled and stored in a tightly closed jar.

**Black sesame seeds:** These are an attractive garnish for cakes and pastries, and savory snack foods.

**Sesame oil:** This is made from the crushed seeds, and because its taste is so rich, is used in small quantities. It also has a low burning point, making it unsuitable for frying by itself. It is added to fried foods as a seasoning, being added at the end so it will not scorch. Its rich amber color and intense flavor make it invaluable as an ingredient in sauces and marinades.

**Sesame paste:** This is also known as sesame "butter," is similar to Middle Eastern tahini, although the Chinese product can sometimes have a more distinct taste and aroma. It is made into a creamy sauce by adding water and sometimes soy sauce or lemon juice, to use as a dressing for cold foods such as shredded chicken, noodles, or jellyfish served as appetizers.

## CONPOY CHING QUA

### CUCUMBER WITH CONPOY SAUCE

*This is a Cantonese recipe that never fails. The cucumber is mild, but the* conpoy *(dried sea scallops) add an interesting taste. This makes a fine appetizer, both relaxing and refreshing at the same time.*

*3 conpoy (dried scallops), soaked in water to cover*
  *for 2 hours*
*2 slices ginger*
*1 tablespoon Chinese rice wine*
*2–3 tablespoons groundnut (peanut) oil*
*1 teaspoon finely chopped garlic*
*1 teaspoon finely chopped ginger*
*1½ lb (750 g) cucumber, split lengthwise and cut into*
  *diamond-shaped pieces*
*1 cup (8 fl oz/250 ml) chicken broth (stock)*
*1 teaspoon salt*
*½ tablespoon oyster sauce*
*1 teaspoon dark soy sauce*
*1 teaspoon cornstarch (cornflour), diluted in*
  *1 tablespoon water*
*2 teaspoons Chinese rice wine*

*SERVES 4–6*

❡ Tear the *conpoy* into coarse shreds and place them, with the soaking liquid, in a dish. Add the ginger and wine. Place the dish on a steaming rack over boiling water and steam for 30 minutes. Remove and set aside.

❡ Heat the oil in a wok or skillet (frying pan) and add the garlic and ginger. When the aroma rises, add the cucumber and sauté over high heat for 1 minute.

❡ Add the broth and *conpoy* with the soaking liquid. Cover and cook over medium heat for 5 minutes. Add the salt, oyster sauce, and soy sauce. Stir in the cornstarch and cook for 1 minute. Add the wine, and serve.

# HO YAU KAI NAN DOU FU

*BEAN CURD AND KALE IN OYSTER SAUCE*

*This is a typical vegetarian dish, but you can cook it many different ways. Here, the bean curd is soft, so stir the kale until tender, to complement it.*

*3 cups (24 fl oz/750 ml) groundnut (peanut) oil*

*1 box bean curd, 6- × 3- × 2-inches (15- × 7.5- × 5-cm), cut into ½-inch (1-cm) cubes and patted dry*

*4 cups (1 qt/1 l) water*

*1 teaspoon salt*

*½ teaspoon baking soda (bicarbonate of soda)*

*2 lb (1 kg) kale or mustard greens, outer leaves and flowers discarded*

*1 teaspoon finely chopped garlic*

*1 teaspoon finely chopped ginger*

*¾ cup (6 fl oz/185 ml) chicken broth (stock)*

*1 tablespoon oyster sauce*

*1 tablespoon light soy sauce*

*1 teaspoon dark soy sauce*

*1 teaspoon cornstarch (cornflour)*

*1 teaspoon Chinese rice wine*

*SERVES 4–6*

❡ Heat 2³/₄ cup (22 fl oz/675 ml) of oil in a wok or skillet (frying pan) until very hot and fry the bean curd until golden brown. Remove, drain, and set aside.

❡ Bring the water to a boil in a large pan. Add the salt, baking soda, and 2–3 tablespoons of the remaining oil. Add the kale and cook over high heat for 5 minutes. Remove, drain, and set aside.

❡ Heat the remaining oil in the wok and add the garlic and ginger. Mix the broth, oyster sauce, soy sauces, and cornstarch in a bowl. Add the broth mixture to the wok and bring to a boil. Add the bean curd and kale, and stir gently to coat the ingredients with the sauce. Add the wine and serve.

*Top: Conpoy Ching Qua; bottom: Ho Yau Kai Nan Dou Fu*

## CHO KU MUN GIT QUA

### BRAISED HAIRY GOURD WITH STRAW MUSHROOMS

*There is no real substitute for the hairy gourd, although cucumber or zucchini (courgette) might just do at a pinch. An ideal companion for the mild hairy gourd is the dried straw mushroom, which is quite strong in flavor.*

*20 dried straw mushrooms, soaked in 1 cup (8 fl oz/250 ml) water for 30 minutes, and drained*
*2–3 tablespoons groundnut (peanut) oil*
*2 garlic cloves, crushed*
*3–4 slices ginger*
*2 cups (16 fl oz/500 ml) chicken broth (stock)*
*1 teaspoon salt*

*1 tablespoon oyster sauce*
*1½ lb (750 g) hairy gourd, skin scraped, and cut crosswise into ½-inch (1-cm) thick pieces*
*1 teaspoon Chinese rice wine*

*SERVES 4–6*

¶ Scrape away any woody parts of the mushrooms and clean. Set aside.
¶ Heat the oil in a wok or skillet (frying pan) and add the garlic and ginger. When the aroma rises, add the mushrooms and sauté over medium heat for 30 seconds.
¶ Mix the broth, salt, and oyster sauce in a bowl. Add the hairy gourd and the broth mixture to the wok. Bring to a boil, cover, and cook over medium–low heat for 10 minutes. Add the wine and serve.

*Cho Ku Mun Git Qua*

# BAMBOO SHOOTS

*Chuk san* is the edible bamboo, of which only the young shoots are eaten. Winter bamboo has long, slender shoots of dense soft flesh, while standard bamboo has squat tapering shoots of layered and more fibrous texture. When harvested, the shoots are encased in a sheath of overlapping coarse leaves, which must be removed before the shoots can be cooked. Bamboo shoots must be cooked for several hours to make them soft enough to eat. They are processed to this stage for canning or sale as fresh

bamboo, and are also pickled in brine or dried and salted to preserve them.

Prepared fresh, bamboo shoots, as whole shoots, slices, or shreds, are now sold in many Chinese greengrocers' or delicatessens. They can be kept in a container of lightly salted water, for a week or two in the refrigerator. More readily available, canned bamboo shoots can be stored in the refrigerator for a week or two after opening. Salted bamboo must be soaked to soften before use, and the water changed several

times to remove excess saltiness. Pickled bamboo shoots are boiled in several changes of water to remove the tartness before using.

Bamboo shoots have a distinct, vegetative taste and strong aroma. They are especially good added to red-cooked dishes, stir-fries, and soups and are a tasty ingredient in many dumplings.

From ancient times, hollow bamboo stems have been used as food carrying and cooking containers, and dried bamboo leaves are used to wrap savory dumplings to add flavor.

*1. sliced bamboo shoots;*
*2. shredded bamboo; 3. bamboo*
*leaves; 4. winter bamboo*
*shoots; 5. fresh harvested*
*bamboo shoots*

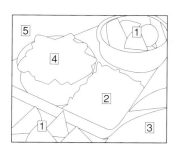

# HEUNG JIN CARE TZE

*PAN-FRIED EGGPLANT*

*Another Sichuan eggplant (aubergine) dish. The vegetable is so versatile and so tasty that it's difficult to make a bad recipe with it.*

*4–6 tablespoons groundnut (peanut) oil*
*1½ lb (750 g) eggplant (aubergine), cut on a slant into*
*    ¼-inch (0.5-cm) thick slices*
*1 teaspoon finely chopped garlic*

*1 teaspoon finely chopped ginger*
*1 cup (8 fl oz/250 ml) chicken broth (stock)*
*1 teaspoon aromatic or cider vinegar*
*1 teaspoon sesame oil*
*1 tablespoon light soy sauce*
*1 teaspoon dark soy sauce*
*1 teaspoon salt*
*1 teaspoon sugar*
*1 teaspoon Chinese rice wine*
*2 tablespoons chopped scallion (spring onion)*

*SERVES 4–6*

*Left: Heung Jin Care Tze; right: Gone Bin Say Kwai Dou*

❦ Heat 1–2 tablespoons of the oil in a wok or skillet (frying pan) and fry the eggplant until lightly browned on both sides. Remove, drain, and set aside.

❦ Heat the remaining 3–4 tablespoons of oil in the wok. Add the garlic and ginger. In a bowl, mix together the broth, vinegar, sesame oil, soy sauces, salt, and sugar. When the aroma rises from the wok, add the broth mixture. Return the eggplant to the wok and cook over medium heat until the liquid has almost evaporated. Add the wine, sprinkle the scallion on top, and serve.

# GONE BIN SAY KWAI DOU

### FRIED STRING BEANS WITH DRIED SHRIMP

*Tell your guests that you're going to serve a Sichuan dish, and they may have palpitations just thinking about the fire. There is nothing to fear with this dish, though, for it is very rich in flavor, but not hot.*

*1 cup (8 fl oz/250 ml) groundnut (peanut) oil*
*1 lb (500 g) string (French, green) beans, cut into 2-inch (5-cm) lengths*
*1 tablespoon finely chopped garlic*
*1 tablespoon finely chopped ginger*
*1 tablespoon chopped scallion (spring onion)*
*2 tablespoons dried shrimp (prawns), soaked in warm water for 30 minutes, drained, and finely chopped*
*1 cup (8 fl oz/250 ml) chicken broth (stock)*
*1 tablespoon light soy sauce*
*1 teaspoon dark soy sauce*
*1/2 teaspoon salt*
*1 teaspoon sugar*
*1/2 teaspoon aromatic or cider vinegar*
*1 teaspoon sesame oil*

*SERVES 4–6*

❦ Heat the oil in a wok or skillet (frying pan) and add the beans. Fry over medium–high heat until they are wrinkled. Remove the beans from the pan, drain, and set aside.

❦ Drain all but 2–3 tablespoons of oil from the wok and reheat. Add the garlic, ginger, and scallions. When the aroma rises, add the shrimp and stir-fry for 30 seconds.

❦ Mix all the remaining ingredients in a bowl and add to the wok. Return the string beans to the wok and stir-fry over high heat until the liquid has evaporated.

❦ Serve immediately.

---

*CILANTRO*
*Cilantro (fresh coriander), yen sai, or Chinese parsley is instantly recognizable by its pungent, piercing aroma when cooked. Its distinctive taste is used to enhance fish dishes, soups, and even salads. The leaves can be steamed or boiled, or simply used as a garnish.*
*In addition to its culinary value, cilantro is prized for its medicinal properties: It is high in many vitamins, as well as chlorophyll, and also acts as a stimulant to the digestive process.*

*Bottom: Chiu Yim Dou Fu; top: Mun Chai Bow*

## CHIU YIM DOU FU

*DEEP-FRIED BEAN CURD WITH CHILI SALT*

*Bean curd is good for soaking up flavors, and this is a good dish to serve when you have leftover vegetables, meat, or fish.*

3 tablespoons salt
1 tablespoon finely chopped chilis
½ teaspoon five-spice powder
3 cups (24 fl oz/750 ml) groundnut (peanut) oil
1 box, 6- × 3- × 2-inches (15- × 7.5- × 5-cm), bean curd, cut
    into ½-inch (1-cm) cubes and patted dry

*SERVES 4–6*

❡ Heat a wok or skillet (frying pan) and add the salt, chilis and five-spice powder. Sauté until lightly browned. Remove from the pan and reserve for use as the dip. Clean the wok.
❡ Heat the oil in the wok until very hot. Add the bean curd and fry until golden brown. Remove and drain on paper towels. Serve with the dip.

## MUN CHAI BOW

*VEGETARIAN TREASURE POT*

*This is a banquet dish with many different names, such as "Eight Treasures." You can make it with any vegetables that seem to fit. Experiment with the basic vegetables I have here, then add or subtract whatever you want.*

3 cups (24 fl oz/750 ml) plus 2–3 tablespoons groundnut
    (peanut) oil
6 pieces bean curd, 2- × 2- × ½-inch (5- × 5- × 1-cm) square,
    patted dry
4 oz (125 g) hairy gourd, skin scraped, cut into 1½-inch
    (4-cm) long pieces
4 oz (125 g) eggplant (aubergine), cut into 1½-inch
    (4-cm) long pieces
4 oz (125 g) string (French, green) beans, cut into
    1½-inch (4-cm) lengths
4 oz (125 g) cabbage, cut into 1½-inch (4-cm) long pieces
6 dried black mushrooms, soaked in warm water for 1 hour,
    drained, and stems discarded
2 garlic cloves, crushed
3 slices ginger
6 sweet bean curd sheets, halved
2 cups (16 fl oz/500 ml) chicken broth (stock)
1½ tablespoons oyster sauce
1 tablespoon light soy sauce
1 teaspoon dark soy sauce
1 oz (30 g) green bean noodles, soaked in warm water for 30
    minutes, drained, and cut into 4-inch (10-cm) lengths
1½ teaspoons cornstarch (cornflour)
1 teaspoon Chinese rice wine

*SERVES 4–6*

❡ Heat the oil in a wok or skillet (frying pan) until very hot and fry the bean curd until golden brown. Remove the bean curd from the wok, drain, and set aside.
❡ In the same oil, fry the hairy gourd, eggplant, string beans, cabbage, and mushrooms for 1½ minutes. Remove, drain, and set aside.
❡ Heat the remaining 2–3 tablespoons oil in a clay pot. Add the garlic and ginger. When the aroma rises, add the vegetables and place the bean curd sheets on top.
❡ Mix the broth, oyster sauce, and soy sauces, and add to the pot. Cover, and cook over medium heat for 10 minutes. Add the green bean noodles and cook for 2 minutes. Stir in the cornstarch and add the wine. Serve in the clay pot.

---

### LOTUS ROOT

*Almost every part of the lotus is used in Chinese cooking; however, lotus root is most often used. It can be purchased in most Chinese groceries, either fresh, canned, dried, or sugared. The root can be used in soups, vegetarian dishes, and, cut in tiny pieces, as a chewy additive to almost any dumpling.*

*For a subtle snack, the lotus root can be sliced crosswise and the pieces marinated in three different savory sauces and then deep-fried until crisp.*

*Clockwise from top right: Sichuan pickled mustard greens, shredded salt-pickled turnip with chili; pickled garlic; pickled mustard greens; pickled lettuce with ginger; salt-pickled cucumber, chili-pickled vegetables; dry-pickled turnip shreds*

# PICKLED VEGETABLES

The Chinese use a varied range of pickled vegetables in their cooking. In the North, where winters can be long and harsh, pickled cabbage is a mainstay vegetable in much the same way as is a similar chili-hot cabbage pickle, *kim chee*, in Korea. In central Sichuan, bitter mustard greens are packed into crocks with salt, garlic, and masses of chili to cure into a pungent vegetable that adds vibrancy to many of their dishes. The Cantonese, exponents of a bland style of cooking, like the pep and saltiness of shredded pickled vegetable in their soups. Sweet pickled bulbs of young leeks or scallions (spring onions), and whole cloves of garlic are a palate stimulating pre-meal snack that goes well with sliced cold meats and other appetizers. Finely chopped pickled vegetable is often the surprise ingredient in a filling or chopped meat preparation, adding a brightness to the flavor and a satisfying crunch to the texture.

Hard root vegetables such as turnips, carrots, and radish are cut into narrow, thin strips, rubbed with salt, sun-dried until they are firm but pliable, and then packed into crocks to cure. Cabbages and other greens are pickled in brine, or in vinegar, with spices.

## TUI YUNG SHEUNG SAW

*CUCUMBER AND MUSHROOM SLIVERS IN HAM SAUCE*

*This is a very refreshing dish for any season. The mixture of vegetables is "relaxing," but the ham prevents it from going to sleep.*

3–4 tablespoons groundnut (peanut) oil
1 teaspoon salt
12 oz (375 g) button mushrooms (champignons), sliced
1 cucumber, about 6 oz (185 g), split lengthwise, seeded, and thinly sliced
1 teaspoon shredded ginger
½ teaspoon finely chopped garlic
1 oz (30 g) Chinese or Virginia ham, very finely chopped
1 cup (8 fl oz/250 ml) chicken broth (stock)
1 teaspoon sugar
½ teaspoon sesame oil
1 teaspoon cornstarch (cornflour)
1 teaspoon Chinese rice wine

SERVES 4–6

❡ Heat 1 tablespoon groundnut oil in a wok or skillet (frying pan). Add the salt and mushrooms, and sauté for 2 minutes. Add the cucumber and sauté for 45 seconds. Remove, drain, and transfer to a serving platter.

❡ Heat the remaining oil in the wok. Add the ginger and garlic. When the aroma rises, add the ham. Mix the broth, sugar, sesame oil, and cornstarch, and add to the wok. Boil rapidly to reduce by half, and add the wine. Pour over the vegetables and serve.

## JAR CHOI YUK SZE

*STIR-FRIED PORK AND PICKLED VEGETABLE ROOT SICHUAN-STYLE*

*This stir-fried vegetable dish is made with chili and a pickled root that is something like a turnip. If you can not find* jar choi, *the picked vegetables, you can substitute turnips. This dish is a delicious accompaniment with noodles, rice, or northern-style pancakes.*

For the marinade:
½ teaspoon salt
½ teaspoon sugar
1 teaspoon cornstarch (cornflour)
½ tablespoon water
For the pork and vegetables:

4 oz (125 g) pork fillet, cut into 2-inch (5-cm) long shreds
½ cup (4 fl oz/125 ml) groundnut (peanut) oil
1 tablespoon shredded ginger
1 teaspoon finely chopped garlic
1 green bell pepper (capsicum), cut into 2-inch (5-cm) long shreds
1 red bell pepper (capsicum), cut into 2-inch (5-cm) long shreds
4 oz (125 g) pickled Sichuan vegetable root, soaked in warm water for 1 hour, drained, and cut into 2-inch (5-cm) long shreds

¼ cup (2 fl oz/60 ml) chicken broth (stock)
1–2 teaspoons chili oil
1½ teaspoons sugar
1 teaspoon sesame oil
1 teaspoon Chinese rice wine
1 teaspoon cornstarch (cornflour)

*SERVES 4–6*

❡ For the marinade: Combine all of the ingredients in a bowl.
❡ Marinate the pork for 15 minutes.

❡ Heat the groundnut oil in a wok or skillet (frying pan) and stir-fry the pork for 1 minute. Remove the pork from the wok, drain, and set aside.
❡ Drain all but 3–4 tablespoons of oil from the wok and reheat. Add the ginger and garlic, and fry. When the aroma rises, add the peppers and pickled vegetable root. Stir-fry over medium heat for 2 minutes.
❡ In a bowl, mix together all the remaining ingredients and add to the wok. Return the pork to the wok and stir-fry over high heat for 1 minute.
❡ Serve immediately.

*Left: Tui Yung Sheung Saw; Right: Jar Choi Yuk Sze*

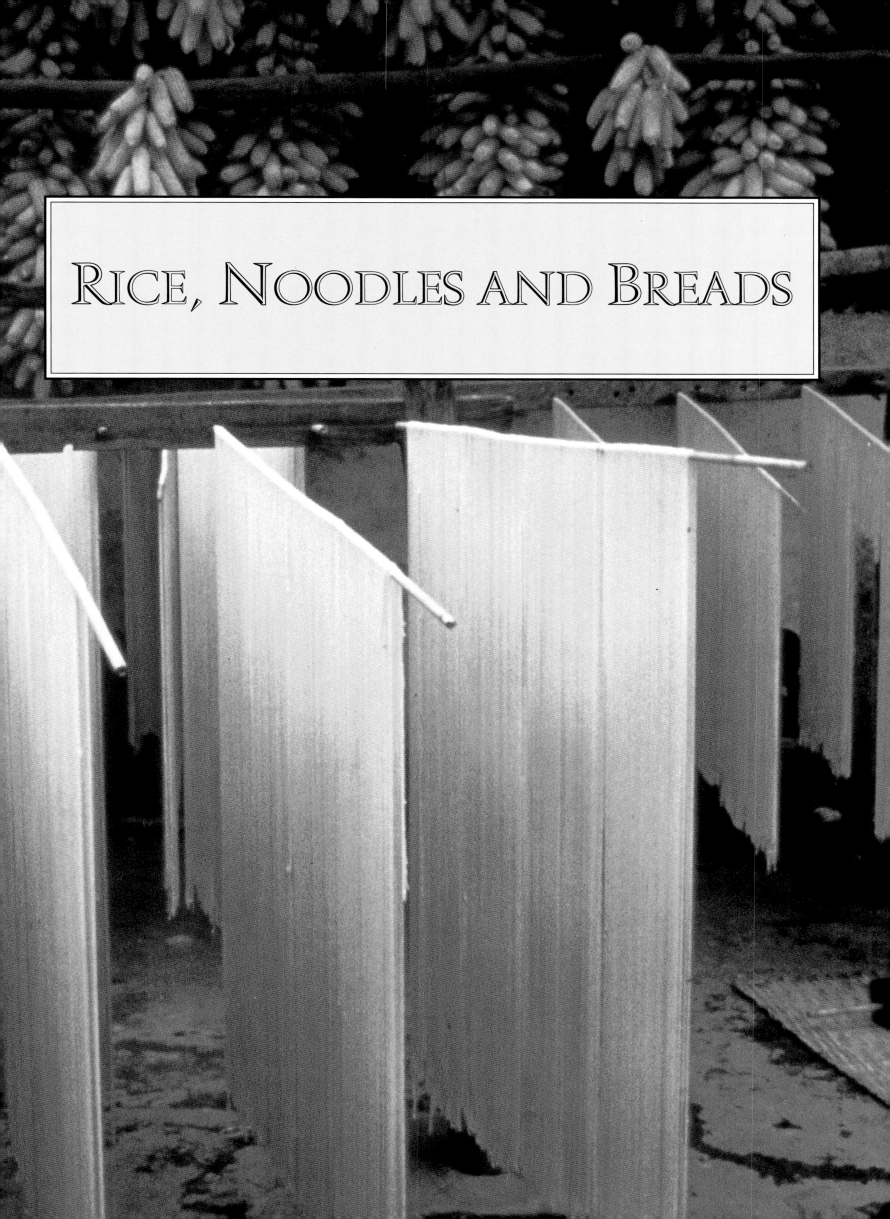

# Rice, Noodles and Breads

# RICE, NOODLES AND BREADS

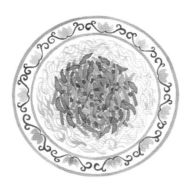

IN THE YEAR 2800 BC, EMPEROR CHIN-NING DONNED HIS CEREMONIAL ROBES, STRAPPED ON A PAIR OF UNCEREMONIAL sandals, walked out to the fields around his palace and dug a hole for an important ceremony. Into this hole he planted a seed, and begged the Lord of Heaven to help make the seed grow. Today, that seed has grown to such proportions that half the world depends upon a single grain: rice.

¶ Rice has, in fact, been cultivated in China since around 5000 BC and today there are more than 7,000 varieties.

¶ In China, rice is more than a food: It is the staple of living that has permeated the language. Rather than saying "Hello," the Chinese greet one another with "Have you had your rice yet?" Throughout China "eating dinner" is "eating rice."

¶ With the exception of northern China, where wheat is generally preferred, rice is used all over China. The reasons are obvious: Rice yields more calories per acre (kilojoules per hectare) than any other vegetable crop, with the exception of potatoes.

¶ White rice is king ("Always clean and polish your rice," said Confucius in the fifth century), though now more and more Chinese are eating brown rice, on which the nutrient-rich hull is left intact.

¶ Noodles have been eaten in China for centuries. Around the fourth century, the writer Shu Hsi stated that noodles were basically a dish of "the common people." In fact, until the Mongol invasion of the thirteenth and fourteenth centuries, noodles were scorned by the gourmets of South China, who believed that the northern Chinese were barbarians. But when the northerners became rulers, their foods suddenly gained a kind of cachet.

¶ There is a huge variety of noodles manufactured in China today, the majority made from wheat flour combined with eggs or water. Rice is used for thin vermicelli and flat "ribbons"; opaque, glassy bean-thread vermicelli is made from ground mung beans.

¶ An enjoyable sidelight to any discussion of Chinese noodles are the "showbusiness" noodle makers. These are the chefs employed by restaurants, large or small, who are skilled at turning a lump of wheat flour dough into loops of thin strands, by tossing them around like hula-hoops.

¶ Although the Chinese are best known for their rice and noodle dishes, chefs also turn out a surprising array of rolls and breads. Mostly they are boiled or steamed, though some breakfast breads are deep-fried. Sometimes the buns are filled with savory or sweet fillings, and others are opened into "pockets" to stuff with stir-fried meat and vegetables. One of the most popular breads from the north is "scallion bread" a curlique of dough filled with chopped scallions (spring onions.)

*Previous pages: Neat strings of noodles hang out to dry in Sichuan Province. Although noodles are more popular in the North, they are eaten all over China in a wide variety of forms—from the ribbon-like egg and wheat variety that resembles Italian pasta, to ultra-fine "cellophane" noodles, made from ground mung beans.* CHINA TOURISM PHOTO LIBRARY/WANG MIAO

*Opposite: A Tibetan woman makes dough for noodles. This nutritious and versatile ingredient can be fried or used in light soups and thicker stew-like dishes, with virtually any kind of vegetable and meats such as chicken, pork, or shrimp (prawns).* LEO MEIER/WELDONS

*Top: Ngau Sung Tong Mai; bottom: Yuk Sze Chau Min*

## YUK SZE CHAU MIN

### PAN-FRIED EGG NOODLES WITH PORK SHREDS AND BEAN SPROUTS

*Did Marco Polo really get his pasta from China? Nobody knows the truth, but the similarity between Chinese noodles and Italian pasta is undeniable. In any event, this is obviously a southern dish, since it calls for egg noodles; in the North, noodles are made from wheat flour and water, but not with eggs.*

For the marinade:
*1 tablespoon light soy sauce*
*1 teaspoon salt*
*1 teaspoon sugar*
*1 teaspoon cornstarch (cornflour)*
For the sauce:
*1 tablespoon light soy sauce*

*1 teaspoon dark soy sauce*
*1 tablespoon oyster sauce*
*2 teaspoons salt*
*2 teaspoons sugar*
*1½ cups (12 fl oz/375 ml) chicken broth (stock)*
For the pork and bean sprouts:
*6 oz (185 g) pork fillet, finely shredded*
*2½ cups (8 oz/250 g) bean sprouts*
*8 oz (250 g) egg noodles*
*1 cup (8 fl oz/250 ml) groundnut (peanut) oil*
*1 teaspoon chopped ginger*
*1 teaspoon chopped garlic*

*SERVES 4–6*

¶ For the marinade: Mix the ingredients in a bowl.
¶ For the sauce: In a separate bowl, mix all the ingredients well.
¶ Marinate the pork for 15 minutes.
¶ In a large pan, bring 4 cups (1 qt/1 l) of water to

## NGAU SUNG TONG MAI

### RICE VERMICELLI WITH GROUND BEEF AND CILANTRO

*Cilantro (fresh coriander) is often called "Chinese parsley," as its leaves resemble those of flat-leaf (continental) parsley. But the two plants are altogether different. Whereas parsley has a clean, almost tea-like flavor, cilantro has a strong, tangy aroma and taste. If you are sensitive to cilantro or object to its scent, you can substitute scallions (spring onions) or parsley in this recipe.*

For the marinade:
*1 tablespoon light soy sauce*
*1 teaspoon salt*
*1 teaspoon sugar*
*1 teaspoon Chinese rice wine*
*2 teaspoons cornstarch (cornflour)*
*2 tablespoons water*
For the sauce:
*1 tablespoon light soy sauce*
*1 teaspoon dark soy sauce*
*2 tablespoons oyster sauce*
*1 1/2 teaspoons salt*
*2 teaspoons Chinese rice wine*
*2 teaspoons cornstarch (cornflour)*
*1 1/2 cups (12 fl oz/375 ml) chicken broth (stock)*
For the beef:
*8 oz (250 g) rice vermicelli, soaked in water for 20 minutes, and drained*
*6 oz (185 g) beef fillet, ground (minced)*
*1 cup (8 fl oz/250 ml) groundnut (peanut) oil*
*1 teaspoon chopped garlic*
*1 teaspoon chopped ginger*
*2 teaspoons red chili, seeded and shredded*
*2 tablespoons chopped cilantro (fresh coriander)*

*SERVES 4–6*

❧ For the marinade: Combine all of the ingredients in a bowl.
❧ For the sauce: In a separate bowl, mix all the ingredients well.
❧ Marinate the beef for 15 minutes.
❧ Heat 3–4 tablespoons of oil in a pan. Fry the vermicelli until brown, drain, transfer to a serving platter, and keep warm.
❧ Heat the remaining oil in a wok or skillet (frying pan). Add the beef and fry for 5 minutes, stirring to avoid sticking. Remove the beef, drain, and set aside.
❧ Drain all but 1 tablespoon of oil from the wok and reheat. Add the garlic, ginger, and chili. Add the sauce and bring to a boil. Return the beef to the wok and add the cilantro. When it returns to a boil, pour over the vermicelli and serve.

a boil. Add the bean sprouts and boil for 30 seconds. Remove, drain, and set aside.
❧ Drop the noodles into the boiling water. When the water returns to a boil, add 1/3 cup (3 fl oz/90 ml) of cold water and cook for 3–4 minutes. Stir the noodles to separate. Remove, rinse under cold water, drain, and set aside.
❧ Heat 3–4 tablespoons of oil in a wok or skillet (frying pan). Fry the noodles until lightly browned, approximately 10 seconds. Remove, drain, and transfer to a serving dish.
❧ Heat the remaining oil in a separate wok or skillet (frying pan). Add the pork, stirring to avoid sticking, and fry for 10 seconds. Remove and set aside.
❧ Drain all but 1–2 tablespoons of oil from the pan and reheat. Add the ginger and garlic. Return the pork and add the bean sprouts to the pan, and stir-fry for 30 seconds. Add the sauce and bring to a boil. Pour over the noodles and serve.

## HAI YUK E-FU MIN

### E-FU NOODLES WITH CRAB MEAT

*You can make your own E-fu noodles, by steaming egg noodles and then frying them. But today E-fu noodles are available in packaged form and are just as delicious. This Cantonese dish is very tasty, with fresh crab meat lending a smooth contrast to the fried noodles.*

8 oz (250 g) E-fu *noodles*
6 tablespoons groundnut (peanut) oil
2 cups (16 fl oz/500 ml) chicken broth (stock)
1 tablespoon oyster sauce
1 tablespoon dark soy sauce
1 teaspoon finely chopped garlic
1 teaspoon finely chopped ginger
6 oz (185 g) cooked crab meat
1/2 teaspoon salt
1/2 teaspoon sugar
1/2 teaspoon aromatic or cider vinegar
1/2 teaspoon ground black pepper
1 teaspoon cornstarch (cornflour)
1 egg white
1 teaspoon Chinese rice wine
4 oz (125 g) Chinese chives, chopped

*SERVES 4–6*

❡ Drop the noodles in a large pan of boiling water, cook until soft, about 3 minutes. Remove, drain, and set aside.
❡ Heat 3–4 tablespoons oil in a wok or skillet (frying pan). Add the noodles and stir-fry briefly.
❡ Mix 1 cup (8 fl oz/250 ml) broth with the oyster sauce and soy sauce. Add to the noodles and cook until all of the liquid has been absorbed. Transfer to a serving dish, cover, and set aside.
❡ Heat the remaining oil in the wok. Add the garlic and ginger. When the aroma rises, add the crab meat and stir-fry for 10 seconds.
❡ Mix the remaining broth with the salt, sugar, vinegar, pepper, and cornstarch. Bring the mixture to a boil and stir in the egg white. Add the wine and pour over the noodles. Sprinkle with chives and serve.

## TAN TAN MIN

### TAN-TAN NOODLES

*The word tan-tan means "carrying on the shoulder." The noodle-seller would carry his boxes of fresh noodles on his shoulder, delivering them from house to house. In this simple but spicy dish from Sichuan, the combination of pickled turnip, scallions, garlic, and ginger gives the noodles a "bouncy" taste—rather like the bouncing footsteps of the* tan-tan *man.*

For sauce A:
2 tablespoons chopped dried shrimp (prawns)
2 tablespoons chopped pickled turnip
2 tablespoons chopped scallion (spring onion)
1 tablespoon chopped garlic
1 tablespoon chopped ginger
For sauce B:
2 tablespoons light soy sauce
1 tablespoon dark soy sauce
1 tablespoon sugar

1–2 tablespoons chili oil
2 tablespoons aromatic or cider vinegar
1 tablespoon Chinese rice wine
1 tablespoon sesame oil
6 tablespoons water
For the noodles:
2 tablespoons groundnut (peanut) oil
8 oz (250 g) wheat noodles
4 cups (1 qt/1 l) chicken broth (stock)

SERVES 4–6

❡ For sauce A: Mix all the ingredients together in a bowl.
❡ For sauce B: In a separate bowl, mix together all of the ingredients until well combined.

❡ Heat the oil in a pan. Add sauce A and cook over medium–low heat for 1 minute. Add sauce B and cook for 1 minute. Remove from heat and set aside.
❡ Bring a large pan of water to a boil. Drop in the noodles and return to a boil. Add ⅓ cup (3 fl oz/ 90 ml) cold water and cook for 3–4 minutes. With a slotted spoon, remove the noodles from the pan, rinse under cold water, and drain the noodles, but do not drain the water from the pan. Return the water to a boil, return the noodles, and cook for 30 seconds. Remove, drain, and divide into 4 bowls.
❡ Bring the chicken broth to a boil. Pour over the noodles, and spoon the sauce on top. Serve.

*Left: Hai Yuk E-fu Min; right: Tan Tan Min*

## JAR CHEUNG MIN

*NOODLES WITH PORK PEKING-STYLE*

*Lesser restaurants will try to scrimp on this dish by grinding (mincing) the pork, but the meat should really be diced into good-size cubes.*

3–4 tablespoons groundnut (peanut) oil
1 tablespoon chopped garlic
2 oz (60 g) bamboo shoots, cut into ½-inch (1-cm) cubes
6 oz (185 g) pork fillet, cut into ½-inch (1-cm) cubes
2 tablespoons sweet flour paste (available at Chinese stores)
2 tablespoons light soy sauce
1 red chili, seeded and cut into small rings
5 cups (1¼ qt/1.25 l) chicken broth (stock)
6 oz (185 g) dry thick wheat noodles
1 cucumber, finely shredded
1 tablespoon chopped scallion (spring onion)

*SERVES 4*

❡ Heat the oil in a wok or skillet (frying pan). Add the garlic, bamboo shoots, and pork, and stir-fry over medium heat for 1 minute. Add the sweet flour paste, soy sauce, and chili, and stir to mix. When the aroma rises, stir in 1 cup (8 fl oz/250 ml) of the chicken broth. Bring to a boil, then simmer for 2 minutes, stirring constantly. Transfer to a bowl and set aside.

❡ In a large pan, bring the remaining chicken broth to a boil, then divide into four serving bowls.

❡ Bring a large pan of water to a boil. Drop in the noodles, and when the water returns to a boil, add ⅓ cup (3 fl oz/90 ml) of cold water. Cook for 8 minutes. Remove the noodles from the pan, rinse, and drain the noodles, but do not drain the water from the pan. Return the noodles to the pan of boiling water and cook for 45 seconds. Remove, drain, and divide amongst the bowls with the chicken broth.

❡ Place some shredded cucumber on the noodles and pour the pork mixture on top. Add the scallion and serve.

---

### STICKY RICE

Glutinous rice, known colloquially as "sticky rice," is a special type of rice with a high starch content — so much so that the grains stick together when cooked. It is used extensively in Chinese sweets, in dim sum dishes, and in several recipes based on curries. Fermented sticky rice is the basis for rice wine, made in distilleries.
Cooking no may, as sticky rice is called in Chinese, is simple. It should be soaked overnight in water with a bit of salt, then drained and cooked like conventional rice.

---

## CHEE MA HAR MIN

*NOODLES WITH SHRIMP IN SESAME SAUCE*

*Nothing could be simpler, more filling, or more delicious than this Teochiu recipe. If you feel like a one-dish meal, then this is the answer.*

For the sauce:
3 tablespoons sesame paste
2 tablespoons light soy sauce
1 tablespoon aromatic or cider vinegar
2 teaspoons sugar
1 tablespoon Chinese rice wine
1½ cups (12 fl oz/375 ml) chicken broth (stock)
1 tablespoon cornstarch (cornflour)
For the marinade:
½ egg white
1 teaspoon salt
½ teaspoon pepper
1 tablespoon cornstarch (cornflour)
For the noodles and shrimp:
8 oz (250 g) uncooked shrimp (green prawns), heads removed, peeled, deveined, cleaned, and patted dry
3½ cups (27 fl oz/840 ml) cold water
8 oz (250 g) egg noodles
4–6 tablespoons groundnut (peanut) oil
4 oz (125 g) button mushrooms (champignons)

*SERVES 4–6*

❡ For the sauce: Mix all of the ingredients together in a bowl.

❡ For the marinade: Mix all of the ingredients together in a bowl and marinate the shrimp for at least 15 minutes.

❡ In a medium-sized pan, bring 3 cups (24 fl oz/750 ml) of the water to a rapid boil. Add the shrimp, cook briefly, drain, and set aside.

❡ Bring a large pan of water to a rapid boil and drop in the noodles. When the water returns to a boil, add the remaining ⅓ cup (3 fl oz/90 ml) cold water. Simmer the noodles for 5 minutes, stirring to separate. Remove the noodles from the pan, drain, and rinse with cold water, but do not drain the pan. Return the noodles to the pan and simmer for 30 seconds. Remove and drain.

❡ Place on a serving platter and toss with 2–3 tablespoons of heated oil. Set aside.

❡ Heat the remaining 2–3 tablespoons of oil in a wok or skillet (frying pan), and stir-fry the mushrooms for 1 minute. Add the sauce and bring to a boil.

❡ Add the shrimp and cook for 30 seconds. Pour the shrimp and sauce over the noodles.

❡ Serve immediately.

*Top: Chee Ma Har Min; bottom: Jar Cheung Min*

# BREADS

In the north of China, bread made from wheat flour is eaten with most meals. This bread comes mainly in the form of buns, made from leavened dough, which are steamed instead of baked. Most buns are small, little more than a few mouthfuls, and often filled with sweet or savory ingredients or with sweet lotus seed paste, egg custard, or mashed sweetened red beans. These filled buns are popular items on the *dim sum* cart. One of the most enjoyable is *cha siu bao*, filled with roast meat in a sweet bean sauce; the top of these buns split as they cook, revealing their sweet red filling.

**Plain steamed buns**, *bao*, or bread rolls: These are used to mop up gravy and supplement the meal in place of rice. A plain *bao* is a simple roll of dough, about 6 inches (15 cm) long, snowy white, and springy to the touch when cooked, fine textured, and dryish to eat.

**Steamed "snail breads"** (*lwo sz juan*): These are a little more complicated to make. They are made by winding fine strips of dough into little bundles before steaming.

**"Silver thread" bread** (*yin sz juan*): This is made by wrapping a bundle of dough strips within a thin sheet of dough. The finished roll is a smooth oval on the inside, with layered threads within. They are sometimes deep-fried, or fried and then glazed with sugar syrup to give them a sticky golden exterior.

**Steamed "flower" buns:** These accompany crisp-fried poultry, and are made by shaping small pieces of dough into disks which are folded in half before steaming. As they expand, the layers open up like a flower bud. A larger version of this folded bun is served with the central Chinese dish, "honey-glazed ham."

**"Family cake":** This is a circular unleavened bread pan-cooked without oil and cut into wedges. It is served as a snack with green vegetables or bean sprouts and is a favorite with children. Similar in preparation is the crisp, chewy, layered "scallion (spring onion) bread," *ts'ung yu ping*. Wander down any small lane in the center of Shanghai and you're bound to come across a vendor with a pile of warm disks of scallion bread ready for an appreciative customer.

**Mandarin pancakes:** When the lacquered amber skin of a Peking duck is carved into bite-size squares, it is packed onto wafer-fine disks of soft bread like small, slightly chewy crêpes called "Mandarin pancakes," *bo ping*, and sometimes "lotus pad" pancakes for their round, flat shape, and are so thin that they are cooked in pairs to prevent them tearing.

**Sesame flavored pocket breads:** These look like flat golden spectacle cases, and accompany dishes of spicy shredded meat cooked with pickled vegetables. The meat is packed into the bread to eat like a sandwich.

**Sweet buns:** Some sweet buns made with a flaky style of pastry using lard as the shortening, are oven-baked, as is the Cantonese "moon cake," prepared to celebrate the moon festival. Other types of bread and cake are deep-fried, including the long, double-layered *you tiao* crullers that resemble elongated doughnuts. They are sliced to float on bowls of breakfast *congee*.

**Sweet "long-life" buns:** These are dough filled with lotus seed paste, formed into peach shapes and tinted with pink food coloring. They are usually served at Chinese New Year.

*1. steamed rolls; 2. stuffed buns; 3. glazed "silver thread" buns; 4. scallion breads; 5. fried you tiao crullers; 6. custard filled buns; 7. steamed rolls; 8. glazed baked lotus cakes; 9. cha siu bao; 10. steamed "snail" bread*

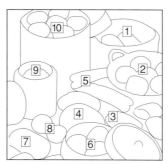

## Ngau Sung Chau Fan

### FRIED RICE WITH GROUND BEEF

*Nothing is ever wasted in the Cantonese kitchen: When housewives trim beef from the butcher, they save the shreds of fat and meat. The same goes for leftover rice: It is saved to be used in a dish like this. Leftover rice is the best kind for frying, since the grains separate when chilled overnight.*

For the marinade:
1 teaspoon salt
1 teaspoon sugar
1 teaspoon Chinese rice wine
1 teaspoon cornstarch (cornflour)
1 tablespoon water
1 tablespoon groundnut (peanut) oil
For the beef:
3 oz (90 g) beef round steak, ground (minced)
3–4 tablespoons groundnut (peanut) oil
1 tablespoons shredded ginger
1 tablespoon chopped garlic
1½ cups (9 oz/280 g) raw rice, cooked and cooled, or 4 cups (10 oz/315 g) cold cooked rice
2 tablespoons light soy sauce
2 teaspoons dark soy sauce
3–4 tablespoons chicken broth (stock)
2 tablespoons scallions (spring onions), chopped

*SERVES 4–6*

❦ For the marinade: Combine all of the ingredients in a bowl.
❦ Marinate the beef for 5 minutes.
❦ Heat the oil in a wok or skillet (frying pan) and add the ginger and garlic. When the aroma rises, add the beef, stirring to separate. Add the cooked rice, 1 cup (2½ oz/75 g) at a time, and continue stirring. Add the soy sauces, chicken broth, and scallions, and stir-fry for 3 minutes. Serve.

## Chai Chau Fan

### VEGETARIAN FRIED RICE

*I've mentioned several vegetables in the ingredients, but you can use whatever vegetables are at hand. What makes the dish memorable are the pine nuts — which add a crunchy texture to this healthy, delicious dish. You can also substitute almonds or groundnuts (peanuts) for the pine nuts.*

*Top: Chai Chau Fan; bottom: Ngau Sung Chau Fan*

4 pieces dried wood ear fungus, soaked in water to cover, drained, stems removed, and diced; with soaking liquid reserved
½ teaspoon salt
1 teaspoon sugar
3–4 tablespoons groundnut (peanut) oil
1 tablespoon chopped ginger
2 tablespoons fresh green peas, blanched or frozen peas, thawed
2 tablespoons carrots, diced and blanched
2 tablespoons button mushrooms (champignons), diced and blanched
1½ cups (9 oz/280 g) raw rice, or 4 cups (10 oz/315 g) cold, cooked rice
2 tablespoons light soy sauce
2 teaspoons dark soy sauce
2 tablespoons roasted pine nuts

*SERVES 4–6*

❦ In a small pan, place the black mushrooms with the soaking liquid, salt, and ½ teaspoon sugar. Cook over low heat until the liquid is reduced to one-third. Transfer to a bowl and set aside.
❦ Heat the oil in a wok or skillet (frying pan) and add the ginger. When the aroma rises, add the peas, carrots, and button mushrooms, and stir-fry over medium heat for 30 seconds.
❦ Add the rice, 1 cup (2½ oz/75 g) at a time, and continue stirring. Add the soy sauces and the remaining sugar.
❦ Add the black mushrooms with their liquid to the wok, and stir-fry for 3 minutes. Add the pine nuts, and mix well.
❦ Serve immediately.

---

### CHINESE WILD RICE SHOOTS

*Gau sun is commonly known as wild rice, although it is not related to rice botanically. Like American wild rice, gau sun is actually a perennial aquatic grass that is found growing wild in pools or low marshy areas.*

*In Chinese groceries, the whole stem is sold individually. The leaves must be discarded and the green zest (rind) peeled. The pith, which tastes something like hearts of palm and has a moist texture, is then cut and shredded for use. Gau sun is usually served stir-fried with beef or pork.*

*While the Chinese never use gau sun as a substitute for rice, there is no harm in adding some to ordinary rice for a different texture. The only caveat is that it should be cooked about one-third longer than rice.*

---

*Top: Bow Fan; left: Dong Ku Gai Lup Fan; right: Sheung Cheung Fan*

## DONG KU GAI LUP FAN

*RICE WITH DICED CHICKEN AND MUSHROOMS*

*What I particularly like in this rather ordinary dish is the extraordinary aroma, which comes from the use of fragrant shiitake mushrooms.*

For the marinade:
*1 tablespoon light soy sauce*
*1 teaspoon dark soy sauce*
*1 teaspoon sugar*
*1 teaspoon Chinese rice wine*
*1¹/₂ teaspoons cornstarch (cornflour)*

*1 tablespoon water*
For the chicken and rice:
*8 oz (250 g) chicken breast, cut into ¹/₂-inch (1-cm) cubes*
*2 cups (10 oz/315 g) long-grain rice*
*1 teaspoon salt*
*2 teaspoons groundnut (peanut) oil*
*4 cups (1 qt/1 l) chicken broth (stock)*
*3 dried mushrooms, soaked for 30 minutes, drained, stems discarded, and cut into ¹/₄-inch (0.5-cm) shreds*
*3–4 slices ginger*
*2 scallions (spring onions), white part only, cut into 1-inch (2.5-cm) lengths*

*SERVES 4–6*

## SHEUNG CHEUNG FAN

### RICE WITH PORK AND DUCK LIVER SAUSAGES

*This dish provides a good excuse to sample some of the various sausages that can be seen hanging in Chinese butchers' shops. The duck liver sausage is soft, the pork is chewy; and both are delicious.*

2 cups (10 oz/215 g) long-grain rice
2 links pork sausage
2 links duck-liver sausage
1 tablespoon dark soy sauce diluted with 1 tablespoon water

*SERVES 4–6*

❡ Wash the rice and drain. Place in a clay pot or saucepan and add water to cover 1 inch (2.5 cm) above the rice. Place the sausages on top and bring to a boil over high heat. Reduce the heat to medium and cook until the water evaporates to the level of the rice.
❡ Cover and cook over very low heat for 10 minutes. Remove the sausages and set aside. Cover and cook over high heat for 30 seconds. Reduce the heat to very low and cook for 10 minutes.
❡ Cut the pork sausages into thin slices and cut the duck-liver sausages into ¼-inch thick pieces. Mix with the rice, add the soy sauce, and serve.

## BOW FAN

### RICE

*Everyone has a favorite way to cook rice, and this is mine. The groundnut (peanut) oil and salt are optional, though I think they add considerably to the taste. You can use Chinese, Indian, or Thai long-grain rice — or whatever type you prefer.*

2½ cups (15 oz/450 g) long-grain rice
1 teaspoon salt
2 teaspoon groundnut (peanut) oil

*SERVES 6–8*

❡ Wash the rice and drain well. Mix the rice with the salt and oil.
❡ Place the rice in a clay pot or saucepan. Add water to cover 1 inch (2.5 cm) above the rice.
❡ Bring the mixture to a boil over high heat, reduce the heat to medium, and cook until the water has almost evaporated. Cover and cook over very low heat for 10 minutes. Turn the heat to high and cook for 30 seconds, then reduce the heat to very low and cook for 10 minutes. Serve.

❡ For the marinade: Combine all of the ingredients in a bowl.
❡ Marinate the chicken for 15 minutes.
❡ Wash the rice and drain. Mix with the salt and oil, and place in a clay pot or saucepan. Add the broth to cover 1¼ inches (3 cm) above the rice. Bring to a boil over high heat, reduce to medium heat, and cook until the broth evaporates to the level of the rice.
❡ Spread the chicken, mushrooms, ginger, and scallions over the rice. Cover and cook over very low heat for 10 minutes. Stir to mix well. Cover again and turn heat to high for 30 seconds. Reduce the heat to very low and cook for 10 minutes.
❡ Serve immediately.

## Noodles

Noodles, being a manufactured ingredient, come in many styles, made from the various grains that grow in China, mainly wheat and rice, as well as ingredients like sweet potato and mung beans.

Noodles are erroneously closely associated with North China, since little rice is grown there and noodles are a basic fare. But no full southern meal is complete without at least one dish of noodles.

Noodles can be cooked in a soup, they can be fried, boiled, steamed, or served as the base for a variety of meats, fish, shellfish, and vegetables. They can be a main family meal or a snack at any time of the day. And at Chinese New Year and other important occasions such as weddings and birthdays, the banquet would be incomplete without "long life" noodles—long strands uncut and carefully unbroken during cooking. Noodles are so popular in many parts of China that whole restaurants are

**Da mee:** Literally "hit noodles," these are made from wheat flour "beaten" out into sheets with a roller and cut into strips.

**Egg noodles:** Made from wheat flour and eggs, egg noodles have a bright yellow color and rich flavor. They are more expensive than the golden noodles of similar appearance, made with lye-water—water boiled with a pinch of sodium hydroxide—which should be labeled "made without eggs." They must be rinsed before use.

**Handmade noodles:** These are produced by skilled noodle-makers who begin with a ball of dough, kneaded to just the right consistency. This is then grasped at the edges by both hands and the center of the ball swung away from the maker to stretch into a long coil. The two ends are brought together in one hand, the other end taken up and the dough swung again. This action is repeated over and over until the dough has been stretched and separated into long strands of snowy white noodles as thick or thin as are required. They need just two or three minutes in boiling water to be ready for the table.

**Buckwheat noodles:** These thin, gray noodles are popular in Beijing, Tianjin, and Manchuria. They are best in soups, but should be boiled for a few minutes longer than egg noodles.

In Sichuan province, noodles are made from a variety of dried beans and from root vegetables such as yams or sweet potato. These yield noodles that are chewy and semi-transparent, with a slippery texture and little taste, but the ability to readily absorb the flavors that surround them. And in Sichuan that usually means fiery hot flavors like the chili-laden sauce that accompanies their popular fine wheat noodles "*dan dan*."

**Rice noodles:** These are soft textured and bland in taste. The best are those bought fresh from the markets and cooked within hours of purchase. Rice dough is sold precut into noodles or in sheets, to cut into noodles of widths to suit the recipe. They require just a minute or two in boiling water, or a quick rinse and then into the wok for stir-frying. The tourist province of Guilin has been noted for its rice noodles for centuries, as is the beer-making town of Shaho in Guangdong (Canton), where they use a formula dating back to the thirteenth century for making rice noodles with their excellent rice flour and mountain waters.

**Dried rice noodles:** These are made of a rice dough, machine rolled or extruded into flat ribbons or fine vermicelli threads. Boiled, the latter are melt-in-the-mouth tender. Crisp-fried they puff into little cumulus clouds of feather lightness for garnishing all kinds of dishes.

**E-fu noodles:** These are egg noodles which have been boiled in chicken-flavored broth (stock), then fried crisp. They are then dried into large airy tangles of gold, which can be found hanging from a rail above any good noodle makers' shop counter.

*1. rice noodles; 2. fresh rice ribbon noodles; 3. dried and fresh wheatflour (Peking) noodles; 4. dried and fresh fine egg noodles; 5. dried and fresh flat egg noodles; 6. fried (E-fu) noodles*

devoted to serving just noodle dishes, usually specializing in one kind of noodle, cooked in a myriad of ways.

**"Family noodles":** These are made with unbleached wheat starch flour simply mixed with water and salt.

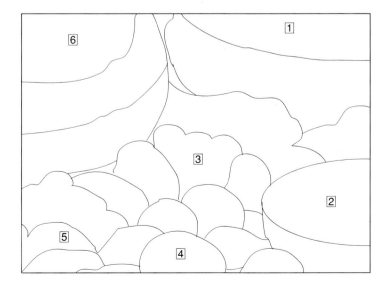

## NGAU YUK CHAU MIN

*FRIED EGG NOODLES WITH BEEF AND BELL PEPPERS*

*This is a Shanghai dish, and the Shanghai name means "Yellow On Both Sides." There are, of course, many ways to fry noodles, but this recipe ensures that they are crispy on both sides, golden brown, and very tasty.*

For the marinade :
½ teaspoon salt
½ teaspoon sugar
1 teaspoon Chinese rice wine
1 teaspoon cornstarch (cornflour)
1 tablespoon water
For the noodles:
4 oz (125 g) beef fillet, cut into slivers
1 cup (8 oz/250 g) egg noodles
⅓ cup (3 fl oz/90 ml) cold water
1 cup (8 fl oz/250 ml) groundnut (peanut) oil
1 red bell pepper (capsicum), cut into 1-inch (2.5-cm) squares
1 green bell pepper (capsicum), cut into 1-inch (2.5-cm) squares
1 tablespoon chopped garlic
6 slices ginger
2 tablespoons mashed fermented black beans
1 tablespoon light soy sauce
1 teaspoon dark soy sauce
1 tablespoon oyster sauce
1 teaspoon sugar
1 teaspoon Chinese rice wine
1½ cups (12 fl oz/375 ml) chicken broth (stock)
1 tablespoon cornstarch (cornflour)

*SERVES 4–6*

❡ For the marinade: Combine ingredients in a bowl.
❡ Marinate the beef for 15 minutes.
❡ Bring a pan of water to a boil and add the noodles. When the water returns to a boil, add the cold water and cook for 3–4 minutes, stirring to separate. Remove, rinse under cold water, and drain.
❡ Heat 3–4 tablespoons of oil in a wok or skillet (frying pan) and fry the noodles over medium heat until lightly browned. Place the noodles on a serving platter and set aside.
❡ Heat the remaining oil in the wok and add the beef, stirring to separate. Remove the beef from the pan, drain, and set aside.
❡ Drain all but 2–3 tablespoons of oil from the wok and reheat. Add the peppers and stir-fry for 1 minute. Add the garlic, ginger, and black beans. Mix all the remaining ingredients in a bowl. When the aroma rises from the wok, add the soy sauce mixture and bring to a boil. Add the beef to the wok and mix well. Pour over the noodles and serve.

## GAI SZE TONG MIN

*EGG NOODLES WITH CHICKEN AND MUSHROOMS IN SOUP*

*This homemade "pasta" dish can be one of the most creative recipes. There are so many types of noodle soup that most chefs put in whatever vegetables, spices, and herbs suit their taste, to create their own personal version.*

For the marinade:
1 teaspoon salt
1 teaspoon sugar
1 teaspoon Chinese rice wine
2 teaspoons cornstarch (cornflour)
1 tablespoon water
For the noodles:
4 oz (125 g) chicken breast, cut into 2-inch (5-cm) long shreds
1 cup (8 oz/250 g) egg noodles
⅓ cup (3 fl oz/90 ml) cold water
2–3 tablespoons groundnut (peanut) oil
1 tablespoon shredded ginger
4 oz (125 g) cabbage, cut into 2-inch (5-cm) long shreds
2 dried black mushrooms, soaked in warm water for 1 hour, drained, stems discarded, and shredded
4 cups (1 qt/1 l) chicken broth (stock)
1 tablespoon light soy sauce
1 teaspoon dark soy sauce
½ teaspoon sesame oil
1 teaspoon Chinese rice wine
1 tablespoon finely chopped scallion (spring onion)

*SERVES 4–6*

❡ For the marinade: Combine all of the ingredients in a bowl.
❡ Marinate the chicken for 15 minutes.
❡ Bring a pan of water to a boil and add the noodles. When the water returns to a boil, add the cold water and cook for 3–4 minutes, stirring to separate. Remove the noodles from the pan, rinse under cold water and drain the noodles, but do not drain the water from the pan. Reheat the water to boiling, return the noodles to the pan and cook for 1 minute. Remove, drain, and divide into bowls. Set aside.
❡ Heat the oil in a wok or skillet (frying pan), and add the ginger, cabbage, and mushrooms. Stir-fry for 30 seconds. Add 1 cup (8 fl oz/250 ml) broth and cook over medium–low heat for 3 minutes. Add the chicken, soy sauces, sesame oil, and wine. Cook over medium heat for 1½ minutes. Divide and place on top of the noodles. Sprinkle the scallion on top.
❡ Bring the remaining 3 cups (24 fl oz/750 ml) of broth to a boil. Pour over the noodles and serve.

*Top: Ngau Yuk Chau Min; bottom: Gai Sze Tong Min*

*Left: Yuk Sze Mun Fun Sze; right: Won Ton Min*

## YUK SZE MUN FUN SZE

*BRAISED GREEN BEAN NOODLES WITH DRIED SHRIMP, PORK, AND WINTER MELON*

*This is an excellent pasta-style dish to go with rice. You can serve it for* dim sum *or as a main course.*

For the marinade:
*1/2 teaspoon salt*
*1/2 teaspoon sugar*
*1 teaspoon cornstarch (cornflour)*
*1 tablespoon water*
For the noodles:
*4 oz (125 g) pork fillet, cut into 2-inch (5-cm) long shreds*
*3–4 tablespoons groundnut (peanut) oil*
*1 tablespoon shredded ginger*
*1 oz (30 g) dried shrimp (prawns), soaked in cold water for 30 minutes, and drained*
*6–8 oz (185–250 g) winter melon, shredded*
*3 cups (24 fl oz/750 ml) chicken broth (stock)*
*4 oz (125 g) green bean noodles, soaked in cold water for 30 minutes, and drained*
*1 teaspoon salt*
*1 tablespoon oyster sauce*
*1 teaspoon Chinese rice wine*
*1/2 teaspoon sesame oil*
*1 1/2 tablespoons cornstarch (cornflour), diluted in 1 tablespoon water*

*SERVES 4–6*

❡ For the marinade: Combine all ingredients in bowl.
❡ Marinate the pork for 15 minutes.
❡ Heat the oil in a pan. Add the ginger, shrimp, and winter melon, and stir-fry for 1 minute. Add the broth. Cover and cook over medium heat for 2 minutes.
❡ Add the noodles. Cover and cook over medium heat for 1 minute.
❡ Add the pork, salt, oyster sauce, wine, and

sesame oil, stirring to separate the pork. Cover and cook over medium heat for 1 minute. Stir in the cornstarch, cook for 1 minute, and serve.

## WON TON MIN

*WON TON AND NOODLE SOUP*

*While this is a soup, it is regarded as a kind of liquid* dim sum *or a full meal. You can have it for breakfast, lunch, or even as a sort of "high tea."*

For the marinade:
*1/2 teaspoon salt*
*1/2 teaspoon sugar*
*1/4 teaspoon sesame oil*
*1/4 teaspoon cornstarch (cornflour)*
For the *won ton* and noodles:
*8 oz (250 g) uncooked shrimp (green prawn) meat, coarsely chopped*
*36 won ton wrappers*
*1 egg, beaten*
*1 3/4 oz (50 g) egg noodles*
*1/3 cup (3 fl oz/90 ml) cold water*
*4–5 cups (1–1 1/4 qt/1–1.25 l) chicken broth (stock)*
*1 tablespoon light soy sauce*
*1 teaspoon salt*
*1 teaspoon pepper*
*1/2 teaspoon sesame oil*
*2 oz (60 g) chives, cut into 1-inch (2.5-cm) lengths*

*SERVES 4–6*

❡ For the marinade: Mix all the ingredients in a bowl.
❡ Marinate the shrimp for 30 minutes.
❡ Place 1 1/2 teaspoons of shrimp in the middle of a won ton wrapper. Brush the shrimp with egg and enclose the *won ton* by pleating the edges of the wrapper together, shaping it like a bag. Repeat with the remaining wrappers and set aside.
❡ Drop the noodles into a large pan of boiling water. When the water returns to a boil, add the cold water and cook for 3–4 minutes. Remove the noodles from the pan, rinse under cold water, and drain, but do not drain the pan. Return the noodles to the pan and cook for 30 seconds. Remove the noodles, drain, and divide among soup bowls, but do not drain the pan.
❡ Drop the *won tons* into the pan of boiling water and cook until they float. Remove, drain, and place on top of the noodles.
❡ In another large pan, bring the broth to a boil. Add the soy sauce, salt, pepper, and sesame oil. Add the chives and cook for 1 minute. Divide the liquid among the soup bowls and serve.

*In rice box: standard short-grain white rice; left: glutinous white rice; center front: rice cakes in bamboo leaf wrappers; upper left: (in bowl) wild rice, (top on platter) brown rice; bowls on right: (top) steamed white rice, (bottom) "sticky rice"*

# RICE

The Chinese favor the short-grained varieties of rice, which cook plump and fluffy, but with just enough stickiness to hold together on the chopsticks. They are particular about their rice and are happy, where economically possible, to use rice from other countries if it is better than their own.

Like many cooking techniques used in China, their method of cooking rice is not only fuel effective, but gives the best results. Rice and a prescribed measure of water is placed in the pot, the water quickly brought to the boil, then the heat turned to its lowest point. The rice "steams" until it has absorbed all of the liquid in the pot and is plump and fluffy without a trace of sogginess. This technique also applies to the now popular electric rice cooker which is also used for boiling soups, simmering *congee* and steaming dishes. A practical appliance, it not only cooks perfect rice every time, but leaves the gas (or, still, in rural parts of China and in most restaurants the charcoal or wood-burning fire) free for cooking other dishes.

Plain white rice is served with almost every day-to-day meal in southern and Central China as the traditional base element of the meal, even if noodles or bread are also served. In the North, however, it is more the reverse, with noodles or bread providing the starch or grain carbohydrate content of the meal. At a banquet or important meal, rice and noodles are generally not served until the end of the main courses, if at all. This signifies that the host has not skimped on his expenditure by including "filling" starch dishes in the menu. On these occasions the rice is inevitably "fried rice" redolent of chopped pork, shrimp (prawns), peas, and egg.

As important a breakfast food as the Western cereal, many Chinese enjoy a filling bowl of *juk* or *congee* at the start of the day. Hundreds of thousands of bowls of rice boiled with water, flavored with scraps of meat (often liver), ginger, fish, and chopped scallions (spring onions) are slurped piping hot from Chinese porcelain spoons in homes, at street stalls, and in restaurants all over China, except in the North where its counterpart has for centuries been made from millet grain.

## CHUNG YAU PAN

*PAN-FRIED SCALLION BREAD*

*This is the favorite dish of many visitors to Beijing restaurants. No matter what else they may order, they often fill up on these delicious scallion rolls. You can, of course, add more onions to taste.*

2 cups (8 oz/250 g) all-purpose (plain) flour
1 teaspoon salt
3/4 cup (6 fl oz/185 ml) cold water
3 tablespoons chopped scallion (spring onion)
1/8 teaspoon five-spice powder
1/2 teaspoon pepper
2 teaspoons sesame oil
1 tablespoon melted lard
2 cups (16 fl oz/500 ml) groundnut (peanut) oil

SERVES 4–6

❡ Sift the flour in a bowl. Add the salt and cold water, and work quickly with the fingers to mix. Knead for about 3 minutes and cover with a cloth. Set aside for 15 minutes.
❡ Mix the scallions with the five-spice powder, pepper, and sesame oil. Set aside.
❡ Divide the dough into 12 pieces. Roll out into 1/4-inch (0.5-cm) thick rectangles on a floured board. Brush with the melted lard and sprinkle with the scallions. Roll up lengthwise and twist to form a spiral. Flatten with the palm.
❡ Heat the oil in a wok or skillet (frying pan). Fry the bread, a few at a time, on both sides over medium heat until golden brown, about 3 minutes. Remove and drain. Serve.

## JING BOU

*CHINESE STEAMED BREAD*

*Northern Chinese have three ways to make bread: steaming, baking, and steaming with quick-frying. Bread isn't really for sandwiches, but it is ideal for soaking up sauces. If you don't care for the sugar in the bread, you can always add a pinch of salt instead.*

5 cups (1 1/4 lb/600 g) all-purpose (plain) flour
1/4 cup (2 oz/60 g) sugar
1 1/2 cups (12 fl oz/375 ml) warm water
1 tablespoon dried yeast
1 tablespoon melted lard
10 cups (2 1/2 qt/2.5 l) water

SERVES 6–8

❡ Sift the flour into a large mixing bowl.
❡ Dissolve the sugar in the water. When dissolved, stir in the yeast. Set aside for 10 minutes.
❡ Add the yeast mixture and the lard to the flour and mix well. Remove from the bowl and knead for 3–4 minutes until smooth.
❡ Roll the dough into a long sausage shape and divide into 24 equal pieces. Flatten each into a thick round shape, about 3 inches (8 cm) in diameter. Press the middle with a chopstick and fold in half. Pinch at the edges to make a bun. Stick a piece of baking parchment (greaseproof paper) on the bottom. Repeat with the remaining dough. Set aside in a warm place to rise for 12–15 minutes.

❡ Bring the water to a boil in a wok or large pan. Arrange the buns in a steamer and set in the wok. Cover, and steam over high heat for 10–12 minutes.

## POK PAN

*CHINESE PANCAKES*

*These are best known with Peking Duck, but the pancake can be used for other dishes as well. For instance, if you have some fish-flavored eggplant from Sichuan, which is quite gooey, you can put some on a pancake and eat it.*

*2 cups (8 oz/250 g) all-purpose (plain) flour*
*¹⁄₃ cup (3 fl oz/90 ml) boiling water*
*¹⁄₃ cup (3 fl oz/90 ml) cold water*

*SERVES 4–6*

❡ Sift the flour in a bowl, make a well in the center, add the boiling water, and mix. Add the cold water a little at a time and stir to mix. Knead for 5 minutes. Cover, and set aside for 25 minutes.
❡ Roll the dough into a long sausage shape. Divide into 12 equal pieces. Roll out each piece on a floured board to form a thin pancake.
❡ Heat a wok or skillet (frying pan). Cook the pancakes on both sides until lightly browned. Cover with a cloth until ready to serve.

*Left: Chung Yau Pan; right: Jing Bou; bottom: Pok Pan*

# NGAU YUK CHUK

## CONGEE WITH GROUND BEEF

*Chicken is not the only accompaniment to* congee. *You can also use beef or pork for variety.*

For the rice:
1 ½ cups (8 oz/250 g) short-grain rice
1 teaspoon salt
1 tablespoon groundnut (peanut) oil
10 cups (2 ½ qt/2.5 l) water
5 cups (1 ¼ qt/1.25 l) chicken broth (stock)
3–4 slices ginger
1 piece dried orange peel (optional)
1 lb (500 g) rump steak, ground (minced)
2 tablespoons chopped scallion (spring onion)
For the marinade:
1 tablespoon light soy sauce
1 tablespoon Chinese rice wine
1 teaspoon salt
1 teaspoon sugar
1 teaspoon sesame oil
2 tablespoons water
1 tablespoon cornstarch (cornflour)

SERVES 6–8

❡ In a large bowl, mix the rice with the salt and oil. Add water to cover ½-inch (0.5 cm) above the rice and soak for 1 hour.
❡ Place the water, broth, ginger, and orange peel in a large pan and bring to a boil. Add the rice and cook over high heat for 15 minutes. Cover the pan loosely, leaving a slit open, and simmer over low heat for 2 hours.
❡ For the marinade: Mix all the ingredients in a bowl. Marinate the beef for 15 minutes. Stir the mixture with a fork for 5 minutes.
❡ Using a teaspoon, scoop the beef into balls and set aside on a lightly greased platter.
❡ Add the beef to the rice and bring to a boil. Divide the mixture among soup bowls, add the scallions, and serve.

# GAI CHUK

## CONGEE WITH CHICKEN

*While this is traditionally a breakfast dish, you don't have to limit yourself. Congee can also be a relaxing late-night supper. Just keep some handy in the refrigerator and, when hunger pangs strike, heat it up for a bedtime snack.*

For the rice:
1 ½ cups (8 oz/250 g) short-grain rice
1 teaspoon salt
1 tablespoon groundnut (peanut) oil
14 cups (3 ½ qt/3.5 l) water
5 cups (1 ¼ qt/1.25 l) chicken broth (stock)
3–4 slices ginger
1 piece dried orange peel (optional)
1 lb (500 g) chicken breast
2 tablespoons chopped scallion (spring onion)
light soy sauce, to taste
pepper, to taste
For the marinade:
2 tablespoons light soy sauce

*Top: Gai Chuk; bottom: Ngau Yuk Chuk*

*1 tablespoon Chinese rice wine*
*1 teaspoon salt*
*1 teaspoon sugar*
*1 teaspoon sesame oil*
*1 tablespoon cornstarch (cornflour)*

*SERVES 6–8*

❡ In a large bowl, mix the rice with the salt and oil. Add water to cover ½ inch (0.5 cm) above the rice and soak for 1 hour.

❡ Place 10 cups (2 ½ qt/2.5 l) of the water, the broth, ginger, and orange peel in a large pan and bring to a boil. Add the rice and cook over high heat for 15 minutes. Cover the pan loosely,

leaving a slit open, and simmer over low heat for 2 hours.

❡ For the marinade: Mix all the ingredients in a bowl. Place the chicken in a dish and marinate for 30 minutes.

❡ Bring the remaining water to a boil in a wok or large pan and place a steaming rack in the middle. Place the dish with the chicken on the rack, cover, and steam for 15 minutes.

❡ Remove the chicken and tear into ¼-inch (0.5-cm) thick shreds. Divide among soup bowls and add the scallions. Pour the rice on top.

❡ Season to taste with light soy sauce and pepper.

❡ Serve immediately.

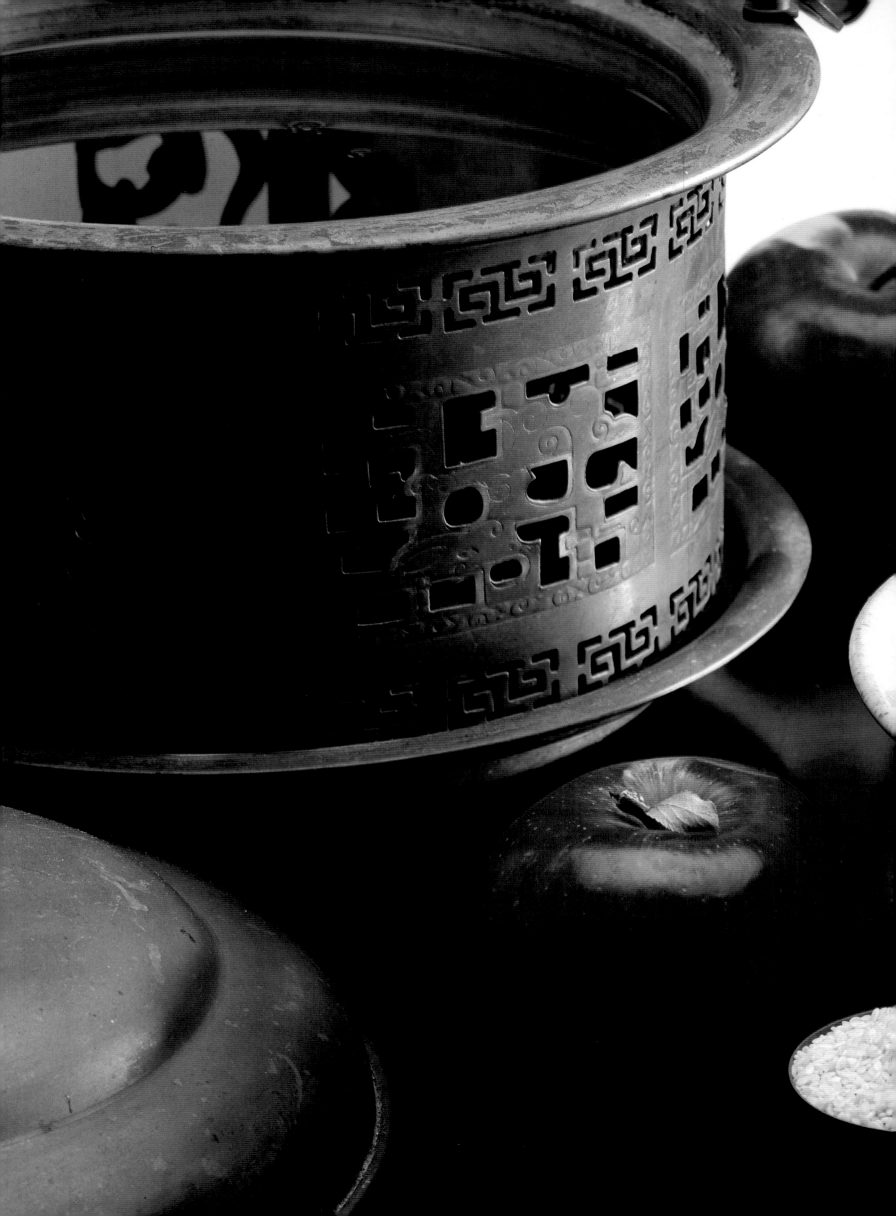

# DESSERTS

# DESSERTS

E XCEPT IN THE NORTH, THE CHINESE HAVE NEVER HAD A SWEET TOOTH. NOTHING MORE IS NEEDED AFTER A FULL MEAL THAN A CUP OF tea, a clear soup, or perhaps some fruit—a few slices of orange, a wedge of chilled melon.

❡ This does not mean that the Chinese do not enjoy sweets. In an average *dim sum* restaurant you might be offered dumplings filled with a sweet custard or a thick, heavily sweetened paste made of boiled lotus seeds or red adzuki beans; glutinous rice dough shaped around a filling of sugar and nuts; wobbly cubes of sweet coconut jelly; or the cooling, popular sweetened bean curd gelatin cubes served with fruit salad.

❡ Cake shops in towns like Suzhou are famed for the variety, colors, and textures of their offerings. A banquet meal will always conclude with a plate of small sweet foods such as tiny pastries: crisp-fried crêpes filled with a sweetened mixture of dates; egg tarts (*darn tat*): rich sweet egg custard encased in light-as-air pastry; or, perhaps, "long-life" buns (*suo tao*) shaped and tinted to resemble peaches.

❡ In the North, desserts play a fundamental role. On the streets of Beijing, Tianjin, and towns all the way to Mongolia, sweet vendors sell apples and berries with a sugar coating hardened into a caramel glaze. A variation on this is found also on the streets in Shanghai. Hot candied fruit is also served in restaurants, and while apple remains the first choice, a wider selection of fruits (in the South perhaps bananas and the intensely fragrant durian) may be offered, with sesame seeds sprinkled into the candy coating. Candied apple fritters are made from slices of apple coated with cornstarch (cornflour), deep-fried, and then fried again with melted sugar. Just before serving, they are plunged into ice water so that the sugar glaze hardens immediately.

❡ A complete texture contrast is found in a dish of sweet white fungus soup and wolfberries, a wrinkled bright red dried berry related to honeysuckle. This imperial delicacy is considered a tonic for the lungs and kidneys. Perhaps the most famous Chinese dessert is based on bird's nest, prized for its rarity and its delicate taste and texture.

❡ An unusual, but highly refreshing dessert, *jeou nang shuei guo keng*, is made from glutinous rice fermented with yeast for a week, then served in a chilled sweet soup with diced fresh fruit.

❡ Sweet warm puddings and creamy desserts are enjoyed in the cooler months. They are often made with ingredients more readily associated with savory food, such as sweet peanut or taro cream. Sweet "sticky rice" packed with candied fruit and nuts is a dessert served at special occasions and goes under the name of "eight treasures rice."

❡ Sweets are also reserved for special family and festival occasions. During New Year, for example, *hai how siu*, a simple concoction of flour, sugar, and sesame seeds, is well known.

*Previous pages: Toffied apples are a toothsome sweet treat not only purchased from street vendors, but also as a delicious end to a meal in your favorite Chinese restaurant.*
BRUCE PEEBLES

*Opposite: Hawkers selling toffied apples in Shaanxi province. Unlike the western tradition, Chinese sweets and desserts are used mostly as snacks, or as* dim sum, *rather than eaten at the end of a meal.* CHINA TOURISM PHOTO LIBRARY/WANG MIAO

# HUNG YAN LO

*ALMOND CREAM*

*Almond Cream is served in most restaurants for dessert. The Chinese prize it for its refreshing taste and the beneficial effect of the almonds on the respiratory system.*

*1½ cups (6 oz/185 g) almonds, peeled*
*1½ cups (12 fl oz/375 ml) water*
*1 cup (8 oz/250 g) sugar*
*¼ cup (1 oz/30 g) rice flour*

*SERVES 4–6*

❧ Pour boiling water over the almonds to cover, and let soak for 2 hours. Drain.
❧ Place the almonds in a blender. Adding 2–3 tablespoons of water at a time, blend 1 cup (8 fl oz /250 ml) of water with the almonds until they are very smooth. Strain through a fine cloth.
❧ Put the almond mixture in a pan and bring to a boil. Add the sugar, stirring to dissolve. Mix the rice flour with ½ cup (4 fl oz/125 ml) of water and slowly stir into the almond mixture to thicken. Return to a boil and serve.

# LIE DUN DARN

*STEAMED EGG AND MILK*

*Even though the Cantonese don't usually eat milk dishes, this sweet dish is always popular in restaurants. You can use evaporated milk, but fresh milk is better.*

*¾ cup (6 oz/185 g) sugar*
*2 cups (16 fl oz/500 ml) milk*
*1 cup (8 fl oz/250 ml) egg whites (about 6–8 eggs)*
*4–6 slices ginger*
*6 cups (1½ qt/1.5 l) water*

*SERVES 4–6*

❧ Dissolve the sugar in the milk over low heat, making sure that it does not boil. Set aside to cool.
❧ When cool, add the milk gradually to the egg whites, stirring to mix well.
❧ Divide the mixture among small bowls. Add 1 slice ginger to each.
❧ Bring the water to a boil in a wok or large pan. Place a steaming rack over it and place the bowls on the rack. Steam for 15 minutes over medium heat.
❧ Serve immediately.

*Top: Hung Yan Lo; bottom: Lie Dun Darn*

*Left: Hung Yan Dou Fu; right: Cho Lie Woo Pan*

# CHO LIE WOO PAN

### PANCAKES FILLED WITH RED DATE PASTE

*This is a popular dessert pancake, a crêpe filled with red dates. In northern China, it is also a dim sum, to be eaten at teatime, and it is also sold by street vendors in Beijing and Tianjin.*

For the date paste:
6 oz (185 g) dried red dates
2 tablespoons lard
3 tablespoons sugar

For the pancakes:
³/₄ cup (4 oz/125 g) all-purpose (plain) flour
1 egg
³/₄ cup (6 fl oz/185 ml) water

Mash the dates through a sieve into a bowl, discarding any skin or pits. Stir enough of the retained liquid into the dates to make a thick paste.

Heat the lard in a small pan, until it melts. Add the sugar and dissolve it over medium heat until the mixture becomes thick and dry. Remove from the heat and set aside.

For the pancakes: Sift the flour into a bowl. Make a hollow in the center and add the egg. Work the egg into the flour and, adding a few tablespoons of water at a time, mix in the water to make a smooth batter.

Coat a skillet (frying pan) with 1–2 teaspoons of oil. Add just enough batter to make a thin pancake. Cook over medium heat until the pancake is quite firm. Turn over and cook the other side. Remove the pancake and set aside. Use the rest of the batter in the same way, adding more oil if needed.

Mix the date paste with the lard and sugar mixture and spread some in the center of a pancake and fold into a rectangular envelope. Seal the edges with wet cornstarch.

Heat 2 tablespoons of oil in a pan. Fry the filled pancakes until lightly browned on each side. Cut into 1-inch (2.5-cm) wide strips and serve.

## HUNG YAN DOU FU

### *ALMOND-FLAVORED "BEAN CURD"*

*The name of this dish is deceptive, as this dish isn't really bean curd at all—it is mock bean curd. It is a common dessert, served in virtually all Chinese restaurants, but rarely at home. Instead of canned fruit salad, you can use litchi (lychee), tangerines (mandarins), or any soft fruit.*

*3 cups (24 fl oz/750 ml) water*
*3 tablespoons powdered agar agar*
*½ cup (4 oz/125 g) sugar*
*¾ cup (6 fl oz/185 ml) sweetened condensed milk*
*1½ teaspoons almond extract (essence)*
*12 oz (375 g) canned fruit salad*

*SERVES 6–8*

Bring the water to a boil in a large pan and add the agar agar and sugar. Lower the heat and cook for 5 minutes, stirring occasionally. Add the condensed milk and almond extract, stirring to mix well.

Pour the mixture into a shallow cake pan. Let cool, then refrigerate until set, about 1 hour. Chill the can of fruit salad at the same time.

When set, cut the "bean curd" into ½-inch (1-cm) cubes and place in serving bowls. Cover with the fruit salad and serve.

*3–4 tablespoons groundnut (peanut) oil*
*cornstarch (cornflour)*

*SERVES 4–6*

For the date paste: Place the dates in a pan, adding water to cover. Boil over medium–low heat until the dates soften. Remove the dates and retain the liquid.

# Fruit

From the freezing deserts of Mongolia to the sub-tropical orchards of Guangzhou, China produces an impressive array of fruit.

In the North, apples, grapes, firm-fleshed pears, peaches, and melons of several varieties, and cherries are all crops which have been cultivated for centuries. Further south, tropical fruits such as pineapples, bananas, coconuts, and the tropical "exotics"—longan, durian, rambutan, mango, jambu (water apple), mangosteen, carambola (star fruit), and litchi (lychee) are grown.

**Apples:** These are grown in the north of China, have little of the crunchy sweetness generally associated with apples, but are esteemed when coated with sugar and served on sticks.

**Durian:** This large, spiny-skinned fruit is prized not only for its unique, almost too sweet flavor, but for its value as an aphrodisiac. This is not a Chinese fruit, but is imported, mainly from Malaysia, as a luxury treat during its short season. Fastidious as most Chinese are in dining, eating durian is an exception. The flesh is simply scooped up with the fingers and popped into the mouth. One caveat about durian: Never drink alcohol with it, as this is said to be a poisonous combination.

**Grapes:** Grapes have grown in China since ancient times, from a native vine, and from the seeds of table and wine grapes brought back by

expeditions westwards by the adventurer Chang Ch'ien in the Han dynasty. Grape juice was an early source of a type of vinegar used for pickling.

**Guavas:** These aromatic fruits, with their rose-hued flesh, grow well in the southern parts of China where they are eaten fresh and pressed for their juice.

**Kumquats and persimmons:** Several fruits are highly regarded by the Chinese for their symbolic association with good fortune. Around Chinese New Year little golden kumquat trees proliferate at market places, as do trays of orange-red persimmons with skin so smooth it almost glows. Their bright color make them the ideal New Year fruit, as it symbolizes joy itself.

**Litchis (lychees):** The exotic tropical fruit of the South include some of the sweetest fruits known to man. Until the early 1980s, one of Hong Kong's most appealing unofficial festivals was the spring Litchi Festival. Families would go into the orchards near the Chinese border where the fruit grew, to fill their bags with the knobbly red fruits with their crisp but jelly-like sweet fruit. Today they rush to the market at the first sighting of new season litchis. They are one of China's few native fruits, though today are raised throughout the Orient. Canned litchis hardly do justice to the fruit, though they are in common use and readily available.

**Longans:** The Chinese call

the longan "the little brother of the litchi." True, this grape-like fruit is smaller than a litchi, but is exceptionally sweet and aromatic. In summer months no fruit salad is complete without them. Dried longan are added, for their sweetness and perfume, to slow-cooked sweet soups.

**Mangoes:** Sweet golden mangoes grow in the far southern sub-tropical region of China, so have been integrated into the Cantonese cuisine, occasionally as an ingredient in stir-fries, and often as a sweet pudding. Few fruits can rival a sweet, ripe mango as an eating experience that borders on the sensual.

**Peaches:** These are one of China's most revered fruits; the name in Chinese means "fairy fruit," since fairies are supposed to live forever and the peach is known in China as the fruit of immortality. The bark, fruit, flowers, and even sap of the peach tree is used by Chinese doctors for a range of diseases.

**Pears:** Marco Polo wrote of the luscious white pears he disovered in his travels through China. Firm and crisp as an apple, the Chinese or Tientsin pear is enjoyed raw, can be shredded into salads where it does not suffer the fate of apples or pears by turning brown, or poached in sugar syrup to serve as a dessert. This buff-green skinned pear is of the same family as the Japanese pear or *nashi*.

**Plums:** These are preferred dried as a salty, palate-

stimulating snack, rather than eaten fresh, and are made into the classic plum sauce to flavor anything from Peking Duck to braised fish.

**Sweet melons:** These are grown throughout China. In the spring, the streets of Beijing and Tianjin are filled with luscious ripe watermelons. Melons similar to the honeydew and cantaloupe (rockmelon) are also grown, but rarely have the sweetness of their Western counterparts.

**Tangerines (mandarins) and oranges:** These have been known in China for 2,500 years, originating in Northwest China. This golden fruit, symbolizing prosperity, is often served after a special banquet. The dried peel of tangerines is used extensively in Chinese cooking, adding a sweet taste and aroma to soups, braised meat dishes, and vegetables, as well as some dishes which use curry spices. Another citrus fruit occasionally eaten in China is the dry-fleshed pomelo which resembles a grapefruit but is not as tart.

*1. oranges; 2. red grapes; 3. durian; 4. guavas; 5. Chinese pears; 6. fresh peach; 7. mango; 8. litchis (lychees)*

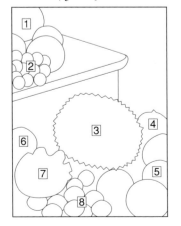

*Rear: lotus seeds in sweet soup; center left: sweet lotus seed paste; upper right: dried whole and halved lotus seeds; lower left: dried sliced lotus root; lower center: candied lotus; lower right: lotus paste buns*

## LOTUS

Almost every part of the lotus is used in Chinese cooking, even the flower, which can serve as a garnish or edible food container.

**Lotus root:** The fibrous roots, transected by a series of neatly spaced holes, are used as a vegetable in soups, stir-fries, and stewed dishes, and are candied as a sweet. As a snack, sliced lotus root can be marinated, then deep-fried until crisp.

**Lotus seeds:** These have medicinal properties, and are considered to invoke good fortune so they are often added to banquet dishes as a sweet conclusion to the meal in a clear sugar syrup, or in a rich soup or braised dish.

During the (Chinese) Lunar New Year, candied lotus seeds are given as a gift or offered to visitors. The cream-colored seeds are sold fresh or canned, and require no additional preparation and little cooking. Dried lotus seeds must be soaked and slow-simmered to soften them. A rich, amber sweet paste of mashed lotus seeds, sold in cans, is the filling for certain special cakes and buns served at *yum cha* restaurants. Its sweetness is often countered by the inclusion of a piece of salted egg yolk.

**Lotus leaves:** These used as a wrapper for steamed foods, add a subtle flavor to a dish. "Sticky rice" is wrapped in lotus leaves, and the famed "beggar's chicken" is usually wrapped in lotus before its clay crust is applied.

*In bowl: canned water chestnuts in syrup; on skewers: water chestnuts on ice; baskets at rear: dried red dates, dried black dates*

## WATER CHESTNUTS AND DATES

### WATER CHESTNUTS

These were first noted about 3,000 years ago in Chinese traditional medicine manuals. Boiled up as a tonic, water chestnuts are supposedly full of nutrients and "cold energy." These ancient fruits may in fact have been the two-horned water caltrop (*ling gok*) that enjoys a long history as a food in China. Water chestnuts, *ma tee*, are small, hoof-shaped bulbs which grow in marshy swamplands. Peeled of its hard, thin brown husk the chestnut is a pristine, plump white disk of crunchy sweet flesh. They have both savory and sweet applications in cooking.

Sliced or whole, they add crunch to stir-fries and casseroles. Chopped, they are the sweet, crisp note in a dumpling filling. They are crushed and dried to a flour which is used as a thickener for dishes like shark's fin soup, and for sweet cakes and puddings.

Water chestnuts are diced into coconut or sugar syrup desserts, but nothing could be more pleasing to nibble on a hot day than a slim bamboo skewer piercing a half dozen iced disks of water chestnut.

### DATES

**Red dates:** Since ancient times the Chinese red date, or jujube fruit, has been used in cooking and medicine. It is called "the food of harmony" as it is said to calm the nerves.

Red dates, with their wrinkled red skin and soft sweet flesh, are added to sweet and savory dishes. Their meaty amber-red flesh has a subtle sweetness and delicate fragrance which can provide interesting flavor highlights in a soup or stew.

**Black dates:** These were originally known in China as "Persian jujubes" for their similarity to the red fruit. They are used in puddings, particularly the "eight treasure" dessert based on glutinous rice.

At the end of a Chinese banquet—and even sometimes mid-way— the host will offer fresh fruit and a platter of small sweet pastries, including a crisp folded crêpe filled with mashed dates.

# BUTT SZE PINK GOAR

### TOFFEE APPLES

*Fun to eat and easy to make, this luscious concoction from Shanghai is enjoyed throughout northern China. Toffee apples are crunchy and nutritious, and have the extra charm of being "frozen" in ice water. Cantonese desserts are nothing to boast about. They are sweet and usually a little gooey, and no Cantonese household would serve them at ordinary meals. Desserts are usually served only at the end of special banquets. You can also find these concoctions as snacks from street vendors.*

½ cup (2 oz/60 g) all-purpose (plain) flour
6–7 tablespoons water
5 green apples, peeled, cored and cut into wedges
3½ cups (28 fl oz/875 ml) groundnut (peanut) oil
½ cup (4 oz/125 g) sugar
1 tablespoon sesame seeds

*SERVES 4–6*

❡ Mix the flour with 3–4 tablespoons of the cold water to make a thick batter. Coat each piece of apple evenly with the batter.
❡ Heat 3 cups (24 fl oz/875 ml) of the oil in a large pan. Deep-fry the apple until lightly browned, about 1½ minutes. Remove, drain and set aside.
❡ Heat ½ cup (4 fl oz/125 ml) of the oil in a medium-size pan. Add the sugar and melt. Add 3 tablespoons of water, stir and cook over low heat until the sugar turns light brown. Add the apples, coating each piece evenly with the syrup. Sprinkle with sesame seeds and serve with a bowl of ice cubes in water. Dip the apple in ice water to harden the syrup before eating.

*Butt Sze Pink Goar*

# TEA AND WINE

# TEA AND WINE

Unlike the Japanese, the Chinese have no tea ceremony. "Ceremonies," a Chinese sage once explained, "are given for history and respect and worship. But to the Chinese, tea is an old friend and old friends do not stand on ceremony."

❡ An old friend, indeed. In China, tea dates back more than 5,000 years, although its exact origins are lost to history. In the eighth century, the *Ch'a Ching,* or "Book of Tea," was written by Lu Yu, who is still considered the greatest authority ever on the subject. He states that tea was introduced around the 2700s BC, when Emperor Shen Nung had a kettle of water on the fire. The dragon who guarded his reign gently pushed a camellia plant (the camellia is a close relative of tea) next to the kettle, and some of the leaves fell in the water. The emperor sniffed the fragrant water, nodded his royal head with pleasure at this new aroma, and drank it. As a beneficent ruler, he decided that such a wonderful brew should be shared with his subjects.

❡ A type of tea leaf was probably known in China during the fifth century BC, as a contemporary of Confucius mentions this "wondrous bud," then called

*t'u.* By the first century, the Chinese character was changed to *ch'a,* the current term for tea.

❡ Tea has always been a revered drink in China: Nobles would give tea to the emperor as part of his tribute, eminent philosophers and poets would extol tea as "better than wine, which loosens the tongue," and it is still part of the marriage custom for the groom's family to give boxes of tea to the bride's family. Taoists said that wasting tea was one of the three most deplorable acts man could commit. The best water for tea invariably comes from the vicinity of Buddhist temples.

❡ Anyone searching for an "original" leaf could go to Yunnan province, where an 800-year-old tea tree still produces leaves suitable for brewing. Workers there climb 60 feet (18 meters) to get the youngest leaves, which are served to tea disciples.

❡ Those in search of the "original" water should go to Suzhou, where more jasmine tea is grown than anywhere in the world. In Tiger Hill Garden, a well dug 1,400 years ago is still in use, and tea made from the well water is served in a pagoda on top of the hill.

❡ The tea plant itself, *Camellia sinensis,* is a flowering evergreen that thrives in tropical and subtropical climates. Left to itself, it will grow to 40 feet (12 meters) but is kept at about 4 feet (1.5 meters) in cultivation. Although China's one-time pre-eminence in tea production was overtaken by India's in the 1940s, tea plantations still dot the countryside with green waves and a heavenly aroma.

❡ The tea plant matures in about three to five years, at which time it sends forth little "flushes" (the tea leaves), which are picked by hand. The best teas come from the youngest shoots: These give prized orange pekoe; from older leaves come pekoe and souchong.

*Previous pages: A busy tea-house in Chengdu, Sichuan province. Tea-houses are the equivalent of bars and cafés, and are places to meet, talk, play cards or chess, read the newspapers, or just enjoy the many teas on offer.* CHINA TOURISM PHOTO LIBRARY/CHEN JING

*Opposite: A woman sips tea from a bowl. Tea in China is served either in this type of receptacle, or in cups fitted with lids to keep the heat in and to stop floating leaves from being swallowed.* CHINA TOURISM PHOTO LIBRARY/CHEN JING

*Giant water pots are a traditional feature of many tea-houses.* CHINA TOURISM PHOTO LIBRARY/WANG SENGSENG

❦ The leaves are processed into black (fermented), green (unfermented), or oolong (semi-fermented) tea. For black tea, the leaves are dried on trays on mesh in troughs, rolled to release their juices, then left to ferment until they turn copper-colored. Finally, the leaves are dried in ovens, at which point they turn black. Leaves for green tea are steamed to arrest fermentation, crushed, and then dried in ovens; they will retain some of their green color. Oolong teas are allowed to wilt and ferment partially, which results in a greenish-brown tea.

❦ The tea is packed in chests that can be very colorfully decorated with paintings and descriptions; some even have poetry about the tea on the label.

❦ But nothing surpasses the beauty of Lu Yu's poetry in the *Ch'a Ching*, in which he describes the pleasures of drinking tea:

The first bowl soothes the throat, while the second banishes loneliness. At the third bowl, I search my soul and find 5,000 volumes of ancient poems. With the fourth bowl, a slight perspiration washes away all unhappy things. At the fifth bowl, my bones and muscles are cleansed. With the sixth bowl, I establish communications with the immortal spirit. The seventh bowl? It is forbidden! Already a cool ethereal breeze begins to soothe my whole body.

**Preparing Tea**

❦ The Chinese believe that the only way to make tea is to infuse the leaves in water. Tea bags, they hold, detract from the flavor of tea (as do milk and sugar), and should never be used.

❦ Ironically, this is not how tea-brewing in China began. Up to the ninth century, tea leaves as such were rarely used. Instead, the leaves were dried and molded into oblong cakes; the cakes were then steamed and pounded into powder. This powder, which is equivalent to the powder in today's tea bags, was either stirred into boiling water, or boiling water was poured onto it from an ewer.

❦ Not until the Yüan dynasty, around the time of Marco Polo, did it become customary to pour water over the tea leaves themselves, allowing them to steep. This method necessitated using a teapot, which was generally small and filled with boiling water.

❦ For a perfect cup of tea, follow these recommendations from an experienced tea merchant, whose first rule is to start with the finest quality tea. Heat water just to the point of boiling in a kettle with a narrow spout, so that as little oxygen as possible escapes (too little oxygen in the water results in "flat" tea). Use a teapot made of glazed porcelain, which can be thoroughly cleaned of any residues after each use.

❦ While the water is heating, rinse the teapot and cups with hot water to warm them. Then fill the pot with dry tea loose leaves (the general rule is one teaspoon of tea per one cup of water). Add the heated water and allow the pot to sit for about 30 seconds. At this point, discard about half the water, swirl the pot and discard all the remaining water.

❡ Let the pot rest a minute or two, allowing the freshly moistened leaves to expand. Add fresh water for the first infusion of tea by adding hot water and allowing it to sit for increasing lengths of time. Never let the tea "stew," but keep changing the water. The tea leaves are usually good for up to eight or nine infusions, although the third and fourth are the best.

❡ The Chinese serve tea in cups without handles, so that they feel the warmth of the tea through the porcelain. The cups may have fitted lids, which can be adjusted to allow a little liquid out, thus straining any leaves before drinking.

**Varieties of Tea**

❡ The Chinese produce more than 300 varieties of tea, with many districts specializing in one variety. Today, Taiwan prides itself on being the repository of China's great tea culture: When the Kuomintang left the mainland in 1949, they brought with them tea branches from all parts of the country.

❡ In theory, there are three types of tea: black, green, and oolong. But in practice, the Chinese mix the types and add other substances for new flavors. "Fragrant tea," for instance, has flowers added. Among the most popular flowers are chrysanthemum, jasmine, roses, and the blossoms of the litchi (lychee) fruit.

❡ In Hong Kong restaurants, *Bo Lai* tea, from the Bo Lay district in Yunnan province, is usually served, unless one asks for an alternative like Jasmine. Iron Goddess of Mercy (*To Kwan Yin*) is served before Teochiu meals in brandy-style snifters. It has an exceptionally high caffeine content. *Woo lung*, a smoky tea, is often served with *dim sum*.

❡ Among the green teas, Black Dragon, actually a cross between green and black teas, is one of the most popular. Cloud Mist is the ideal afternoon tea. It is grown high in the mountains of Jianxi province and the leaves are picked by trained monkeys.

❡ A favorite tea in Hong Kong is jasmine tea (*mook lai fai*) from Fukien. This is aromatic and strong, consisting of Dragon Well tea and jasmine flowers. *Heung Peen* is a fragrant expensive tea, while *Swong Yuk* is a rare tea made from young mulberry leaves.

❡ Tea leaves should be stored in an airtight container. Keep the container in a cool, dry, dark place and the tea should keep its flavor for several months.

**Tea Knuckle Language**

❡ Visitors to Chinese restaurants are often curious about the "knuckle language" heard when tea is being served. When the waiter has almost finished pouring tea into a cup, the recipient forms a fist, puts the heel of the fist on the table, and taps the table three or four times with the knuckles.

❡ The origin of this tradition comes from legend. Apparently an emperor wanted to see what his people really thought about him, so he donned ordinary clothes and took his courtiers on a tour of the city. When the residents continued to kowtow to him, he admonished them, saying that he was to be treated like just another citizen. But at a tea-house, when the Lord of Heaven began to pour tea into their cups, they were astounded at such behavior. Since they were forbidden to bow to their emperor, they secretly put their hands on the table and "bowed" with their knuckles.

❡ Today, this custom simply shows respect for the person who pours the tea—and a simple thanks.

## WINE AND BEER

❡ Except for the teetotal Chinese Muslims, who account for about four percent of the population, the Chinese revel in drink. Ancient poets, artists, and storytellers extolled drunkenness as a panacea for the world's worries. One Taoist group from the third

*Although Chinese wines are many and varied, they are usually made from glutinous rice rather than grapes and taste very much like sherry. Chinese spirits are extremely strong and should be drunk only in strict moderation!*

BRUCE COLEMAN LIMITED/MICHAEL FREEMAN

century called itself "the immortals of the wine cup." And then there is Liu Lung, the poet who traveled around the countryside in a donkey cart, totally inebriated. He was followed by two devoted servants: One carried his wine jar, the other carried a spade—which was to be used in case he died and needed a quick burial.

¶ Nowadays, of course, overindulgence in drink is as unacceptable as overindulgence in food. Eating is *yin*, drinking is *yang*. Harmony and moderation are expected in both.

¶ Traditionally, Chinese rice wine is the first choice at birthday parties for patriarchs and public figures, at banquets, and also at home. While it is considered invigorating for the heart, liver, hair, and brain, rice wine has a sharp, almost scorching taste and an alcohol content that rarely rises above 20 percent. Some Chinese department stores stock up to 100 different varieties, from the most popular (*Shao Hsing*) to such oenological curiosities as Dragon Flea Tonic, Pure Bamboo Leaf, and Chrysanthemum Bubble.

¶ Another variety of wine is *maotai*, from western China. This is made from millet and wheat, with an alcohol content of about 26 percent. Decidedly different is *kaoliang*, a clear wine made from distilled sorghum. Unlike rice wine, it is about as potent as vodka but smoother in taste.

¶ While rice wine is the most famous drink associated with China, the country also enjoys a long tradition of brewing beer. The first mention of beer goes back 3,000 years, and today virtually every province produces its own brands. *Tsing Tao* beer, made near Guangzhou and said to be brewed with the best spring water, is among the most prized.

**Grape Wine**

¶ Western visitors to Chinese restaurants are frequently surprised to find grape wine on the menu, but this is hardly alien to the Chinese. Chinese oenologists have discovered records of grape pips planted at the imperial court in 128 BC, almost 200 years before Bordeaux and Burgundy grew their first wines. Originally planted as a fruit, their potency was soon in vogue in northern China.

¶ Grapes were originally restricted to a small section of northern China, where it was considered an exotic "foreign" drink introduced from what are now the Turkic countries of the old Soviet empire and Persia. Simultaneously, wines made from fruits and honeyed wine, like mead, were favored for special festivals and imperial banquets.

¶ Rice wine though, was made throughout the more populous rice-growing regions of southern China up through through the Yangtze valley. It was cheaper to drink, it was easy to make (by simply leaving leftover rice in a barrel to ferment), and it finally displaced grape wine as the *vin de pays*.

¶ German missionaries planted a reasonable Riesling. The vineyards were in areas of northern China, such as Shandong, where the climate is similar to the South of France or California. Cuttings of many European vines were imported and vineyards established but during the tumultuous events of the twentieth century, the vineyards fell into disrepair and were abandoned.

¶ Since the early 1980s, however, cuttings of many European vines have been cultivated in the North of China. Riesling and Chardonnay are produced, and have a crisp taste and fragrant aroma.

¶ Two major brands are served at both Chinese and European restaurants. Great Wall wine uses "dragon-eye" grapes (a native variety that dates back to earliest times) to produce a fruity light taste. "Dynasty," a white grape wine that is made from a blend of pinot and dragon's eye grapes, is equally light with a fine aroma.

¶ Drinkers in Chinese restaurants are likely to consume brandy or Cognac with their meals. But younger Chinese gourmets prefer their own Chinese grape wines, which blend in well with the subtle Cantonese cuisine.

**Fermented Millet**

¶ Visits to rural communities in Sichuan, Tibet, and parts of Xinjiang may evoke images of a bunch of teenagers all drinking a chocolate soda out of the same glass with straws. The glass in this case, however, is a tube of bamboo, the straws are paper or bamboo, and the drink is fermented millet.

¶ Millet is the basis of China's most famous drink: *maotai*. This was the drink that sealed Chinese-American friendship when Richard Nixon and Mao Ze Dong toasted each other with it. The drink is more interesting historically than oenologically, though it does have a punch and tastes like a cross between sharp vodka and schnapps.

¶ The fermented millet drink called *tongkha*, made by the Tibetan and Sichuan peoples, is more like beer. It is made from raw millet, yeast, and water and is a milky-white color. It has a mild taste, but after a night of drinking one feels a pleasant wooziness.

# INDEX

# ACKNOWLEDGMENTS

Weldon Russell Pty Ltd would like to thank the following people for their help with the production of this book:

Boyac Decorative Furnishings; Corso de Fiori; Imperial Peking, Rose Bay; Gallery Orientique; Hale Imports; Redelman Furnishing Fabrics; Royal Doulton; St James Furnishings; Waterford Wedgwood

FOOD PHOTOGRAPHY

*Andrew Furlong (photographer) and Marie-Hélène Clauzon (food stylist)*: pp. 18–19, 25, 26–27, 28–29, 32–33, 36–37, 40–41, 42–43, 46–47, 90–91, 92–93, 94, 95, 98, 101, 102, 103, 104, 105, 106, 108–109, 110, 111, 112–113, 116, 118, 119, 184, 186, 190–191, 193, 196, 197, 199, 200, 202–203, 204, 206–207, 212–213, 214–215, 217, 220, 222–223, 226, 228, 230–231, 232–233, 238–239, 240–241, 245

*Mark O'Meara (photographer) and Penny Farrell (food stylist)*: pp. 52, 54, 57, 58, 60, 62–63, 64, 66–67, 72, 74, 75, 78–79, 80, 83, 84–85, 86–87, 124, 125, 126, 127, 130, 132, 133, 134–135, 136, 137, 138, 139, 140, 142–143, 144–145, 150, 152, 153, 155, 158–159, 160, 161, 162–163, 164, 167, 168–169, 170, 172–173, 175, 176, 177, 178–179

*Bruce Peebles (photographer) and Jacki Passmore (food stylist)*: endpapers, pp. 22–23, 30, 34–35, 38–39, 44–45, 59, 61, 65, 72, 77, 82, 96–97, 99, 100, 107, 114–115, 117, 128–129, 131, 141, 154, 156, 165, 166, 171, 174, 185, 187, 188, 192, 194, 195, 198, 201, 205, 218–219, 224–225, 229, 243, 244

| OVEN TEMPERATURE CONVERSIONS | | |
| --- | --- | --- |
| °Celsius | °Fahrenheit | Gas Mark |
| 110°C | 225°F | 1/4 |
| 130 | 250 | 1/2 |
| 140 | 275 | 1 |
| 150 | 300 | 2 |
| 170 | 325 | 3 |
| 180 | 350 | 4 |
| 190 | 375 | 5 |
| 200 | 400 | 6 |
| 220 | 425 | 7 |
| 230 | 450 | 8 |
| 240 | 475 | 9 |